FAITHFUL COMPANIONS

The Alliance of Man and Dog

FAITHFUL COMPANIONS
The Alliance of Man and Dog

Valerie Porter

Methuen . London

First published in Great Britain in 1987
by Methuen London Ltd
11 New Fetter Lane, London EC4P 4EE
Copyright © 1987 Valerie Porter

Made and Printed in Great Britain
by Richard Clay Ltd, Bungay, Suffolk

British Library Cataloguing in Publication Data

Porter, Val
Faithful companions : the alliance of man
and dog.
1. Dogs 2. Human-animal relationships
I. Title
304.2   SF426

ISBN 0-413-14390-2

To Bazz,
the kind-eyed mongrel
who always understood

Contents

List of Illustrations

Acknowledgement and thanks for permission to reproduce the photographs are due to the Australian Information Service for plate 1a; to the Merigal Dingo Education Centre, Bargo, NSW, Australia, for plate 1b; to Ken Walters for plate 1c; to Clem Haagner/Ardea London Ltd for plate 2a; to Jean-Paul Ferrero/ Ardea London Ltd for plates 2b and 3a; to Harry Kerr/Times Newspapers Ltd for plate 3b; to *The Field* for plates 4a and 8a; to Chris Smith/Associated Newspapers for plate 4b; to Nicholas Brown for plate 5; to Chris Harris/Times Newspapers Ltd for plate 6b; to the *Southdown Observer* for plate 7a; to Denzil McNeelance/Times Newspapers Ltd for plate 7b; and to Brian Shuel/Guide Dogs for the Blind Association for plate 8b. Plate 6a is Crown Copyright.

Acknowledgements

My thanks are due to the many people who have told me about their dogs. I am also particularly grateful for the patient help and advice given so generously by: Clarissa Baldwin of the National Canine Defence League; the staff of Battersea Dogs' Home; the Delta Society; the Guide Dogs for the Blind Association, in particular the Wokingham Training Centre and Mr and Mrs M. Grantham and Miss V. Till; Hearing Dogs for the Deaf; The Kennel Club; Marilyn Marchant at the People's Dispensary for Sick Animals; Dr Roger Mugford and his associates at the Animal Behaviour Centre, Chertsey; the Royal Air Force Police Dog School, Newton; the Royal Society for the Prevention of Cruelty to Animals; the Society for Companion Animal Studies; Surrey Police Dog Training Centre; Sussex Constabulary; Dr Alan D. Walker and Spillers Foods Ltd; Dorothy Walster, Scottish Health Education Group; and Berenice Walters, Merigal Dingo Education Centre.

Introduction

Wherever you find man, there too you find the dog, close at his heels. No other creature has voluntarily lived with us for so long and so willingly; no other creature has fulfilled so many helpful roles, nor offered itself so completely as a companion and comforter, nor been so grossly abused. Why is the relationship special and how has the alliance endured for so long in spite of frequent human failure to honour it?

As man's constant companion for ten thousand years, the dog has shared in human life to such a great extent that sometimes the differences between the two species become blurred. There are so many similarities, and therein lies the secret of the bond: each recognizes a kindred spirit in the other.

The original aim of this book was to take a fresh look at the alliance – an objective review of man and dog – and the closer I looked, the more intrigued I became by the reality of the dog, the essential *caninity* that we so often ignore in our age-old determination to humanize this most malleable and versatile of animals. Everyone who has a dog 'knows' dogs but in truth we have hardly begun to know them, even after thousands of years of domestication. We boast of our superiority but dogs are often more generous, more responsible and more honourable than human beings and they can teach our society a great deal about living together with mutual respect and toleration.

Like us, the dog is a social animal. Co-operation is the essence of a successful society and the dog's wild relatives and ancestors, especially the wolf, have bequeathed to the dog its great sense of responsibility to others. I make no apology for including quite a detailed look at how the wild canids organize their co-existence, because their society mirrors our own and can perhaps show us where we are going wrong.

We bold and arrogant humans stride this earth as if it belongs to us, using its resources for our own selfish ends and exploiting all other forms of life in order to sustain our own. And we find ourselves lonely. We have abused the living world so consistently, so wantonly and for so long that nearly every living creature fears us and flees from us if it can. We are isolated, cocooned in our own humanity. Among all the creatures of the earth, only the dog understood our loneliness and took it upon itself to help – to be a bridge that could link us again with the rest of life and with each other.

ONE

The Day of the Dog

Daybreak. The kennel hounds are wide awake and active; they know there will be a meet today. They have shaken the sleep and straw from their coats and joined their various voices in a ritual pre-dawn singing, a hymn to the new morning and a confirmation of pack bonds. Now they prepare noisily for the first competitive situation of the day: breakfast.

The farm collie long ago left her warm straw bed and has already chivvied the cows into the collecting yard. The large, recumbent mongrel in a country cottage kitchen stretches his legs a little, relishing the overnight warmth of the Aga near his box in the corner, aware of the hour and the imminent sequence of familiar morning stirrings in the cottage. A suburban Alsatian dozes a little longer in his basket before the alarm clock irritates the family into action. A fat, slightly smelly, arthritic and much loved terrier snores gently on the worn patchwork quilt, keeping an old lady's feet warm and giving her the comfort and purpose of a shared life. Another night has been safely survived by some of Britain's six million dogs and the people on whose behalf they have remained partially vigilant throughout the hours of darkness, always aware, even in sleep, of the vibrations of life around them.

The cottage mongrel, still lying comfortably on his side, prepares for his first task of the day. He stretches his legs again, the movement flowing along the length of his back and arching his neck. Then he is on his feet for a real stretch, forelegs out, chest to the ground, hips in the air, tail up and arching, chin reaching out – a moment of sheer pleasure which brings on a yawn. He leans forward to stretch his back legs and spine. Then he indulges in a waking shake, a leisurely scratch, and perhaps an indolent grooming with teeth and tongue here and there.

These movements, he knows, will have been registered subconsciously by the sleeping couple upstairs.

The mongrel is quite a subtle dog. If they do not wake up soon, he will have another yawn, a noisy one this time, and another scratch. His hind leg thuds gently on the floor as it misses his customary itch and, as he knew he would, he hears the first sounds of wakening above him. His tail is already waving slowly from side to side as the man sits on the edge of the bed upstairs, ruffling his hair and yawning.

The kitchen door opens. Man and dog greet each other, the man absent-minded in his sleepiness, the dog dignified as befits his size, security and equality, but warm too, expressing his affection without affectation or display, as one friend might welcome another. The man opens the back door before he riddles the stove, and the dog sets about the important business of reading the night signs in his territory. A cat would pause on the threshold, twitching its nose, testing the air, before it ventured forth, but the dog goes straight out, impatient of caution. There is work to be done. The family dog is a responsible animal and takes his role seriously. It is important to *know* what has happened out there during the night. His hackles rise when he smells traces of a nocturnal fox.

The woman has prepared the mongrel's breakfast when he returns. He greets her with more obvious affection – a little noise in his throat and a quick lick in return for a hug, a chest-rub and a chat. Rituals. Then the couple are busy with themselves, preparing for a human working day, and the dog, relishing his milk, does not directly participate in their routine but is a part of it all, just by his presence, making sure they swing smoothly into their morning. Each knows what has to be done. If the dog had been absent overnight in search of his bitch, the couple's morning would be disrupted and the routine upset simply because he was not there to watch.

The mongrel, naturally, hears the postman's van long before the couple hear it. He gives a little 'gruff' as his ears prick in anticipation, both firmly up but slightly tilted at the tip. The Alsatian and collie of his parentage are in perpetual conflict about his ears.

He waits by the half-glazed door until he judges the postman is able to hear him, then he begins his vocal challenge, the barks deep and regular at first, increasing quite quickly to a higher, faster crescendo that almost lifts his forefeet off the doormat. The woman puts a restraining hand on his ample scruff as she opens the door, wondering (as it is Monday) whose round it is this week. The dog has his favourites, and one particular dislike. She relaxes her hold when she hears Tom's cheery whistling in the lane and the dog's chorus becomes talkative and welcoming. He knew, of course, that it was Tom by the tone of his driving, but it is as well to keep everyone alert.

Early in the afternoon woman and dog head off for the woods, she with eyes and ears alert to the wildlife, he with nostrils flared and receptive, head often down, a million sensations being absorbed through all his senses. His world is unimaginably richer than hers; her mind is too occupied with human concerns to let her be flooded with the realities of the rest of the living, pulsating world around them. The dog, like a child, has plenty of space for it all; his energies throb through every nerve-ending and he drinks in immediate information through every pore. He is aware, without crystallizing the sensations, of every detail of their walk; he knows what living creatures have passed this way, or near it, in the twenty-four hours since yesterday's walk; he knows of the life-and-death dramas enacted between owl and vole, weasel and rabbit, blackbird and worm. He does not need to witness the past to know it. The woman, more observant than most people and more attuned to the natural world, recognizes very little. She sees the present but fails to notice most of it and she has only the slightest notion of the immediate past. Perhaps she catches the whiff of a deer but she cannot place its musk, cannot immediately visualize the creature as the dog can, cannot determine how long ago it passed this place, or what its mood was or what it was doing. She hears the tiny rustle and high, thin, almost inaudible insult of a shrew under the leaves but she does not hear the higher sounds or the more distant sounds that reach the dog's infinitely more sensitive ears.

However, she sees the approaching walker and dog in the distance before the mongrel is consciously aware of them. Her eyes can make out details of form – another woman, in drab colours to blend with the background, a black Labrador at her heels. It is too late to turn down another path. She sighs. The dogs both relish a scrap and are too equally matched to have sorted out an acceptable ranking yet. They have met twice before and have barely been restrained from active conflict. One day they will have to be allowed to sort it out for themselves but both women are upset by dog-fights and find it difficult to face the inevitable. She is a little resentful: she and the mongrel have walked the woods and fields for half a dozen years without meeting other people or other dogs. The Labrador and his owner are newcomers, intruders. She feels that, and the mongrel senses her feeling.

Both women clip the leads to their dogs' collars. The path, fortunately, is wide enough here for them to pass by with only vigorous displays of hackling, strutting and snarling from the dogs. The women glance at each other apologetically as they pass. One day we'd better let them. . . .

Perhaps, though, she will revert to old habits and walk the mongrel only at dawn and dusk, when other people are not abroad. Yes, she tells herself comfortingly, the dog enjoys those times more anyway.

The suburban Alsatian (an out-of-date name for the German shepherd dog but less of a mouthful) has a more chaotic start to the day but every piece of the chaos is routine. Adults and children flounce and shout and lose their clothes, burn the toast, fight for the bathroom, grab a quick breakfast, hurry, rush, fret, and disappear about their daily business one by one. The dog is largely ignored but nonetheless acknowledged, something to trip over, something to toss a crust to, something to blame for a missing sock, something essentially *there*. Not for him a leisured survey of his territory as a first priority – nobody thinks of letting him out until the chaos has subsided, the children have headed for school, one or other of the adults has grumbled off to work, and the crockery is clattered into the sink. The Alsatian is content to wait: he knows the routine. First there will be a perfunctory walk on a lead down the road – a chance for him to sniff the markers and add his own messages and a chance for his human companion to draw breath between the chaos of breakfast-time and the stress of the rest of the day.

The highlight of the Alsatian's day comes later – a walk in the park and a chance to run, to meet other dogs, other people. His country cousin has the greater freedom outdoors but perhaps for that reason the exhilaration is less intense. The mongrel has endless fields to explore, rabbits to chase, weasels to affront, crows to berate, pheasants to stalk, but only meets other dogs occasionally, and rarely new ones. His social life is less stimulating than that of the park dog; his territory is far larger and less intimate.

The working collie has no time for social life or boredom. She is in partnership with her owner; she knows perfectly what is expected of her and that she fulfils her role as she should. She shares that satisfaction with other working dogs: she is a vital part of a team and, whether or not her owner expresses it, she knows her work is valued and appreciated. On the farm there is always something happening and plenty of life – cows, bellowing and going about their own reassuringly regular routines, visits by the milk lorry or the feed merchant, reps and postmen to chase, chickens to be controlled, mergansers to be chastized, cats to be kept in their place. The collie has a multitude of tasks on the farm and needs no bidding to carry them out. To a large extent she is in control of her own life, though the rules were long ago laid down by her owner.

The social life of a kennel dog is very different. It is part of a pack of its own kind; it is constantly reacting to other members of the pack, always alert to the ever-changing relationships within the group. Each hound's action is a reaction to other hounds. Dogs living in kennels do not have the strong personal bonds with individual human beings which for many other dogs are more important than their relationships with others of their own species. Hounds remain faithful to their pack, and the pack is canine.

The old lady sleeps late in the mornings. There is nothing much to get up for. The twilight of her life is quiet and she lives in her own small world in which her overfed, under-exercised terrier is an equal but a child. She depends on it for so much. Above all it is good company; it is a listener, a guard, an ally, alert to her emotions and needs. Without the dog she would rise even later and be quite content to stay in a chair by the fire most of the day, but the dog needs to be looked after and that gives her a purpose in life. The dog needs her. She likes to feel its weight at the end of her bed; she likes to hear its snuffling which obliterates the silence of loneliness. She likes to caress it and talk to it, and she is reassured by the way it looks up at her with bright little eyes, never ignoring her or humouring her as people might. In hard times she feeds the dog before she feeds herself and it always grabs the warmest spot by the fire – a fire she might otherwise neglect because the money for coal is precious. She will suffer discomfort herself but she could never deprive her dog.

The little terrier, the suburban Alsatian, the working collie, the kennel hounds and the country mongrel all share at least one highlight in the day: dinner. Whether it is tinned meat, cooked tripe, raw beef, biscuits, kennel carcase or carefully balanced dry chow, dinner is an important daily ritual. The food may disappear in seconds (though smaller dogs are rather more dainty) but there is the anticipation of it, the watching for tell-tale signals before its preparation, the drooling, the certainty of being fed and the pleasure of cleaning up every last scrap in and around the dish. With luck there might be a marrow-bone afterwards. A dog can do a lot with a bone as well as grind teeth on it. A bone can be possessed, attacked, rolled, probed, buried, protected, lost, found again, dug up – oh, there is life in a bone!

At the end of the day the routines continue: a warm doze by the fire while the humans wind down, a last let-out for a compulsory barking at the night, the pleasure of one's own private bed in which to turn and turn before settling to relax and dream with twitching paws and little whimpers. But a dog is never completely asleep; it must always be ready for action, alert to its human companions, on guard against strangers in the night.

TWO

Secret Lives

Anyone who has ever lived with a dog knows all about dogs. Dogs are such honest animals; their faces are open and expressive, their natures are obvious. There is a childishness about them; they enjoy themselves – they love life and they share that joy with us. Cats, on the other hand, are private creatures, intriguing in their independence, but a dog tells everything and shares its every experience and emotion with its human companions.

Or does it? Like cats, dogs have a whole secret world of which humans, even the most observant and empathetic, are largely ignorant.

Jimmy, a typical Australian suburban dog, is a well-loved golden retriever with a pleasant temperament and eyes brimming with kindness and honesty. He is an ideal family pet, well-trained and obedient, playing with the children, friendly with all he meets. Like many of their neighbours, Jimmy's owners like their dog to have his freedom and in the evenings he is released from the confines of house and back yard so that he can enjoy himself out on the streets with other local dogs.

He has a regular group of canine companions, though they are a loose-knit set. Usually there is a German shepherd or two, assorted terriers large and small, collies, mongrels, kelpies, a greyhound, a standard poodle and of course a couple of Labradors. As dusk falls, the group gathers, the secret world of the dogs takes over and the family pet becomes a member of a pack.

There are several smallholdings within a few miles of the streets. During the night a valuable herd of Angora goats is mauled and half a dozen lacerated creatures are left wounded and dying in the paddocks. The smallholder naturally blames it on dingoes – all Australians blame the dingoes. Jimmy is home long before dawn, clean, gentle and cheerful. He eats his breakfast with relish as usual.

On the other side of the world, in a quiet Sussex valley, a couple of Great Danes living on a farm are, as usual, left to their own devices during the day. They, too, are family pets, much loved and well cared for. They are country dogs, mother and son, well behaved with the horses, cattle and sheep kept on the farm. Everyone in the valley knows them: they are often seen ambling in the fields, vaguely and lazily chasing rabbits, wandering into the village to investigate the dustbins or persuade the butcher to part with a titbit. Children greet the big dogs as equals and they are affable to all and sundry.

It is about ten o'clock in the morning when one of the valley's dairy farmers notices a lamb in his ten-acre meadow. 'Rob's fencing's down again,' he thinks to himself. The lamb is not bleating for its mother, nor are any other sheep in sight. Then he notices what might be a little dried blood on its chest. 'Must have come through the barbed-wire,' he tells Rob on the telephone. 'Looks okay though – probably just a scratch.'

Within a few minutes Rob comes to check the fencing. The sheep seem quite peaceful but they are strangely silent as he leans over the gate. Normally they greet him and come up for a chat. Then he notices a ewe lying up by the hedge. He goes over to her but she does not move. She is dead – she has been disembowelled.

Automatically he begins to count the quiet flock. At least a dozen are missing. He runs towards the next field and there he finds carnage. Dead and injured ewes and lambs slump in the grass and under the hedges, or stand immobile and shocked. Hanks of wool are strewn about the field like rubbish after a pop festival. He returns to his Land Rover and tears back to the farmhouse for help.

The dogs, meanwhile, have moved to a second flock a few fields away. While Rob and the vet are frantically tending the injured in the first flock, several hastily summoned local farmers begin a grim-faced hunt. They are armed. They see the dogs from a distance, tearing joyfully into another ewe. There is no sound, either from the dogs or from the sheep, who seems resigned to her fate. The men race across the fields but the dogs flee into the woods.

The Great Danes are unmistakable. Their owner is contacted and comes immediately but the dogs have vanished.

Meanwhile Rob and the vet are overwhelmed by the number of victims and the nature of some of their wounds. Very few have been killed outright but many should be dead. Great hunks of flesh have been ripped from their flanks, sometimes exposing the bones. Ewes have their sides slashed open, and their heavy fleeces hang down on flaps of loose skin. Without the protection of the fleece, the damage would have been even worse. Limbs have been torn off living lambs, faces mauled, throats gashed. Many animals have been hamstrung. Several sheep have to be destroyed: they are beyond saving.

Later in the day the dogs' owner finds them resting peacefully by a stream in the woods. They greet him in the usual loving manner, with a glad wag of the tail and a gentle, friendly lick on the hand. He strokes their heads. 'I can't do it myself,' he says, not meeting their gaze, 'but it must be done.' He caresses them while the vet injects them and the tired, contented bodies slump heavily to the ground. The blood of thirty or forty sheep is still drying on their paws, their chests and their chins.

They were big dogs and the damage they caused was enormous, but even a small Jack Russell can murder a sheep, especially with a little help from its friends. Any dog can. Perhaps it all starts as an innocent game. Perhaps an elegant Afghan hound is enjoying a rabbit chase and finds herself among sheep. The sheep, as sheep will, bunch and run. The hound bounds after them – bigger rabbits, more fun. The sheep seem to join her game, running as she chases and never disappearing inconveniently down a burrow. She catches up with them easily; she snaps playfully at a rump and snatches a mouthful of wool, not really intending to do so. The next snap meets something more solid and the game hots up, the snatching and snapping become as important as the chasing . . .

She has never done it before. She's well-trained (for an Afghan), never even looks at sheep when we are out for a walk. She wouldn't do anything like that. Not *our* dog.

In an average year, more than ten thousand farm animals are

attacked by dogs in Britain. Only one in three of them survives the attack. These are the incidents which are reported to the police; there are probably as many again which go unreported. Nearly all the culprits are pet dogs.

Many people let their dogs out for the day while they are at work. Perhaps they feel guilty if the dog is not as free as they are, to come and go as it pleases, or perhaps they simply do not care enough about the dog to give it the company and exercise it needs. Of course, they say, their dog causes no harm. It knows all about traffic, doesn't cause accidents. It is streetwise.

There's that Labrador at the village dustbins again! He's a well-fed dog but he cannot resist a leisurely scavenge. The bin clatters to its side, yielding its contents. Chicken bones. Bacon rind. Fish skins. Dog's dinner, dog's delight. Dog's nature.

The Labrador has more serious matters in mind. He devours a quick snack, licks his chops and moves on down the pavement, checking the scents and frequently cocking his leg. His progress looks random but he knows exactly where he is going. This morning he caught the whiff of a bitch on heat, three miles away. (No, his owners have not had him castrated – they don't like the idea, makes the man of the house feel uncomfortable just to think of it.) The bitch is not ready yet but the Labrador intends to stake a claim in good time. Several other dogs have the same intention and are already hanging around outside the bitch's home. (No, the bitch's owners have not had her spayed. They don't really want puppies, but doesn't spaying make dogs fat and lazy or something? Expensive, too.)

Each dog keeps his distance, sizing up the rivals. In social terms it can be a difficult situation. In the wild they would be members of a single pack, and would know their pecking order within it. They might test the next dog up the hierarchy now and then but would know precisely what his reaction and power would be. But this collection of domestic dogs, gathering from a wide area, is not a pack. Each comes from a different pack (usually a human family) and there is tension. Several know each other from past encounters in similar situations but meet only rarely. There is uncertainty. They are strangers at a party with no host to make the introductions; they are in an unnatural situation.

The Labrador checks out the opposition, shrugs, and sets off for a more promising venue. He crosses the heath and visits the kennels well away from the village, two miles by road along a single-track lane and a rutted old greenway – but the dog knows a much more direct route. The kennels are always potentially interesting: new dogs arrive every week, especially in the summer when their owners deposit them for two or three weeks.

The kennel inhabitants are always under emotional and social stress. The environment is alien; the territory is not their own; the other residents are strangers, including the humans. For a territorial pack animal and creature of habit such as the dog, the situation is bewildering and frightening. His own pack has cast him out; he does not know the rules and rituals of this new pack and most of the other members seem to be equally unsure. There is plenty of whimpering and howling, or silent dejection. Dogs are capable of grief.

As it turns out, there are no interesting bitches in the kennels on this occasion. The Labrador watches and sniffs from a distance, hidden in a little copse on rising ground downwind. A new promise reaches him. He lifts his muzzle higher to confirm the scent and follows the airborne aroma for a mile and a half to a cottage set among fields. Soon he finds her trail of urine markers on the ground. She has been wandering freely in the fields and woods.

His luck is in. The bitch is free-roaming and he knows her. It takes him a couple of hours to lure her away from the house into the woods but she is not quite ready for him yet. She is still edgy and snappy, flirting a little but spinning round to face him with a growl whenever he places a paw on her rump.

He visits her daily until she changes her manner. Now it is she who leads him away from the house. They frolic for a while, she leading him further and further into the woods. All the while he is almost intoxicated by her scent and the taste of her. At last she is ready; she stands motionless when he rests his chin on her and the moment is right. She draws her tail aside.

Several hours later the Labrador takes himself to the local police station. They know him well there; they telephone his owners, who save him the trouble of a walk home. It works every time. His family was well aware that he was bitching seriously: he had hardly touched his food for days and he had that distant look in his eyes. They did try and restrict him, tying him on a long leash in the garden, but it seemed so unfair on him; he looked into the distance with such longing, lifting his nose and twitching his nostrils and, every now and then, raising his head in a long and mournful howl that seemed to well from his very soul. So they let him go, knowing he would come home each night. When he was younger, they had denied him such freedoms, aware of the aggravations a roaming dog can cause, but they became more confident in him, trusting his road sense, his stock sense and his extreme shyness of guns and traps (the keeper wired the area against foxes) and they began to feel guilty at depriving their companion of one of his greatest joys in life, the freedom to wander and socialize with his own kind on his own terms. They were willingly manipulated; they respected their dog, as he did them, and it seemed presumptuous to curtail him.

Maybe, but maybe not. A dog is a good learner and one of the most adaptable species on earth, but fundamentally it is a dog, not a human being. It has its own concepts of acceptable behaviour which are often *not* acceptable to human beings, especially those who do not particularly like dogs. For thousands of years dogs have associated with humans and have been trained to follow certain human rules but no amount of training can alter the basic nature of the animal. Dogs are dogs, and in an environment in which humans seem to assume they have the right to dominate all other creatures in the interests of human well-being, it is for the dog owner to control the dog so that its behaviour is acceptable to the rest of human society. No one can expect a healthy, self-respecting dog to remember its artificial manners when it is beyond the immediate influence of its owner's presence and is not seeking to please or appease that owner. A dog's 'acceptable' behaviour is no more than an imposed veneer. Among its own kind it observes canine standards and the unnatural veneer of human training can easily crack in circumstances that trigger natural, doggish reactions. A free-ranging dog is an individual, no longer constrained by its humans.

It works both ways. People adapt their own behaviour to their dog, especially in the privacy of the home. They understand the dog's expectations and often play up to them; they indulge in physical romps or slightly ridiculous conversations which they would be much too embarrassed to carry on with other humans.

In assuming ownership of dogs, people must surely also accept not only responsibility for the animals in their care but also responsibility towards society in general insofar as other people are affected by the dogs' behaviour. In the same way, parents take responsibility for the behaviour of their children.

Bitch owners tend to be more responsible, not necessarily because of a social conscience but because of the potential problem of unwanted pups. Due to the seasonal nature of their oestral cycle, bitches are perhaps less inveterate wanderers than male dogs, but pairs of bitches love nothing better than escaping for a hunting escapade and a mother-and-daughter pair seems to be particularly adventurous.

The human preference for male dog or bitch is subject to many factors, both practical and psychological. Very often, people keep bitches because their own parents happened to do so, or perhaps because they are offended by a dog's more blatant sexuality and potential aggression. Others prefer males precisely for their more aggressive image, or because they do not want the hassle of bitches on heat, or again simply because they always had males. There are countless other factors and a whole thesis could be written on the subject.

Sir William Beach Thomas, addressing his own (male) spaniel Whuff through the pages of *Atlantic Monthly*, wrote: 'We most of us prefer to keep male dogs rather than female for reasons more elemental than psychological, and I have suggested that yours is the more reasoning and more sentimental sex; but the other has certain superiorities, both mental and physical. The bitches I have hunt better than the dogs, are keener and more persistent. They possess more instinct and less reason or imagination. Perhaps the same is true in our own species . . . It is my experience that you, Whuff, excel any bitch in this gift of imaginative sympathy. You feel as we feel, and all the more deeply that your energies are not diluted by the abstract.'

Many working dogs are female; for example, some shepherds find bitches are much steadier and more intelligent than dogs, and many a shot or a keeper prefers a bitch in spite of the inconvenience of her almost wilfully coming on heat on the first day of the shooting season.

Spaying or castration, incidentally, may remove the risk of unwanted pregnancy and reduce the reasons for straying, but dogs, whatever their sex or reproductive state, are all capable of anti-social behaviour be it worrying livestock, raiding dustbins, defecating on the pavement or unwittingly scaring passing motorists or dog-wary children, and it is hardly fair to blame the dog for its owner's irresponsibility.

The big, shaggy cottage mongrel is still young enough to enjoy the chase. He had startled the roe deer on a woodland ride and its flashing white rump now bobs tantalizingly ahead of him. He relishes stretching his legs and feeling his own fitness. In excitement he gives little high-pitched yelps now and then, sounding more like a small terrier than a crossbred Alsatian. Normally an obedient dog (he is also half collie), he is deaf to his owner's calls and whistles. Like any dog, or any child, he shuts off his senses to all but the important matter of the moment and it can honestly be said that he did not hear the summons.

He knows he can never catch up with the deer but his pleasure is purely in the pursuit. It is the same with rabbits. The first time he caught a rabbit, he was disappointed because it ran no more despite his efforts to reactivate it. Squirrels are different; he respects their bite and if he catches one, which is a rare event, he kills it instantly, tossing its body into the air. It is the same with rats. His only true enemy is the fox: the smell of one sends his hackles up and his throat rumbling, and he will chase its trail seriously, but he has only once caught up with a fox – quite a young one which found itself cornered against the forestry wiremesh. There was a fight; the fox went for the dog's eyes and he still has a scar running from the corner of one eye down his muzzle. He flicked his head clear, just in time.

The deer is neither enemy nor prey. It simply gives him an excuse to test his running skills and stamina as it dodges between the trees. There is a mutual understanding: the gap between them never varies. If he is lagging, the deer slows her pace and the proper distance is restored. In the end he is always the first to tire and then he wallows in a black-mudded pool, panting and happy. He'll find his human companion again when he is ready to do so. All that calling and whistling is an unnecessary disturbance to the peace of the woods.

Humans often misread their dogs, largely because they cannot 'think dog'. How many humans have tried living at dog level, literally, even for a few minutes? How many have spent a day on all fours looking at the world from the point of view of a dog, or a child? Dogs are humanized, expected to react in certain ways as a human might, but humans are much more destructive and deceitful than dogs. In the deer chase, perhaps a man would have found more satisfaction in the kill than the pursuit, and certainly the deer would have mistrusted his intentions. Most creatures have learned to fear man, and they flee from him, leaving him a little lonely.

THREE

Running Wild

All over the world, though perhaps less now in Britain than elsewhere, dogs have become half-wild and live on their wits in the cities and in the countryside. There is a stage in between, like the domestic dogs of Australian suburbia which are family pets by day and hunting packs by night, or like the roaming British Labrador seeking dustbins and bitches, but there are also the truly feral dogs – dogs with no owners which form loose-knit city packs, scavenging for their food, mating freely with each other, sleeping under houses and sheds or digging out their own burrows, and the wilder rural packs that have much less to do with mankind.

Twenty-five years ago there were nearly twenty-five million domestic dogs in the United States – dogs which could claim to have owners – and almost half of them lived in cities. By the 1970s the population had risen to about thirty-three million, and up to forty per cent of city-dwelling American families had at least one dog. In addition to that huge number of claimed dogs, there were countless strays wandering the streets, often fed regularly by those who befriended them but did not own or take responsibility for them. Urban dogs, by their ubiquity, had quite an influence on urban ecology and on public health.

Alan Beck, now working in New York's Department of Health, made a study of semi-feral and free-roving dogs in Baltimore, Maryland, a city with a population today of about two million people. By observation and recording, he estimated that there were up to a hundred thousand dogs in Baltimore at the time of his study in the early 1970s, at a density of up to eight hundred per square mile, and that there was one free-roving dog for every nine human beings in the city. He studied the behaviour of dogs of all kinds, whether obviously owned or not.

The dogs observed as 'free-roving' during the survey included domestic pets let out for unsupervised runs morning and evening (at least a third of the city's family dogs were given this freedom). In lesser numbers there were escaped pets, abandoned pets whose owners had moved elsewhere, pets stolen by children and then released or escaped, and, to a small extent, animals born in lie-up dens under porch steps, in alleyways, on derelict sites, etc. Pups born to ownerless strays, however, had a very low rate of survival.

Dogs were in evidence on the streets at all times of day and night, whatever the season, except during the overwhelming midday heat of summer when dogs and humans sought cool refuges. In those warm months, most dogs were about the streets between 5 and 8 a.m. and 7 and 10 p.m., reflecting a common habit of people who let their pets out before and after they were absent at work for the day. It was noted that even ownerless dogs, living rough, followed this crepuscular pattern of activity and free-running rural dogs are also at their most active early in the morning and at twilight.

Much of the 'active' period was in fact spent resting or dozing. The free-running dogs tended to have a home range of about a tenth of a square mile (0.26 km sq.) which included outings to open fields and also vital feeding areas like garbage alleys. Rubbish bins were of great importance: they were easily tipped over. Rubbish in plastic bags enabled the dogs to carry the entire package to a secluded area where they could then rummage at leisure for the good bits.

Many of the strays also fed well through the kindness of local residents, especially in the lower income areas where people would regularly put out food for a particular dog, or for the dogs in general – much like people put out food for wild birds. Up to twenty per cent of residents in these areas regularly or occasionally fed strays but in middle-class areas hardly anybody indulged them.

Thus food seemed to be no problem for the urban strays. They found shelter in shrubberies and overgrown sites, in derelict buildings or ones in the course of erection, in communal hallways, or under the porch steps that are a feature of so many American homes. Parked cars could provide useful shady retreats and in hot or wet conditions dogs were often seen sleeping on gravestones or dumped mattresses to insulate themselves from the ground. City tips provided all sorts of hiding places, of course.

During the morning peak activity period about half of all the dogs seen were alone, a quarter were in pairs and most of the rest were in groups of three, four or five; very occasionally larger groups of less than twenty would come together. On the whole the strays did not seem to form cohesive packs and groups seemed to be very fluid: their numbers and membership varied, they often congregated almost incidentally (perhaps around a bitch on heat) and disbanded as suddenly as they had come together, or were dispersed by incidents involving people and vehicles.

There was plenty of teamwork – for example, larger dogs would knock over bins for smaller dogs, or a group would feed in shifts so that some dogs were always on the look-out. On the whole the strays had little fear of humans and would even mate in the street regardless of pedestrians or traffic. A large percentage of deaths were from traffic accidents and if a car came at a dog at any speed the animal tended to cower rather than flee, almost as if the car was a dominant dog it wished to appease. Cars were the commonest cause of injury, and were second only to disease as the cause of death: it was estimated that nearly twenty per cent of the entire dog population were killed in road accidents every year.

Another 'predator' on the dogs was the Municipal Pound, which in one year rounded up eleven or twelve thousand live dogs as well as collecting the fifteen thousand dead ones found in the streets. Most of the captured dogs were injured or sick; barely five hundred were reclaimed by owners. In some areas local people would chase dogs into hiding if they saw the dog-pound vans around, because they knew that most unclaimed pound dogs would be gassed later on, if not sold to laboratories. The gassed dogs ended up as chicken and pigfeed supplements and their fat was rendered down for soap-making.

All the rubbish-tipping dogs, whether owned or genuine

strays, created certain public health problems since scattered rubbish, besides looking unsightly, encourages secondary scavengers like rodents, cockroaches and flies. Strangely, none of the dogs ever even tried to catch a rat. They chased off cats, which stalked rats although they rarely captured them, and thus gave rats an even quieter life among the bins. Moreover, the strays also chased off human rat-catchers!

During the year of the study about seven thousand Baltimore citizens were bitten by dogs – a bite rate of about seventy-four per ten thousand people, which was almost double the American average. This may have been because Baltimore had such a large, free-roving dog population. The most usual victims, as in other cities, were children under fifteen years old and the bite rate in general doubled during the summer because there was more street activity, both human and canine. People on bicycles frequently had trouble with dogs, and very occasionally a pack of dogs had attacked zoo animals or children. The authorities were alarmed at the increasing trend among city dwellers to own large, aggressive dogs for self-protection against violent crimes. The thought of packs of Rottweilers and Dobermann pinschers on the loose is more than a little frightening.

There were other problems which both pet and stray dogs caused in the city. Dog faeces caused offence and were potential health hazards; dog-worms could infect children playing where dogs had fouled the ground; *Salmonella* organisms could be transmitted to humans by flies feeding on dog faeces, which are almost as attractive to house flies as rubbish bins. The faeces also attracted rats. Dog urine seemed to account to a limited extent for the spread of leptospirosis to humans, and dogs could also act as hosts for other diseases, although these were on a very minor scale in the human population.

Then there was the nuisance value of dogs – chaos in traffic, for example, and the cacophony of chain-reaction barking whenever dogs live in dense populations. Many people found that the city's free-roving dogs were an additional source of anxiety in an urban life already full of stress, but, as can be seen from the voluntary feeding of strays in some areas and their protection from the dog-catchers, other citizens welcomed the presence of the dogs. Whatever steps the authorities took were bound to upset somebody, one way or another.

Baltimore's dogs were free-rovers or strays; they were rarely truly feral. A feral animal is a domesticated species which has taken to the wild and can successfully survive and reproduce without the help of humans. Indeed, feral animals usually fear humans. They have lost the domesticity or tameness which generally means a lack of such fear.

A stray dog might become a feral dog, and indeed types such as collies, Dobermanns and German shepherds are more likely to than most. However, all over the world feral dogs have had a continuous existence for centuries. Even in such a recently 'civilized' land as the United States, feral dogs were very probably present before the white man first stepped ashore; the Indians had their own domesticated dogs.

Ferals catch the blame every time, everywhere, when livestock are attacked but in fact feral dogs live largely on small mammals, carrion and rubbish. William H. Nesbitt, later Manager of the Hunting Activities Department of the National Rifle Association of America, carried out a five-year study of feral dogs in a national wildlife refuge in Illinois. He followed the development of a litter of weaned, feral, collie-type puppies which formed the nucleus of a pack for the period of his study. At first the pack included a setter-pointer cross of the same age as the puppies, an adult female mongrel, and an adult male collie, both the latter about ten years old. One of the three original puppies soon became pack leader but at the age of two he was found shot dead and his sister took over the role. The third member of the litter had broken away by then to run as a pair with another dog.

When a female in the pack was in pup, she would whelp alone in heavy cover but did not dig a den. Her behaviour with the litter was much like that of a wolf: as the pups neared weaning age, she would increasingly leave them so that she could run with the pack for a while. Sometimes another member of the pack would stay near the litter to keep an eye on them for her. At first the pups were quite vocal but became markedly less so by the time they were a year old; the adult dogs rarely used their voices. The pups entered the pack when they were about four months of age but their survival rate was low and the pack size remained fairly consistent at what was apparently an ecologically efficient number. Naturally the newly entered youngsters were the lowest in the pack hierarchy, which showed clearly in the single-file formation adopted by the pack on the move: leader at the front, pups tagging along at the rear after the lowest-ranking adults. Quite often the leader would scout ahead, then return to the pack and give them a short vocal signal or gesture which activated them to move off together.

All the dogs in the pack were in very good health all year round, apart from occasional ticks. They took immediate evasive action at the sound of human voices and their pack movements were often influenced by human activity as well as by other wildlife, food opportunities, etc. Much like the urban free-rover, they tended to be most active at dawn and dusk and also nocturnally – times of least human interference. They would take cover if necessary in woodland or shrubbery but otherwise travelled along easy routes like roads, deer paths or crop tracks. Their area covered about ten or eleven square miles (28 km sq.), which was almost the full extent of the refuge, an area bounded by fencing, a highway and a lake. The region was varied: it included arable fields, cattle pasture, plantations, hardwood forests and ponds, and it was teeming with deer, small game and waterfowl.

Typically of canids, the dogs were flexible opportunists (a quality which has helped them to be such a successful species). They made the most of small game, carrion, road casualties, crippled deer or injured waterfowl, fruits and a little vegetation, and occasionally they scavenged from the refuge's rubbish-tip. They never attacked livestock, though three calves were killed by free-roving pet dogs wearing collars.

On the whole, therefore, the pack did a good job of cleaning up in the area and were for that reason an important part of its ecology. They were not the rogues that feral and genuinely wild carnivores are so often said to be.

The Australian dingo has teased many an investigator. Some

say it is a feral animal – once a partly domesticated dog even if it was a very long time ago – and others claim it is truly a wild species which has never been domesticated. Many serious researchers have become confused about its origins. It has been linked with mesolithic skeletal remains; it has been recognized in an almost complete southern Australian skeleton of an eighteen-week-old male dingo carbon-dated to 3,000 BP (Before Present), and it has been hinted at in skeletons five thousand years older on the same continent, but it has not been found in Tasmania or New Guinea: like most Australian fauna, it seems to have developed in total isolation. Unlike the marsupials, the dingo probably arrived in Australia not more than nine thousand years ago, a long time after the flooding of the Torres and Bass Straits which cut the continent off from the rest of the world. It is claimed that man was established there thirty thousand years ago, arriving by sea, and that the dingo also came by sea but twenty thousand years later. Did it come as a domesticated dog? If not, how did it get there – surely not by swimming all that way?

The dingo is very different to most domestic dogs (*Canis familiaris*) in some ways but very similar in others. It is a handsome, pure-looking dog in which one can recognize ancient breeds like the basenji and pharaoh hound. There seem to be distinct types adapted to particular terrains: the northern or tropical dingo is strong, muscular and short-haired; the southern mountain dingo is thickly coated and fox-like; and the desert type is smaller and finer than either. All have a strong, broad skull between erect, forward-pointing ears which are particularly expressive and independently mobile.

Like the basenji, the dingo does not have a 'doggy' smell but it does sometimes have an almost cat-like smell if it is excited or during the breeding season. It licks itself clean like a cat and it uses its paws as hands, dealing very effectively with door handles and gate latches. It is as agile as a cat, too, good at springing and climbing (with a passion for being on top of things), and it is an accomplished escape artist.

The dingo shares another unusual characteristic with the basenji: neither of them really bark like dogs. They howl, or yodel. In fact the dingo has a wide range of vocal communications. It *can* bark – one gruff woof – but rarely does, and it can more characteristically sing, 'crow', purr (a vibration of the lips and a rattle of the teeth) and – well – *talk!*

There is perhaps one particular quality that distinguishes the dingo from the average domestic dog. The dingo has a free spirit. It can be successfully trained to a high standard by an understanding and patient human, as Berenice Walters, who has done so much to re-educate her fellow Australians about the worth of the dingo in her battle to reclassify it as a national dog to be proud of rather than a noxious animal to be shot or poisoned on sight, has proved time and time again. She has shown that dingoes are exceptionally intelligent and sensitive – far more so than most dogs – and that they can reach the very highest levels in obedience training, outclassing even the standard winners like German shepherds, once their nature is properly understood and respected. The key to successful dingo training is, she says, 'regular and continuous socializing, regular and varied short training sessions with plenty of praise and play, patience and diplomacy, and a sense of humour. The fostering of a close relationship with this highly intelligent and social breed is essential. Beware of boredom and over-training; his spirit is easily squashed.'

It is for that very spirit that the dingo wins its many admirers. A dingo tries to own a human, as much as a human tries to own it. The dog 'punishes' its human for wrong-doings or intolerance – not aggressively but by gentle reproach or withdrawal. A dingo will not be dominated: it insists on its independence and is never a puppet but always an equal. Mrs Walters, whose close observations of dingo behaviour serve to illuminate all dog behaviour, tells a story which owners of certain 'problem' dogs should note.

Peter, one of the group of dingoes at her Merigal Dingo Centre in Bargo, New South Wales, had always tended to show dominance to people, particularly during the breeding season, and Berenice always treated him with special care and respect. In spite of her understanding, Peter challenged her twice and knowing that, as usual, it was her human failure rather than his, she paused to wonder what she was doing wrong. She realized that she was in fact being much too respectful. Whenever she entered the enclosure Peter shared with his family, she would approach each dingo personally to greet them, carefully stepping around any animal that was in her path; going to them, instead of waiting for them to initiate the greeting, she was acting submissively. So she changed her ways and made a practice of entering the enclosure and going about her business there without paying her respects and without sidling around recumbent dogs. It worked. In two days Peter began to welcome her himself. She can now play with him, rolling him over, leaning on him, scratching his stomach, but she is always aware of his dingo caution and makes sure that he never feels trapped or belittled.

Dingoes do not fawn or cringe; they do not long to please as most dogs do but they take pleasure in human company and they do enjoy pleasing. The leader of Berenice's dingo colony for several years was a very fine dog called Napoleon who was very much a member of the Walters family and took all the prizes at his dog-training school. Napoleon had an absolute sense of fairness and honesty and he was accepted by all the pack as the 'alpha' male – the top dog and leader – a position he held without any need for aggression. Among the members of his human family, he would react to family stress by directing their attention to himself in order to defuse the situation. Like all dingoes, he was a cautious animal and very sensitive: if he was in the presence of someone he disliked he would quietly withdraw. (Dingoes have been tested for work with the army and the police and, though they are excellent for tracking work and obedience, they prove to be far too unaggressive for any guard work.) His sensitivity, coupled with Berenice's own sensitivity and willingness to understand, gave them a degree of mute communication which must be the envy of all dog owners and most human partners.

It is up to the human to earn a dingo's confidence, and even then it will retain its dignity, expecting your behaviour to be in accordance with its own standards. Most dingoes do not express their love in the way that dogs do, but they let their companions know in many small ways that they share mutual respect and affection – a quiet gaze, or a brief rest of a trusting chin. Even then, except in the rare case of a dog like Napoleon, a dingo will not come at your call until he is ready to do so. Nobody owns a dingo.

Napoleon loved nothing more than to sleep on Ken Walters' bed, curling there to share his body warmth. The Aborigines whom the dingo first befriended always slept with the dogs as living blankets and asked nothing more of them. There is a pleasant tradition that a group of these early Australian settlers, wearily longing for a sight of land after too long at sea in their quest for a new home (the Aborigines were the world's first seafarers), had a dingo bitch with them standing boldly at the boat's prow and it was she whose sensitive nose first told them that land was near. Another story envisages a man, his wife, his dog and the dog's wife on such a voyage. Realistically, it is hard to imagine a dingo standing boldly in a boat: it would more than likely distrust its sea-legs and go to ground under the nearest cover. Yet the stories do imply that the dingo was brought to Australia by man and, if that is the case, it must have already been at least partly domesticated. One theory suggests that those mariner dingoes were in fact New Guinea Singing Dogs but as yet no one has unearthed evidence of any dogs at all, singing or otherwise, in New Guinea earlier than fifteen hundred years ago.

N.W.G. Mackintosh, Challis Professor of Anatomy at Sidney University, has studied dingoes and puzzled over their origins for many years. His belief, supported by Aborigine mythology and art, is that the dingo arrived in Australia by sea about nine or ten thousand years ago and that it was never really domesticated or enslaved by the Aborigines but merely tolerated as a camp scavenger and dog blanket – a companion and cohabitant but not a utility dog. He claims that the dingoes were never used to help with hunting and really served no 'useful' purpose at all. He also claims that they were and are unable to be domesticated or made obedient.

That is one point of view and others (especially Mrs Walters) would argue strongly against it on many counts. For one thing, does a dog have to 'useful'? Is not that belittling the special relationship between dogs and humans? Secondly, Mrs Walters has certainly been able to train dingoes. It's a matter of taking the trouble to understand the dingo, to respect it as an individ-

ual, and to realize that, like all dogs, each one *is* an individual
and generalizations about training methods or character or
abilities simply cannot be made. Human attitudes, reactions to
and relationships with individual animals make all the difference in whether or not such relationships are 'successful', if
successful means mutual. To too many people the only successful relationship is one in which the other animal does what is
expected of it, to the benefit of its exploitive 'master'.

A book by Vero Shaw written a century ago described the
dingo, or 'Warrigal', as the native dog of Australia and said that
it was consistent in all parts of Australia except with regard to
size. It was reddish-brown in colour, with a darker shading
along the back and tail, and that tail was very like a fox's brush,
even to its white tip and the way it was carried 'floating loosely
behind' as it ran (a characteristic, incidentally, of wild canids
like the wolf). The occasional curly tail was said to betray
crossing with the local collie types that were the only European
dogs taken out to Australia in the early days. It was these dingo/
collie crosses that were considered to be the worst sheep-killers
at that time. The dingo was known for its cunning; for example,
a pair would employ the typical fox tactic of playing together
like kittens in the sight of, say, young calves, until curiosity
overcame a calf's caution and its mother's admonitions and it
wandered over to investigate. The dingoes smartly went for its
throat, either killing it or severely wounding it before the herd
came to the rescue. Then they simply withdrew until, in due
course, it was safe to claim their carcase. This tale does not ring
entirely true in the light of present knowledge, nor does it do
anything at all for the genuine nature of the dingo which Mrs
Walters is trying to show. In fact dingoes very rarely attack farm
livestock; they much prefer small game like rabbits, and most
livestock attacks are carried out by free-roaming domestic dogs.
However, dingo *crosses* can be a problem with livestock.

Even a hundred years ago, long before Mrs Walters carried
out her patient dingo training to prove that dingoes are dogs
and not vermin, it was stated in Vero Shaw's book that dingoes
were 'very easy to domesticate', but that 'their nature makes
them, if out of your sight (they will be quite good while you are
with them) untrustworthy'. They never attacked humans, how-

ever desperate, and were the bravest of fighters if attacked by a brace of Kangaroo dogs: the dingo dies fighting, and with never a whimper. Another writer of the same period, W.K. Taunton, dismissed all notions of treacherous natures: his own dingoes were always trustworthy and very handsome. Yet they had been classed as vermin even then, accused of creating havoc among the flocks. Large numbers of dingoes were destroyed annually and in some parts of Australia the native 'wild dog' was already becoming scarce.

Today the dingo is still fighting against too many years of prejudice. It is a noble dog and it deserves a great deal better than to be shot on sight by nearly every Australian in the country. Its numbers have been decimated by the widespread and deliberate use of aerially-dropped poisoned baits. How can man do that? The dingo could teach us so much.

Ironically, if men had not tried so hard to eradicate the dingo they would not have needed to introduce myxomatosis to control the all-devouring rabbits, which are the dingoes preferred prey. Rabbits are making a come-back again, but there are too few dingoes left to control them and, once again, these merry vegetarians are becoming a serious pest.

The free-spirited dingo is possibly the purest breed of domestic dog known today, surviving insulated from other dog breeds for thousands of years on its private continent, but its type can be found in many a guise among the ferals and strays of south-eastern Asia and particularly in the chain of lands from Australia to India. It seems that, given a few generations, most feral dogs will eventually resemble a dingo to some extent, if only in colour. The basenji and other African camp-following dogs are not truly feral, but they do share many of the dingo's characteristics. The real ferals include the pariahs and pye-dogs of Asia and the Middle East, the New Guinea Singing Dogs and, in America, the Indian dogs.

The New Guinea dog is useful to the Papuan natives: it can be eaten, it helps with hunting, and it is a good guard dog. Like the dingo, it runs the risk of disappearing because of random cross-breeding so that pure specimens become more and more rare, but at least it is not mercilessly persecuted like its Australian cousin. As its name implies, the dog is a howler, and it is a resident of the highlands.

The term pariah is as often as not an adjective loosely applied to dingo types and any feral domestic dog – it is generally descriptive of a way of life rather than a type of dog. The pariahs are 'useful' dogs: they are scavengers and they act as living waste-disposal units, cleaning up the debris of human communities. They are classified as untouchables, which, although the term may seem derogatory, effectively gives them a protected status. Nobody owns them. Although quite uncared for, they are unmolested and they survive by their wits in areas where people do not have enough for themselves, let alone anything to spare for a dog. 'Pariah' comes from a Tamil word identifying one of a very low caste in southern India and the interchangeable term 'pye-dog' comes from the Hindu word 'pahi', outsider.

Families of pariah dogs may have lived semi-wild for hundreds of years and they can be found all over Asia Minor and southern Asia and sometimes along the eastern Mediterranean coast. There are various types among them and some have possibly been developed into specific breeds like the Sinhala hound of Ceylon, the Thai dog and the Canaan of Israel. The Canaan has the look of a dingo and, like the dingo, it regards itself as an equal rather than a subordinate in its human family. It responds very quickly to training and seems to enjoy learning the most complicated routines and tricks. It also seems to be exclusive: a Canaan will only mate with another Canaan, and most bitches are faithful to one dog.

British people who have lived in India and Thailand tell many a story of pye-dogs. Even normally devout dog-lovers avoided the pye-dogs or pariahs just as the locals did, for the dogs, not surprisingly, were usually a sorry sight, half-starved, filthy, mangy, and there was a very real fear of rabidity. The artist D.V. Cowen tells a more encouraging tale of her time in Bangkok. She had often caught a glimpse of a cowering, skeletal, almost hairless pye-dog scurrying away from its nightly refuge under her house. (Like most local buildings, the house stood on six-foot concrete pillars to lift it out of reach of various unwelcome creepie-crawlies.) She began to put out a plateful of food for the dog in the evenings, and the plate was always empty by morning. 'After a few nights,' she recalls, 'I remained under the house until the dog arrived – but I stayed some distance from its plate of food. Its anguish was clear: food, but this alarming creature standing in sight. I called it softly and talked encouraging nonsense. The food won and over the next few evenings I moved nearer until eventually he ate while I held the plate, and there was even the faint suspicion of a tail-wag. A few hairs were starting to grow, golden brown and coarse. Then came the time when I touched him. The nervous quiver changed to delight when I stroked him, talking gently.' (Was it ever thus, with the first dogs which befriended man?)

From then on, although their relationship developed slowly, the dog's appearance changed rapidly. His coat became thick and healthy; his abject, skinny, tucked-down tail began to curve gaily over his back and to wag freely in greeting. He began to linger around the house by day as well as by night. He even submitted to a bath, though with looks of anguish and plaintive accusations of betrayal, and then, freed of a constant swarm of ticks and fleas, he raced around the garden with yelps of delight, shaking himself dry and finally standing there handsome, golden, full of well-being and – yes – pride. Thereafter he learned how to play and how to enjoy life.

Very few pariahs have such opportunities. Many of them live in burrows if they cannot find refuge under buildings. They keep near human settlements for preference and often form family packs with definite territories. A tamed pariah, if anyone has the patience to befriend it, can be a very good household watchdog.

The Thailand dogs are generally very dingo-like. Morphological comparisons by L.K. Corbett show that the Thai dogs are more similar to dingoes than to other domestic dogs, particularly in their skull characteristics, body measurements, breeding patterns, coat colour and social structures. Corbett has been on the trail of dingo-like dogs in Burma, China, Indonesia, Laos, Malaysia and the Philippines as well as Thailand, concentrating on small rural villages and adjacent beaches and hills, watching the dogs and interviewing local people about their relationships with them. In all these areas the great majority of dogs were, like the Australian dingo, various shades of ginger. In many of the populations the bitches had only one season a year and all within a well-defined period, whereas most domestic dogs show no seasonal pattern and bitches usually have two seasons a year. The Thai dogs were particularly interesting because they had remained largely pure; there are hardly any domestic dogs in rural Thailand with which they could have interbred.

Corbett also noted, from fossil bones, that prehistoric Thai canids were almost indistinguishable from their modern counterparts and that they both had affinities with wolves. His work continues, with the aim of showing that the dingo is not just an Australian dog but that its type is widespread in Asia, and indeed in Africa where the basenji is so dingo-like in many ways. It may well be that the prow-proud dingo said to have sailed with Aborigine mariners to Australia more than nine thousand years ago was in fact an Asian dog carried as food on legs: dogs were commonly eaten throughout Asia, and in the Pacific islands they were considered a delicacy rated even better than pig-meat or poultry. Or perhaps they came as guard dogs: in rural Asia many are still sought after as village guards and as hunters. Or were they of cultural importance? In Borneo today, when a man dies his dog is killed and eaten and the remains are ceremoniously buried with its dead owner's body; death is seen as a new journey, into the after-life, where a man needs to be accompanied by his dog.

So the ginger dingo-like dogs are not confined to Australia, nor even to Asia. The well-known naturalist W.H. Hudson wrote in the early years of this century about the 'Little Red Dogs' he saw sauntering self-importantly in many parts of England. His first meeting with a Little Red Dog had been in Buenos Aires – bushy tailed, foxy about the head, intensely devoted, full of self-importance, and full of cunning. 'His red colour is, indeed, the commonest hue of the common dog, or cur, wherever found.' The little red dog was common in London until the nineteenth-century muzzling laws, which led to the virtual disappearance of London's large population of curs and mongrels, the dogs of the poor which largely fended for themselves in the streets of the city, in true pariah style, scavenging, begging, tricking kind-hearted fools into giving them a meal or a bone – confidence tricksters supreme.

In Mexico the Little Red Dog was responsible for carrying men's souls to heaven, and the red dogs over whom Mowgli triumphed in Rudyard Kipling's imaginative jungle epic were the Indian dholes which turned out to be the most courageous creatures of the jungle, much braver than the other, larger animals they had to face. The dhole is a true wild dog. There are no wild dogs left in Europe now – they have been extinct for centuries – yet they linger on in legend, with ghostly packs of wild hounds racing through the night over Dartmoor or the Yorkshire wolds and in many of the wilder forests of central and northern Europe.

The Wild Dog: it fascinates not only the story-teller but also the naturalist. Indian naturalists used to class the red dhole as the 'natural hound', the 'original dog', so much more coura- geous and noble an ancestor for the domestic dog, they thought, than what they saw as the sneaking foxes, jackals, coyotes and wolves that might also claim ancestry. The dhole was even said to hunt and kill tigers, and according to Kipling a tiger will 'surrender a new kill to the dhole'. In fact, tigers so dislike the dhole that they become nervous of any dog. One Captain Williamson was shooting in India, accompanied by a spaniel which 'came to a stand over a bank, wagging its tail, with ears up, and his whole frame in a state of ecstasy'. The captain assumed the dog had found a hare but when he joined the animal on top of the bank he found himself three yards from a tiger. Made brave by his master's arrival, the spaniel gave a bark and dashed at the tiger – which fled, with the little dog in gay pursuit.

Dholes live and hunt in packs. Their highly socialized lives centre on co-operative hunting and communal care of the young. (Among dingoes, the father considers the pups to be just as much his responsibility as the mother's.) The packs are extended families, usually half a dozen or a dozen animals. Twenty would be a large pack.

Like the dingo, the dhole is severely persecuted by man. It looks something like a pariah dog, except that it carries its tail straight and low in true wild fashion. Generally dholes are red, shading to cream on the underparts, but in the Himalayas they tend to a light brownish-grey. The animal is about a yard or metre long, with a dark tail half as long again, and it weighs the same as an average border collie. It is found all over western Asia and in most of its range it is an endangered species, traditionally regarded as man's rival and enemy and now facing the added problems of habitat destruction and fast-dwindling prey populations which have been recklessly slaughtered by man (the only predator who decimates prey). Already the dhole has completely disappeared from many of its natural and traditional habitats.

It is a fairly quiet animal on the whole but it can growl, whine, snarl, howl, whimper, scream, whistle and yap. It does not practise the prolonged loud barking of a dog. The 'whistle' (easily imitated – three short toots blown across a rifle cartridge) is an assembly call.

The dhole's main prey in India is the cheetah and various deer and antelope. The pack will also chase hares, wild pigs, wild goats and sheep. Occasionally they might take domestic livestock. They prefer to eat their own kills but will take carrion as well, and they eat very quickly – it's better to gobble the meat fast than to squabble over it – bolting down chunks of meat with skin, hair and soft bones intact, all in a mouthful.

Pack hunting is adapted to prey species and terrain. It is a largely silent affair except for some excited whimpering near the end, though they do yap a little to keep in contact when working in heavy cover. They tend to disembowel the victim while it runs and they take biting hunks out of its flanks and thighs. Once the prey comes to a standstill, they continue to attack by circling it at speed, lunging from all directions and thoroughly confusing the victim into believing they are countless. They can continue this type of attack even in water: they are good swimmers and love a good wallow. Hunting is normally by day, especially early in the morning or towards evening. Like dogs, they are therefore crepuscular.

Like dogs, too, a dhole wags its tail when pleased. There is very little quarrelling in the pack, though the pups squabble while they rough-house. They are quite curious about smaller domestic dogs and will follow them, with no aggressive intent, or will even temporarily link up with pariahs for a hunt, but no cross-breeding has been recorded.

With humans, despite the endless persecution, a dhole is bold but would never attack, even in a pack, unless rabid. They eventually retreat from man but with some reluctance. In the jungle hamlets they are almost made welcome: the residents let the dogs make a kill then they drive them from it and take the meat for themselves.

A dhole cub can be tamed but it will always be shy and cringing, never really at ease, though Mr E.R.C. Davidar, a naturalist who has studied the dhole for many years, has a hand-raised cub which is very social and outgoing. However, it is easily disturbed by unfamiliar noises or activities.

The wild Cape hunting dog has been as misunderstood and maligned as the dhole but the van Lawick-Goodalls' very readable chapter in *The Innocent Killers* has helped to re-educate some people and there are several other learned studies of the animal's behaviour. It is a very gregarious species, quite widely spread throughout Africa, with certain geographically varied types. Its Latin name is *Lycaon pictus* (*lykos* is Greek for wolf) and it has very canine behaviour. It is a blotchy dog – black, brown, yellow and white splodges and random markings, with a noticeable white plume at the tip of its tail. The pack is well co-ordinated, based like the dhole on a family unit, and the dogs communicate with a variety of vocalizations – alarm barks, contact calls and a 'twitter'.

The social structure of the pack is unusual. All the males are related to each other; the females come into the pack from other families and become quite aggressive to each other once they join the pack. As a result of fights between the females, there are usually more males in the pack than females. The males make excellent uncles, willingly helping to raise any cubs that are born. There is usually only one litter a season, for only the most dominant female will be mated. If another female wants to breed, she must migrate to another pack. Thus only the 'best' female in a pack becomes a mother. When the females come into season, the arguing becomes even fiercer than usual. There is also a male dominance hierarchy but it is far more subtle than that of the females.

A pack is not exactly territorial, though it will be rather more possessive of the area around the cubs' den or burrow. Except when the cubs are very young, the dogs are largely nomadic, following the game.

Harmony in the pack is maintained by the observation of ritual procedures – a very canine (and human) method of maintaining the peace. For example, there is a ritual pre-hunt greeting ceremony with plenty of excited mouth-nudging and lip-licking between the members, accompanied by little whines, whimpers and squeals. Domestic dog owners will recognize this behaviour. It is an adult version of basic puppy behaviour: rather like young gulls, pups are fed with regurgitated food as they are weaned, and any member of the pack will happily feed the pups in this way. Those left behind to look after the pups during a hunt will also be fed, and pups and their guardians are always given first feed at a kill if they are nearby. There is often quite heated competition for the right to look after the communal pups.

The co-operative spirit is essential to the pack's successful hunting, which is done largely by sight. They tend to hunt in file, with the pack leader at the head. The first aim is to select a weak or young animal from a herd (usually impala or gazelles), separate it, and then run it out until it is overhauled. Selection is made by stalking quite openly; unlike cats, the dogs do not depend on surprise and dash but are prepared to keep on running until the prey is caught. The file formation enables fresh dogs to take over the lead when necessary, though relaying is not very common, and it also means that if the prey doubles back, changes direction or moves in a circle, dogs further down the line can quickly cut across and take up the chase. (Does this remind you of sheepdogs?) The dogs can keep up a speed of perhaps 35–40 miles an hour (60 km/hr) over a distance of three miles (five kilometres) or more, and their kill is normally achieved within half an hour of the original pre-hunt rally. They tend to give up the chase after two or three miles (four or five kilometres).

At the moment of success it is common for one dog to seize the prey by the nose or upper lip, another by its tail, while the rest of the pack rapidly disembowel the victim. Some packs will tackle animals as large as wildebeest and a few specialists will tackle zebra, but this seems to be a family tradition handed down in the pack through the generations. Being such highly socialized animals the hunting dogs are as capable of handing down ancestral knowledge as we are. They are also admirably generous within the pack and take pains to avoid contact with other packs so that friction does not arise. It seems that these highly gregarious hunting dogs have evolved a most successful way of living in harmony.

FOUR

Wild Ancestors

The dog family, the Canidae, includes jackals, coyotes, wolves and foxes as well as wild dogs and the domestic dog. Coyotes and jackals belong to the same genera (*Canis*) as wolves, dingoes and domestic dogs, but foxes are in different genera (mostly *Vulpes* and *Dusicyon*). At present there is perhaps still a little confusion about allocating the canids between genera; for example, the four wild dogs (Cape hunting dog, dhole, raccoon dog and bush dog) are each classified separately, as are the long-legged Maned wolf and others. Nonetheless, they are all canids and all have certain 'doggish' behaviour traits and physical characteristics. However, the domestic dog can only interbreed (circumstances permitting) with another member of the *Canis* genera – wolves, coyotes, dingoes and jackals, which all have the same number of chromosomes ($2n = 78$) – and in theory they can produce fertile offspring. In practice, however, although there are many known cases of domestic dogs breeding with all the *Canis* cousins, and of successful mating in captivity between wolf and coyote and between jackal and coyote, there are no known examples of wolf/jackal crosses. In the wild such crossbreeding would be very unlikely, partly because their breeding seasons do not overlap.

Dogs have also been known to interbreed with the *Dusicyon* foxes of South America, although fertility in the offspring is reduced. These foxes have slightly fewer chromosomes than the *Canis* family ($2n = 74$ to 76) but considerably more than the *Vulpes* foxes ($2n = 34$ to 40) which include our common red fox. Hence a viable mating between the local fox and your dog is most unlikely.

All members of the dog family, or at least those which have been closely studied, help each other in the care of their young.

Aunts, uncles, last year's young and various in-laws co-operate by guarding and feeding the litter, training the growing cubs or pups and generally being tolerant and encouraging towards them. In some species of carnivore, the reverse would be the case: litters are slaughtered and eaten by adults who are not the parents and even in some cases by the father or, exceptionally and under stress, the mother herself.

These canine family helpers increase the survival chances of the litter and also help to strengthen the pack bonds that are so vital to the more highly social canids like the wolf. Wolves will help care for cubs which are in no way related to them and this quite unusual magnanimity is one of the factors which has made the dog so important to man.

Unlike the wolves and wild dogs, coyotes are more often solitary than co-operative. They do sometimes form small packs, especially if last year's young have stayed on to help with the new litter, but at an early age coyotes tend to be naturally more aggressive towards each other than wolves and the most usual social unit is a breeding pair. If there is a pack, it is always a family affair and is centred on the breeding female. Unrelated loners sometimes combine for a co-operative hunt or even for company but these liaisons tend to be temporary.

Circumstances may dictate whether or not a pack is formed. If the local prey is a large herd species like deer and elk, pack hunting is more productive, but if the prey is smaller mammals, hunting is a solitary occupation and packs are unnecessary. This social elasticity enables a predator to be flexible and coyotes will eat almost anything from insects and rattlesnakes to bison, fresh meat or carrion, and plenty of fruit and grass.

The coyote, a North American species, is just about the only wild canid which is actually extending its range. Although it can be quite a serious threat to sheep farmers, it is now protected in several states and its control by hunting or trapping is regulated in most other areas. Few wild canids have those sorts of privilege.

Like other canids, coyotes indulge in a variety of group howls but the coyote's howl is not like that of its relatives. It utters a string of sharp, high yips followed by a long wail. It can also bark, and has quite a complex range of vocal communications.

There are very specific sounds between parents and young indicating messages like 'Food's ready', 'Freeze', 'Keep low', 'Hide', 'Run for it', 'Follow me', etc., and the parents are quite strict in enforcing obedience to these signals. The cubs' survival depends on it.

Calls are used to defend a territory, which is also urine-marked (another typical canid habit), but the animals only seem to be territorial in the denning season or if food supplies are short. Scent posts are visited and overmarked by other coyotes and every passer-by makes a detour to the scent posts.

Some coyote postures are clearly dog-like. An aggressive, dominant animal raises its hackles, pricks its ears, bushes out its tail (holding it horizontally rather than vertically) and snarls its lips to display its canine teeth. The unwilling object of its aggressive threat clamps its tail between its legs, keeps its head low and presses its ears back and down; it hunches, bristles and cringes but at the same time it opens its mouth wide to show a full set of teeth right back to the grinders.

Females attract a string of admirers when they are in season and seem to select whichever male is nearest at a particular moment, while the rest stand back and watch. She will copulate several times during her heat but it may not be quite as random as it seems. The 'nearest' male may in fact be the same one on every occasion – the one which has managed, by hook or by crook, to be in the right place at the right time, and it may also be that the female helps him be there. In due course other bitches become attractive and all but one of the males drift away in search of them. For the last few days of oestrus the pair are alone and the remaining male is the most likely father, even if his mate has been less than selective. They then set about the important business of choosing a territory and digging out a cubbing den, and they remain together to raise the litter. The father, like the mother, regurgitates food for the young ones as they are weaned and the pups encourage him to do so by licking and clawing at his lips. This is common to many other members of the dog family. Later, fresh carcases of mice, rabbits and other small prey are brought to the cubs by the parents.

The father plays an important role throughout, helping with the long and complicated business of education and training, assisting with feeding and grooming, moving the young to a new den if necessary, guarding them while the mother takes her turn at hunting, and he tends to remain with the family until the next breeding season when, presumably, he has the advantage of familiarity over the many new males which will court his mate. In the meantime, at least some of the pups will have set off on their own by about November or December, and only the fittest of them will survive.

Like wolves, coyotes normally consider domestic dogs to be their enemies except at breeding times. A domestic bitch on heat, or a dog which has caught the smell of a coyote bitch in season, will 'go wild' for a while and may very well mate with a coyote. Wherever coyotes are found, so too are 'coydogs' or coyote-dog crosses, most of them fertile. Coyotes do not breed with foxes, but nor do they seem to be in conflict with them like dogs. Surprisingly, coyotes get on particularly well with badgers and will even co-operate with them for rat-hunting.

As usual among the wild canids, the coyote's worst enemy is man – man with dogs, firearms, traps, poisons, motor vehicles and all the rest of his armoury. But coyotes, unlike their relatives, have managed to survive the onslaught and have even benefited from it by becoming generally bigger, faster and more clever and adaptable than ever.

Jackals, too, are persecuted and are maligned as lowly scavengers, pariah-like. The species belongs to Africa, southern Asia and south-eastern Europe and there are several different jackals – Golden, Silver-backed, Side-striped, Simien. Like other wild canids they have large, pricked ears, good running legs and straight brush tails. It is true that they are efficient scavengers but they also hunt live prey. They have interesting social behaviour which is based on pairs rather than wolflike packs.

The Golden jackal is the most common and has been more closely studied than others. Although it is also known as the Asiatic jackal, it is well distributed throughout north and east Africa, the Middle East and southern Asia. It has a foxlike face and its colouring is generally a rather dirty yellow but it varies according to locality. The van Lawick-Goodalls and H. Kruuk

have made close observations of the Golden jackal in the wild
in northern Africa, and I. Golani and A. Keller looked at specific
individuals living among the dunes on the coastal plains of
Israel.

Jackals tend to live in pairs, and certainly a pair is more
efficient in hunting than a solitary animal, although they frequently hunt alone. Like other canids, adults regurgitate food
for puppies and their mothers, and food is also stored in caches.
The diet is very varied, according to opportunity: they will eat
fruit and invertebrates as well as amphibians, snakes and other
reptiles, small mammals, and young gazelle or deer. In fact
scavenging is usually only a minor activity, except where the
animals live in proximity to man. The subjects of the study in
Israel, for instance, depended mainly on the local kibbutz's
rubbish dump, edible refuse on the beach and wild grapevines
growing on the dunes.

Jackal pairs often remain together for several years and the
initial bonding begins several months before mating takes place.
A prospective couple will indulge in mutual grooming, and
often urinate one after the other on the same spot. This type of
urination is especially common after the excitement of a chase
or a fight, and both of them may add a good scrape to disperse
their scent-marks and draw visual attention to them.

Jackal pups show early signs of individuality and a dominant
animal is already apparent by the time of weaning. Dominance
is expressed by 'body-slamming' – a hefty thwack at a lesser
jackal. The first signs of real aggression among the pups become
apparent soon after weaning and by the age of four months
their rough play can easily end in fighting. Female pups often
stay with the parents and act as helpers with next year's litter.

A submissive jackal, in typical canid fashion, will crouch,
undulating its body, flattening its ears and perhaps wagging its
tail. Quite often a third jackal will tag along with a pair but a
paired female may not tolerate potential rivals. She will slam
them with her hindquarters, spinning on her front legs as she
does so. The loser slinks off, tail between legs. Aggressive
animals raise their hackles and pucker their mouths in a snarl,
much like any other canid, but if the subject of the aggression
pretends to be disinterested – looking away or sniffing the

ground – the situation seems to be defused and both animals ignore each other. The same result usually occurs if one of them exhibits submissive behaviour like a drooping tail, flattened ears and drawn-back lips, or lies on its side with its tail wagging furiously. Again, the behaviour is very dog-like.

Jackals also enjoy a good howl together and the howl tends to go through phases, starting with a long and continuous monotone, then an undulating howl, then a series of staccato sounds. Young animals or helpers will join a pair's howl but usually remain seated and only contribute to the third phase, at a high pitch.

The most interesting and misunderstood of all the canids is the wolf. Once upon a time, wolves were spread over an enormous geographical range in a variety of sizes, adapting to all kinds of ecological circumstances. But all over the world wolves have been persecuted and maligned even more than the wild dogs and the jackals and coyotes. Recently, however, close studies of wolf behaviour have revealed what the American Indians and the Eskimos have always known: the wolf is an animal which deserves considerable admiration, both as an individual and as an example of social organization and harmony.

The first myth which needs to be destroyed is that wolves attack people – all those lonely travellers trembling in the dark, wild forests. They do not, unless they are rabid. In fact many cases have been reported of wolves doing no harm at all to men who are injured and alone in the wilderness, however hungry or numerous the wolves might be. They are curious about man, certainly, and keep him under close observation, which might be somewhat unnerving, but they wish him no harm at all and do not attack him, although, being sensible opportunists, they will eat a human corpse, like any other carrion. Even a trapped wolf often submits quietly to the hunter and the Eskimos tell stories of how easy it is for a man to go right into the den of a wolf and remove a cub while the parents stand back and watch with sad resignation at the betrayal. There is a contract between wolf and man, but man breaks it – man, the only species which sets out to eradicate other species and other races, a creature so at conflict with itself that it cannot live in harmony with life but causes all living creatures to flee.

For centuries it is the wolf, not man, which has been portrayed as evil – the ominous grey shadow, yellow eyes gleaming in the night, slinking among the trees and devouring men, women and children. Werewolves, and the big bad wolf who persecuted three little pigs and nearly ate up Little Red Riding-hood, are entirely false images of the wolf. The Freudian aspects of the stories make it clear that these 'wolves' were human. What has the wolf done to earn man's fear and loathing?

Rabies is one of the major culprits. A rabid animal – be it wolf, dog or human – will attack anything in its sheer terror. Britain is now well protected from rabies, thanks to the very strict controls on animal importation, but every now and again cases are reported of people who have been bitten by a rabid animal abroad and returned home to die. In 1986 a woman died of rabies in Sussex after being bitten by a dog in Africa; and ten years previously a chef, bitten by a dog while he was visiting Bangladesh, died in a Manchester hospital. It is a very terrible death and during the inevitable course of the disease human beings act exactly like rabid wolves: they are terrified of water, they foam at the mouth, they bark hysterically and howl, they attack and bite people, and their frenzied strength is unbelievable. It is almost as if they have truly become wild animals – frenzied wild animals out of control, mad, uninhibited, vicious and extremely dangerous, acting completely out of character. They behave like werewolves, or rabid wolves, but not like wolves.

Rabies is caused by a virus which attacks the entire nervous system and destroys brain cells and sanity before it kills. Towards the end of the sixteenth century there was a dramatic epidemic of rabies in wolves and in men which brought terror, agonizing death, rampant superstition and tragedy to a wide area of France, Germany and central Europe. According to Andrew Allen's article 'Rabies and the werewolves of old' in *The Field* of 18 June 1983, a hundred thousand people were burned on mass bonfires because they were 'werewolves': they not only acted like rabid wolves but they really believed themselves to be wolves, and they roamed the countryside howling, foaming at the mouth, breaking into cottages and attacking and eating people.

Rabies in man is known to generate hysteria in unaffected contacts who can develop all the symptoms of rabies purely through fear of it, even to death. As if the combination of actual and psychological rabies victims was not enough, it is now believed that another frenzied agent was at work in sixteenth-century Europe. For half a century the continent was in the grip of a 'little Ice Age' of bitter winters and miserable summers. All over Europe the wheatcrops rotted in the fields, year after year, and black rye bread had to become a staple food. But the succession of wet, cold seasons had provided an ideal breeding ground for rye ergot, a fungus (*Claviceps purpurea*) which, unwittingly devoured by the people along with their daily bread, led to hallucinations, delirium and a burning gangrene known as St Anthony's Fire. This epidemic enormously exaggerated the already terrifying effects of rabies, and the 'werewolves' ran riot. By 1590, real wolves began to come right into the towns, eating people alive. No one knew whether they were wolves or human werewolves, but they were certainly rabid.

Those years were only a peak of the fear. The wolf had long before been victimized by man: the two species were similar and in competition with each other. Ever since the Great Ice Ages wolves had hunted the same prey, rather more efficiently than man; they had a highly developed social structure and a degree of plasticity that only man could equal. Both were powerful predators, with excellent social organizations and sophisticated means of communication, and with greater intellectual powers than any other species, although man was always ahead on that score. The wolf had the advantage of a wonderful sense of smell, speed, pack technique – natural weapons with which to succeed in hunting – and strong, bone-crushing jaws with which to make the most of any carcase. Man, on the other hand, had the better eyesight, adroit hands, a greater ability to plan ahead. Wolves, however, are excellent learners: one experience can be enough to teach them a lesson for life and they may use such lessons to modify their subsequent behaviour. They are quite capable, too, of acting with purpose, making plans and working out problems with insight.

At first, when men were few, widely scattered and nomadic, there was no rivalry between wolf and man. Indeed, wolves could benefit from man's inability to eat every scrap of a carcase and men could learn from the wolves' hunting tactics of driving prey into inescapable situations. Even in more recent times the early buffalo hunters who wrought such havoc among the great herds of North America had nothing but respect for the wolves and accepted the packs that trailed with them. Nor did the Eskimo resent or fear the wolf; it was not seen as a rival predator until the white man brought along all his phobias and superstitions and placed a bounty on the head of the wolf. Before that, Eskimo hunters viewed the wolf with admiration and without animosity, impressed particularly by its intelligence and the success of wolf society. They also pointed out that no one can generalize about 'the wolf'. Every wolf is an individual character, both physically and in temperament and skills, reacting in different ways according to different situations and pressures.

Most 'scientific' studies of wolves have necessarily involved captive animals, where the territorial restrictions, the lack of free interaction with others of their kind and the enforced proximity to humans may well give rise to misleading observations and interpretations. However, there are those such as Greg Tah-Kloma, a young Chimmesyan Indian college graduate in British Columbia, who have lived alone for very long periods in the wilds where they have been accepted by local wolves. By combining their observations with those of trained ecologists, animal behaviourists and zoo or reserve personnel, a clearer picture emerges of the beautifully complex, subtle structure of wolf society. From it one gains greater insight into the mind and ways of that domesticated wolf, the dog.

Female wolves are ready to mate at two years old but males will not do so until they are three, which means that they are that much stronger and more mature as partners and fathers. The females come into season only once a year, and pairing usually begins a month or two before this late winter oestrus. Once mated, wolves are monogamous but they do not mate until the pair has a breeding territory. Without a territory, a wolf remains celibate but is still a welcome member of the 'family'. Widowed wolves tend to live out the rest of their lives as celibates.

In the restricted context of captivity, there is considerable fighting within the pack at pairing time. If pairs cannot move away to establish a territory of their own for breeding, only the dominant male and dominant female will mate and this right is naturally strongly contested.

In the wild, subordinate pairs normally leave the pack to den and may become separated from the main group if local food is scarce and the pack has to travel to find prey, in which case the parents stay with their litter and provide for the young by catching smaller prey. If food is abundant, however, the whole pack will remain in the area and may help in providing for the new cubs. When winter approaches, the supply of easily caught young prey animals is less and less reliable and the wolves need to hunt in packs again, and at that stage a separated family may travel to rejoin its original pack or may form a new family pack of its own.

An average wolf litter might number perhaps five or six cubs, depending on factors like population pressures, health, local climate, food supplies, etc. The young are born in a den, excavated with great industry and forethought by the mother. She often chooses a natural lintel such as a root or rock at the entrance and then tunnels in a considerable distance, sometimes dog-legging the route to give greater protection from the elements and possible predators. Secondary tunnels act as escape routes in case of danger or cave-ins. At the heart is the whelping chamber.

The young remain underground for about a month after birth, as blind and helpless at first as any dog puppies and dependent on their mother's milk. Her mate brings her food and, as the cubs grow older, both parents feed them regurgitated meat. Gradually they emerge from the den and gradually they extend their range from it, during which time various aunts and uncles often take their turn looking after the litter. It is in the first two months of their lives that the major pack bonds are formed: the family unit automatically becomes the nucleus of the pack, and the pack is the essence of wolf society. It is an extended family – very human.

Wolves are rarely alone. From the moment of conception they share a uterus, and then the den, with their litter-mates, and most wolves will be part of a pack or at least of a pair for most of their lives. There are lone wolves – outcasts at the bottom of the pecking order, perhaps aging, once-dominant wolves ousted by a fitter rival, or more often temporarily single young males who have left their family pack to seek a territory and a mate – but even the loners often tag on to a pack, although keeping their distance.

The size of the pack varies during the year and according to available prey and terrain. Within it there is a particularly dominant wolf – either male or female – and there is also a ranking order between males on the one hand and females on the other. The strength of the leader's personality often dictates the stability of the pack. Many packs are only loosely affiliated but a very dominant animal, which has proved itself to be of value as a wise leader, may well keep the group together much of the year, especially in game-rich areas, and those who leave at whelping time tend to den fairly centrally and rejoin the pack later. Such a leader, effectively a benign dictator, may well be mimicked by the rest of the pack who react to its every mood and decision with alacrity. A strong leader will also prevent serious fighting within the pack in the way that a mother controls her squabbling cubs. A real fight is rarely necessary since the rules of behaviour are so sophisticated. The social language of wolves covers every nuance of feeling and intention, and to ensure appropriate social behaviour, not even a glance is necessary from a strong leader: its will and mood can be conveyed very clearly by subtle body language which will be read instantly and correctly by even the most insensitive wolf in the pack. Appeasement is an important contribution to general harmony and a harmonious pack will be more successful in its two main concerns – hunting, and raising the young.

A good leader is not necessarily the strongest or largest animal but the one which is the best organizer, with the most cunning and the confidence to expect respect. Leaders are chosen for personality not brute strength, something which dog owners and trainers might well bear in mind. Berenice Walters, observing her dingoes, reports a situation which would be typical of a wolf pack. When the dingo leader, Napoleon, died suddenly from a snakebite, the whole group immediately became distressed and insecure. They badly needed a leader. Then his aging mother, Dora, took charge. She came into the house, went straight to the spot where Napoleon had died and, with what Mrs Walters describes as 'quiet resignation', bent down and rubbed her cheek and neck where he had rested. Mrs Walters continues: 'Then, with great dignity, her eyes and deportment mirroring the tragic loss of a highly respected leader, and the enormous responsibility that was now thrust upon her, she straightened up and slowly, with resignation, walked outside, head and tail up, ears hard pricked. The eyes of every dog were focussed on her.'

Dora was aged, frail, arthritic and almost toothless but she was accepted by the entire pack as their new leader. They submitted to her authoritative manner instantly, although they could not have feared her physically. Even the big, aggressive cattle-dogs acknowledged her and gave her their complete loyalty. The slightest hint of a growl or a curling lip was enough to drop them in their tracks.

In a captive wolf pack the dominance patterns are more exaggerated than in the wild. Erik Zimen, of West German's Bayerischer Wald national park, found that an individual wolf's status was constantly changing in subtle ways. Very broadly, there were separate social ladders for males and for females, with a dominant 'alpha' male and 'alpha' female at the top of each ladder, and these two alpha wolves were the only breeding partners. There was little or no serious aggressive behaviour between the sexes; on the whole all the non-alpha males were friendly and submissive to the alpha female, and likewise the females to the alpha male. All the wolves were friendly to cubs, and vice versa, and the cubs were generally friendly with each other. The friction points occurred between wolves of the same sex, particularly where the current pecking order was challenged and particularly near the mating season.

The wolf pack's social structure is dynamic, constantly being adjusted, sometimes imperceptibly, sometimes more blatantly. An individual wolf is always tempering its relationships with every other member of the pack and such adjustments can be influenced by the season of the year, increasing maturity of the individual, or some purely personal chemistry of like or dislike – a very human characteristic. There are also alliances between friends and one may well defend another who is being threatened.

Among such social animals, play is as important a part of daily life as is the serious business of hunting. Through play the animals get to know each other and for co-operative hunting packs this familiarity is essential. Each member needs to know how other members are likely to react in different situations, what their particular skills are and how dependable they are as hunting associates.

In a typical play activity the leader will seize an object – a bone, a piece of meat, a stick – and will bound around holding it high in the air and teasing every member of the pack with it. There is plenty of mock chasing but no one tries to seize the trophy and when it is finally dropped by the leader it is forgotten. The whole ceremony is a reforging of pack bonds. The same performance takes place among dingoes and among tamed wolves.

Wolves are excellent communicators and very aware of the tiniest innuendo in their colleagues' behaviour. Like the Cape hunting dogs, wolves perform elaborate and loving greeting rituals but not only as a hunting preliminary. The greetings are exuberant whenever pack members meet each other, even after only a short separation. Again, every dog owner will recognize the behaviour: tails wag enthusiastically, a forepaw is put on a friend's neck, two animals will rear up with paws on each other's shoulders, licking each other's lips (and the same treatment is given by a wolf to a favourite human). All this is usually followed by a bout of play, leaping away from each other in a good-humoured game of chase-me-Charlie. Wolves have a great sense of fun and it is not unknown for them to play practical jokes on each other.

They use a wide range of sounds, movements and stances to communicate with each other, with some of the most subtle conversations conducted by mutterings and squeaks at frequencies almost inaudible to a human. There is a great variety of tone to cover every possible situation – the leader's instructions to the pack (attack, retreat, assemble, disperse and so on) or the conveyance of pleasure, sadness, affection, rejection, agreement, disagreement, friendship, antipathy, acceptance and gratitude. Wolves can express a full range of emotions, from fear and jealousy to joy and contentment, through all sorts of whines, whimpers, growls, snarls, yelps and occasional single gruff barks – although they do not use barking as dogs do to express so many messages. Perhaps dogs have learned that humans, being less subtle in their understanding of animal language, need the more obvious messages of barking.

A common signal is chomping the teeth. This is usually a sharp warning if the mouth is open, but if the lips are closed and the chomp is muffled, it is a signal of greeting. Most characteristic and emotive of all is the chorus of howling in which each wolf sings at a different pitch. The howl is another vital unifying ritual, used to re-establish contact in the pack, to gather before a hunt or to advertise the pack's presence to other wolves in the vicinity so that confrontations are avoided. Interpack squabbling is not sought and, given the chance, packs will quietly slip away from each other. Scent-marking, largely by the leader, reinforces other packs' avoidance of the area.

Body language gives even more dimension to communication, with the added advantage of being recognizable at some distance. Strong signals include crouching, flexing the knee joints, flicking an ear (a backward flick during a stalk might mean 'Wait – don't move', to those who are following, for example), tongue flicking, lifting the front lip, tensing the back, raising hackles, holding the tail high in dominance or low in submission, or wagging it in anticipation. Muzzles are wrinkled as 'smiles' of pleasure. Like a dog, a wolf often yawns if it is embarrassed. The eyes, too, are expressive: the degree to which the lids are open or closed conveys a message to another wolf. Only the bold will stare, for example. Bared teeth are normally a threat but it depends on the posture of the lips. A dominant threatener puckers his upper lip so that the canine teeth are exposed – an expression which some call the 'small-mouth threat' and which is seen in other canids. An animal which is to some degree frightened or is submissive will open its mouth

quite wide and use more facial muscles so that all its teeth are
exposed.

When a pair of wolves seek to join a pack, they will typically
meet first with the leader. The newcomers will approach very
cautiously, with their tails, ears and bodies held low as if they
were trying to reduce their size. The leader, alive with dominance, stands tall with head and tail high, hackles slightly
raised along the neck (but not the spine – that is a sign of fear),
mouth closed, and a deep hum in its throat. At perhaps 10 feet
(3 metres) apart – wolves have individual 'approach' territories –
all three animals will raise their tails and emit a highly personal
musk from the anal glands, easily sensed by wolves but barely
perceptible to humans. This is both a friendly greeting and a
confirmation of personal identity: 'This is who I am, and I come
in friendship.'

The leader, hackles still up, takes the initiative and checks the
smell of the saliva around the newcomers' lips and the scent of
their excretory organs before it allows a reciprocal sniff-over.
There is plenty of urinating and checking. Then the dominant
animal will probably snarl, quite viciously, at the wolf of its
own sex. The appropriate response is for the pair to show total,
instant submission, rolling on their backs to expose their vulnerable bellies while the leader stalks around them on stiff legs.
This very dog-like behaviour is also enacted between wolves of
different packs but since wolves are so adept at social reaction,
it is very rare indeed for any actual fighting to take place: an
intruder will slip away in an apologetic, submissive crouch.

If, after the initial meeting, the pair are allowed to join the
pack, the leader does nothing to prevent other members from
attacking and harrassing them until they are firmly established
near the bottom of the pecking order and are absorbed into the
everyday scheme of things. Such a scene may be re-enacted
several times in late summer, when mated couples return to the
pack, often with their own litters. The hierarchy must be
readjusted each time but in a well-established pack old levels
are quickly resumed. The cubs will have been training for pack
duties all summer, learning how to track and stalk, practising
vigilance, becoming familiar with smells of all kinds and learning how to kill. (Captive wolf cubs have to be taught to kill by

their human captors – a very difficult task; it is not an innate impulse or skill.) After they join the bigger pack they begin to learn about social niceties, about teamwork in hunting and what their particular roles will be. The hunt is a classic example of disciplined co-operation and in its early stages it is like that of other pack canids. There is a similar excited rallying once the prey has been located – plenty of gossiping and licking and general friendly excitement and encouragement, tails well up and everybody ready for the action. They set off in single file; the leader is not necessarily in the van but its tail is the only one fully raised and the pack knows who is in charge.

The sense of hearing is more important during the hunt than the sense of smell. Also, a wolf's binocular vision is poor and they therefore lack a good sense of perspective; nor can they identify detail at a distance. Although their eyesight is good enough for hunting in open country, in the forests hearing and smell are much more useful.

The first task of the pack is to choose a likely victim and separate it from the herd. Wolves are more likely to 'go for the jugular' when they close in, rather than bite hunks out of thighs and bellies, though if the prey is large the aim will be to hamstring it to make it more manageable – a technique used for centuries by Afghan hounds and salukis coursing in pairs.

After the kill the pack gorges and each member takes food back to the cubs and mothers left at the dens, some to be regurgitated and some to be buried in caches near the den. Unlike foxes, wolves only kill to eat and never simply for sport.

There was a time when the wolf was found almost world-wide, in every climate and on every terrain, exploiting the widest variety of ecological niches, just like man. Today there are only two species of wolf – the large gray or timber wolf (*Canis lupus*) of the north and the endangered red wolf (*C. rufus*) of the south-eastern United States. The gray wolf includes many subspecies suited to different regions of the northern hemisphere, from the large, shaggy tundra wolves to the small, light wolves of the deserts and steppes. Wolves became extinct in Britain two centuries ago but they are still to be found, in greatly reduced, and reducing, numbers, in some of the forests of eastern Europe, the wildernesses of North America and Asia, and a few mountainous and desert refuges in the Mediterranean area and the Middle East.

And they are still to be found, many believe, in the domestic dog, *Canis familiaris*, which some call *Canis lupus familiaris*. It is strange that wolves and dogs do not seem to recognize their affinity. They will mate – and husky bitches in the northern world are sometimes given every opportunity to mate with a wild wolf by owners who value the pups of such a cross – but a wolf is likely to attack and eat a dog (though they can live together quite amicably in captivity) and dogs are readily trained to kill wolves. Yet a wolf would rarely attack another wolf or a human being. Perhaps the wolf feels more on a level with man than with dogs. Wolves, like dingoes, consider themselves to be man's equal and would have been his friend if man had allowed it.

FIVE

Dog Meets Dog

What about the social behaviour of domestic dogs, then? The wild canids seem to have certain characteristics in common, be they wolf, jackal, coyote or wild dog. Does the everyday mutt exhibit similar traits? Or has domesticity changed all that?

Watch two dogs, particularly two strange males, meeting for the first time on neutral territory. If they spot each other from a distance they may pause. They might even crouch, or drop right to the ground, as if observing and stalking prey. A dog which feels it is intruding might finally approach with his head averted, ears down and eyes almost closed (a direct gaze can be taken as a threat). Such a dog might then become apparently playful, coming close to the resident dog and then suddenly leaping up in the air. The intentions are friendly. Or the dog dropped to the ground might wait while the other approaches slowly, halting now and then and wondering at the creature that has flattened itself. Once upon a time that drop might have served a useful purpose: it was concealment from prey or from an animal whose intentions towards it were uncertain. Now it is a formality, a convention. As C.J. Cornish put it in *Animals at Work and Play*: 'It is not polite for one dog to omit the form of pretending that the other is a big, strong, important person, against whom he must take precautions. A breach of canine etiquette might, and sometimes does, lead to a fight.'

Or the dogs might march slowly and deliberately towards each other, stiff-legged, heads up, ears up, tails up, hackles rising, standing even taller as they draw near. By the time they meet the air will be electric with tension. They stand alongside each other, nose to tail, almost quivering, their tails perhaps slightly and stiffly waving at the tip, perhaps a low muttering in the throat developing into a snarl, with ears going back like a bad-tempered horse and lips curled to show off a fang. In this situation, if neither dog relaxes or shows signs of submission, there is very likely to be a fight – a great deal of noise, furious sounds of snapping, snarling threats, and, probably, very little actual physical damage other than a torn ear and a wet scruff. They will go for each other's neck and shoulders, trying to dodge the other's snapping teeth and aiming to get a good hold so that the rival cannot bite back. The intention may be to force the opponent to the ground (gaining a submission like any Black Belt or wrestler) but fights rarely reach this stage. Humans usually intervene anyway and often it is tension in human companions which sparks off the fight. However, breeding makes a difference: a terrier fight, for example, is usually serious and can be to the death. Sheepdogs are bred to threaten rather than actually attack so a serious fight is less likely. Hounds are least likely to fight of all: they are bred for kennel life, where peace needs to be kept; also those droopy ears and flews are too easy targets.

A real fight is far less common between wolves than between domestic dogs because of the pack structure and the careful avoidance of confrontation between packs. Every wolf in the pack knows every other wolf and it usually takes just a curl of the lip and a stiff, upright stance to encourage a subordinate into a submissive posture. If there is a fight, it will be preceded by stiff-legged behaviour very like that of dogs, with the tail-tip wag, growling, snarling, etc., but in the actual fight the wolves tend to dart in and out, slamming against each other with their hindquarters, and they go for each other's legs rather than scruff when they use their teeth. Sometimes a dominant wolf, having already persuaded a subordinate to roll over submissively, may pin it to the ground and perhaps even put his jaws round its throat, though without doing any harm.

Two dogs which know each other and have therefore begun to sort out their relationship will, like the wolves, react according to that relationship. They may simply growl and move apart if they can do so, though on leads or on a narrow path this can be awkward. Or the more self-assured dog will growl and place its forepaw on the back of the other, which keeps its tail and head down to avoid provocation or may roll on its back with puppy-like yelps and little play snaps while the top dog stands over it. All the canids, including dogs, show submission by reverting to puppy behaviour – crouching, sitting, rolling on the back, yelping; the intention is to appeal to the more dominant dog's natural tolerance of puppies.

Dominance between dogs is not necessarily governed by size and physical strength. Like the wolf, a dog can retain its higher position by force of personality and skill. Many terriers are, by their very natures, self-willed and determined, and seem to have little thought for their size. Even a tiny Yorkie will do its best to boss a large German shepherd or a Great Dane. The bigger dogs are often nonplussed by such behaviour, for the small creature looks like a puppy but certainly does not behave like one. The larger dog experiences conflict: it would not seriously threaten a puppy (though too bumptious a youngster will be quietly put in its place and would immediately become excessively submissive, trying to lick the adult around the lips to stimulate regurgitation). A small, aggressive terrier, however, has no intention of showing such meek reactions and it also has the advantage that it can easily get under the bigger dog's feet. It is quite common to see a large, normally dominant dog looking totally bewildered in such a situation and almost seeming to lose sight of the cheeky little creature that is presuming to stand its ground so cockily and yapping so infuriatingly. And of course the terrier, if not put in its place, is that much more confident at the next meeting. In the world of the dog, outward appearances are nothing. You are as big as you believe.

Another submissive gesture common to the canids is tucking the tail between the hindlegs. This effectively masks the glands that issue an animal's personal smell, and the gesture is almost a denial of self-existence. The sense of smell, of course, plays an important role in canine social behaviour and scent-marking with urine and faeces is practised to some degree by most of them. Males in particular choose to urinate against vertical markers – the traditional lamppost of the city dog, or trees, rocks, bushes, grass tussocks and old carcases in a more natural setting. Such posts are also used for defecating (some choose the most uncomfortable positions poised over a thistle, for example) and dogs, like wolves and jackals, often scratch near their marker, which draws attention to it. The very act of leg-cocking by a male is a good long-distance signal: other dogs can see from a long way off that he *is* a male, and the more exaggerated his lift the more dominant a dog he is likely to be.

Leader wolves mark out the family territory around the den by topping up urination points on their boundaries. Other wolves will respect these territorial limits. The Indian Greg Tah-Kloma, who was befriended by a huge female pack leader, realized that she had accepted him when she made a point of urinating in his camp-site, covering most of his personal belongings with her personal smell so that the rest of the pack could accept his presence but would also understand that only she was allowed to be his friend. Farley Mowat, in his book *Never Cry Wolf*, described how he camped in the Canadian Arctic within the territory of a wolf family with the intention of studying and befriending them. He was ignored and as an experiment Mowat, after drinking plenty of tea, marked the boundaries of his own camp, an area of about three acres – it took him all night. The resident male wolf returned from a hunting trip and immediately discovered the new boundary. He checked the markers carefully but, being generous in the manner of wolves, he acceded the claim and calmly urinated along the outside edge of the site to re-delineate his own territory. Note that he did not overmark Mowat's contributions. A dog would have automatically overmarked and so would a jackal. For example, dogs, especially males, being exercised in a park investigate every possible scent-marker and overmark it with their own urine. It is a great incentive to leg-cocking. But the park is no single dog's exclusive territory and scent-marking in this context is more a matter of 'Dog was here' than 'This belongs to Dog'. Many pet dogs will 'beat the bounds' last thing at night in their own gardens by scent-marking the territory with a few well-placed leaks.

Some say that a complex message can be read into scent-marks and it is true that they reveal the marker's personal identity, sex and oestral state, and there is probably some indication of mood, health and diet as well, but there are other ways of communicating more complex messages. For example, two familiar dogs meet quite briefly on a walk with their respective owners. They may only touch muzzles, no more, but an assignation has been made. An hour later each dog slips quietly away from home and they meet up for a few hours of hunting, scavenging or simply meandering about the countryside like a couple of schoolchildren playing hooky. Some dog owners firmly believe that their animals keep a diary: 'Tuesday – meet that spaniel under the old oak, noon,' 'Thursday, meet Fred Terrier behind the barn for ratting.'

Communication is an essential skill among animals that live sociably. The wolf pack, as we have seen, communicates in numerous ways – body language, vocal sounds, smells and so on – and this is vital to co-ordinated hunting, which is organized down to the last detail. Certain members specialize in locating the prey herd; others take responsibility for moving the herd in a controlled way, either to drive it into an ambush or to select weaker animals and separate them from the protection of the crowd so that they can be run down by good runners and finally attacked by the killers. The herding part of the hunt requires considerable skill, understanding of prey psychology and co-operation between the herders – qualities which can be seen in good working collies under the guidance of a shepherd who knows his sheep and dogs.

The aim of the hunt, whatever its social niceties and value in forging pack bonds, is to acquire food. Food is a serious affair for any animal, on four legs or two, but quite apart from its practical value in keeping a creature alive it also adds dimension to its social life. When a hunt is successful, wolves usually gorge themselves to repletion and carry rations back to the dens. They cache a certain amount of fresh food near the den in regular hiding places so that nursing mothers or cub guards can help themselves when they need it, and they also react to real or pseudo begging behaviour, by cubs or other submissive wolves, who nuzzle their muzzles and lick at their lips and the corners of their mouths to encourage regurgitation of food.

Although originally such gestures were for the sake of survival, i.e. nutrition, they developed into ritual activities which indicated friendship and submission. Two dingoes on good terms with each other indulge in plenty of such nuzzling. Dogs do, too, with each other (especially if mating) and also, in a

more displaced way, with humans. Dogs very naturally lick
people's faces and tame wolves often stand on their hindlegs,
paws on a human's shoulders, and 'kiss' with their tongues.
Licking is also part of grooming and some of the canids (though
not often dogs) indulge in mutual grooming sessions, nibbling
and licking each other especially around the muzzle and ears.

Another food-related ritual in dogs is bone burying, reminis-
cent of the wolf's meat cache. Occasionally a dog will remember
to unbury a bone as well! A burial spot is carefully chosen,
preferably unwatched; the dog half-cringes with the bone in its
mouth, looking around to see if it is being observed. It digs out
a suitable hole (a compost heap is ideal), then covers the bone
by pushing earth over it with its nose – exactly the method used
by a wolf with its cache. If a crow or similar bird goes anywhere
near a dog's bone, even if it is flying overhead quite innocently,
the dog will hackle, growl and bark it away much as any jackal
or wild dog would swear at vultures. Even a town pet can
recognize a carrion competitor in feathers.

A wolf returning from the hunt will carry quite large trophies
back to the den – perhaps half a leg of deer – and it characteristically holds its head and tail high as it bears the unwieldy
burden, rolling its eyes to see who is watching. The posture
may be the most practical way of carrying a cumbersome trophy
for some distance but it looks boastful and jaunty, and the
behaviour is echoed in the way a pack leader struts around the
pack with an object in its mouth – be it meat, bone, stick or, in
a 'tamed' pack, any object it can steal from the house. Lois
Crisler, who kept wolves in a very large enclosure in the United
States, was on particularly good terms with the female pack
leader, who had daily access to the Crislers' cabin. It was the
wolf's joy to seize an item – perhaps a cushion, a rubber glove,
a dishcloth – then scamper out to the enclosure with her head
and tail up, and flaunt the trophy at every member of the pack.
A general game of tag would ensue during this morning ritual
but no other animal would grab the object nor touch it once it
had been discarded at the end of the game. The ritual seemed
to serve as a reminder of who was the leader, and the game of
chase, like all play, served to reinforce the pack bonds.

Dogs, too, love to parade in this way with a seized trophy,

none prouder than the homeward-bound mongrel carrying its master's walking-stick and negotiating its unwieldy length carefully through the gateway, head up, tail high and eyes gay. The errand dog is not now such a common sight but they too had that same proud stance as they carried a basketful of goods home from the village shop, defying all the street curs to seize it from them and divide the spoils. The way they bore the basket made it plain that they were inviolate and not even the most aggressive bully would attempt to snatch the prize. Meat, bread and purse full of change always arrived home safely.

Possession of an item like a bone often alters the relationship between two dogs momentarily. If a more lowly dog already owns a bone, a more dominant dog does not grab it from him nor does the owner act submissively and yield it as one might expect. If the other dog approaches too close, overstepping the invisible 'distance territory', the possessor may react quite aggressively. But a 'neutral' bone will automatically be ceded to the more dominant dog.

Pack behaviour in domestic dogs is most obvious among kennelled hounds. They sleep all in a heap; they join together in dawn howls, especially on the morning of a meet (very wolf); they hunt as a unit; they behave much more distantly towards humans; they abuse a newcomer with almost unacceptable persecution. Like wolves, if one dog does something, everyone else tends to join in as well, be it lying down, running, stretching or whatever.

Despite their unnatural confinement, hounds do not often fight each other, at least not seriously, which is partly because they manage to sort out hound to hound relationships much as wolves do and partly because they have been selectively bred for their ability to kennel amicably. No huntsman wants to work with quarrellers. Moreover, the physical appearance of the hound reduces the risk of fighting: its long, dropped ears and flabby flews are easy targets for a pair of determined jaws, and hounds, on the whole, are not masochists. Of course – and it bears constant repeating – every dog, like every wolf, is an individual and it is dangerous to generalize even within a breed.

Kennel managers normally keep male and female hounds separate so that mating can be controlled, a practice which reduces any quarrelling that could arise from pairing competition. Wild canids, dingoes and basenjis have only one season a year but domestic dogs have two and they start mating earlier too. Whereas a female wolf is two years old before she breeds, a domestic bitch can mate at a year old. In theory, a bitch allowed to mate freely could be responsible for anything up to twenty thousand descendants in her lifetime.

Kennel bitches are given private quarters for whelping and, like any other bitch, they may make a gesture at nesting. If a house bitch is given the most desirable whelping box you can conceive, she will often still have a good scrabble at its base to make it more comfortable for her pups. She has been deprived of the chance of digging out her own secret den but she can still give it the finishing touches.

Wolf cubs, and those of all the wild canids, are born in dark, secret places where they tend to hide for the first few weeks. A puppy also has the urge to find a dark refuge and a pup which has been taken away from its mother and its familiar surroundings to make a new life in a new home deserves a warm, dark place in which to hide while it comes to terms with all the alarming changes in its life.

Cubs go through their period of maximum social bonding while they are still in the depths of the den. After the first week or two their mother begins to leave them alone to go off for a hunt or simply to stretch her legs or refresh herself with adult company, and the cubs have very little contact with other adults at this early stage. It is now that a new pack begins to develop. The cubs are socializing almost entirely with each other and the bonds are formed.

John Scott and John Fuller closely studied and compared breeds of dogs over several years, and reported in their book *Genetics and the Social Behaviour of the Dog* that puppies, too, are most susceptible to social contact at a very early age. They are born blind and completely deaf, with only a very limited sense of smell but a good sense of taste and sharp reactions to cold and pain. They are primarily tactile (even taste relies on touch to begin with – you can't taste milk unless your tongue is in contact with it). The new puppies live haphazardly; they have limited mobility and seem to rely on chance bumping them up against those vital nipples.

Only when the eyes open does life take on more dimensions. On average (but depending on the breed) pups open their eyes by about the thirteenth day and suddenly the puppy becomes a highly adaptable creature. During the following week or two everything begins to happen rather fast. Teeth begin to come through by perhaps the twentieth day; the tail wags a little (cocker spaniels' tails earlier than other breeds, and thereafter they never stop!); the pup becomes aware of its littermates as individuals and begins to form relationships with them. Development is rapid and this is a crucial period in the puppy's education about living with others, that is, being part of a pack.

The bitch, left to her own devices, weans her pups when they are between seven and ten weeks old. Like the wolf she will, if left to herself, regurgitate her own food for the pups, but more often than not her owner intervenes to provide puppy-food which, as far as the bitch is concerned, is just the same as other adult wolves in the pack regurgitating for the pups.

During the weaning period pups learn to use definite places for defecation (the nest itself is never soiled because the bitch herself keeps it clean) and they are stimulated to use these places by the smell of previous defecations – early scent-posts. House-training a puppy should therefore be a simple matter. It will hold tight if confined to its 'nest' overnight (which in fairness should be a very short night). Up to about twelve weeks old it may want to defecate or urinate as often as every couple of hours while it is awake, and the understanding human will anticipate its needs and lead it to an appropriate place in good time, particularly immediately after a meal.

At twelve to fourteen weeks old a kennel puppy will begin to venture away from the 'den'. By fourteen weeks it has virtually determined its behaviour patterns for life and if it has not been used to frequent contact with humans it will tend to be nervous and shy. A puppy kept with its littermates will not bother much with vocalizing but a puppy alone in a strange environment will yelp with increasing frequency up to the age of about seven weeks; thereafter it quietens down until by twelve weeks it is quite quiet even in a strange place. However, at younger than about seven weeks it does not seem to mind being in a new locality. It seems that six or seven weeks is a crucial period when new situations cause great distress.

A young cub or puppy in the wild would be in serious trouble if it found itself alone or away from the familiar den – no wonder it yells for help. Also, being a litter animal, isolation is a terrifying experience and even adult dogs often bark endlessly if they are shut up alone. Given company, human or otherwise (even a friendly pony or a chicken perhaps), the dog will quieten down. Dogs essentially need company, just as wolves do.

A three-week-old puppy is prepared to investigate, with due caution, a human being who sits quietly near its nest. If the person keeps quite still, imposing no threat, the pup will have a good exploratory sniff with its rapidly developing sense of smell and will possibly wag its tail with pleasure. It will also check out any new object in much the same way, human or not (the pleasure is not in recognition of humans). A moving person is a different matter: sudden movements or noises can cause considerable alarm and indeed the mother encourages these reactions because a frightened puppy can take avoiding action in the face of potential danger.

If a puppy is handled regularly from an early age (say three weeks) it quickly becomes reassured and loses its fear of humans but the older a puppy is on initial contact, the greater and more long-lasting its fear. The wild instincts, even after ten thousand years, are not far beneath the surface. Fourteen-week-old puppies reared in their own paddock without any human contact are almost like wild creatures: they show extreme fear of people and will not approach them voluntarily even after a week or two. They can be forced into some kind of tameness by being kept enclosed without means of escape and fed only by hand so that they cannot avoid human contact. Puppies which are isolated from all contact, human or canine, become so emotionally disturbed that they freeze when finally introduced: they do not even try to run away but are abject in their terror.

From the many experiments carried out by Scott and Fuller, it seems that a puppy's crucial period for forming social relationships other than with its suckling mother is from about three or four weeks old. If a puppy has no regular and affectionate contact with humans during this socialization period, there is a possibility that it will never be able to form a good bond with people. If it is isolated from its own kind too early, then it will become entirely humanized and will always have difficulty in forming relationships with other dogs. Ideally a dog needs to be able to get on with both humans and dogs and it needs the opportunity to form ties with both species during the critical socialization perioid. Such relationships, or the ability to form them, will then be lasting.

The next critical period is at six to seven weeks old when the puppy develops a strong sense of place and becomes very attached to familiar surroundings. Any move elsewhere is likely to be quite traumatic at that stage but the phase passes and weakens.

Of course all these timings are average; they vary between breeds and between individuals. The major universal fact seems to be that dogs, like wolves, are highly sociable animals. They constantly react to other dogs, and people, and they react even more strongly to the absence of other dogs or people. Dogs are natural companions: they cannot be understood in isolation because their behaviour is based on reactions to others. They need company, even if it is only for squabbling with.

The husky dogs of Greenland, for example, live in 'packs' where some very wolflike behaviour can be seen and also some behaviour which is more doggish. In the early 1930s the well-known naturalist Niko Tinbergen spent some time in the Arctic and observed the huskies. It was their pack behaviour that he found most interesting.

He noted that within each pack, i.e. team of dogs belonging to a particular hunter, there were continual arguments but the pack had its own territory and all members of the pack, except youngsters, forgot their arguments and joined forces to defend it against other packs. Within the territory, individual pack members were free to go where they pleased; they did not have their own areas. They wrangled constantly among themselves over other matters, reaffirming social rank at every opportunity. The leader was usually a strong male who had a favourite bitch as his second in command, and woe betide any careless dog who came between them in the team. He was completely dominant in the pack and all other dogs conceded to him at the merest hint of a growl or a frown. At the bottom of the pecking order there was a wretched creature which kept its distance from the rest and seemed to live in abject terror of them all. Wolf packs always have a scapegoat of this kind, on which any wolf can vent its annoyance, and in the domestic dog it can happen that an animal walked in the park, for example, is regularly abused by all other dogs, although he seems to have done nothing to deserve such treatment. His submissiveness increases with every attack and his owner's trepidation at such incidents enhances his scapegoat role. It can become so unpleasant for dog and owner that they walk only in areas where they do not meet other dogs, which cannot help the dog to re-establish its confidence. Owners have been known to try other remedies in desperation, such as dowsing their dog liberally with an unpleasant smell to mask its own personal scent and thus, they hope, escape detection for a while until its confidence is regained. However, in all aspects of its life a dog that has once been conditioned to fail is very difficult to motivate to achieve success.

Scapegoats are often particularly willing to befriend humans; perhaps the first domestic dogs were scapegoats rejected by their packs. Yet even the scapegoat joins the rest of the pack against strange dogs in defence of the communal territory and will be allowed to do so, whether wolf or husky.

Tinbergen noticed with some amusement the way neighbouring husky packs behaved. At a mutual boundary there was no attacking but the males, especially the respective leaders, would growl and very deliberately cock a leg to scent-mark the boundary. Unless one side or the other wantonly trespassed, there was no fighting and the general feeling was of enjoyable tension. At times this became so unbearable for the strutting pack leaders that they found relief by taking it out on the nearest lowly member of their own pack – acting very like an irritable human kicking the cat. This displaced action occurs in many other species: I watched a squirrel lunge at a tame pheasant which had persistently tried to get near some peanuts spread on the ground in my garden; startled and offended, the pheasant backed off and happened to espy a harmless moorhen lurking nearby on which it took out its offended pride by promptly sending it scuttling off.

On the whole the husky packs respected each other's territories and relative peace was maintained but occasionally there would be a real transgression. Tinbergen's group upset the status quo a little because they had a refuse dump by their camp. A neighbouring dog could not resist the occasional raid, coming across furtively with much glancing over its shoulder and evidence of guilt, with a submissive companion in tow. If they were spotted by the resident dogs the culprits would flee; there would be a chase, in complete silence until the intruders had reached their own territory and then they would start yapping like yard-dogs challenging passers-by. The affronted pack would remain on its side of the boundary, shouting back defiantly. The more dominant of the intruders, to regain face after this ignoble retreat, would then turn on the underling, whose offended yelping would excite every pack in the village until there was a general collective howling session involving every dog in earshot.

In the humanly defined restrictions of husky society, the pack's territories were small because their food supply was ensured by the Eskimos and was on the whole adequate. The dogs did not need space in which to hunt, but in most species food naturally affects the size of a territory. A wolf pack's hunting range may cover many square miles in areas where game is less than abundant and generally only one pack hunts in a range. It is thought that both boundary scent-marking and howling serve to keep neighbouring packs apart so that confrontation and competition are avoided. Like the huskies, wolves do not intrude into neighbouring territories and they always prefer avoidance to conflict.

The young huskies, however, did not seem to be aware of territorial limits for the early months of their lives. As pups they tended to remain close to their mothers and therefore within the pack's area but as they become more independent they seemed to wander where they pleased. If they happened to be trespassing they were chased off, yelping, but they never seemed to learn from experience. However, they did learn eventually and, in the case of male pups, very abruptly. Tinbergen took particular notice of two males which matured at about eight months old and became interested in bitches. Within a week of coming of age, the young huskies suddenly began to join the pack in territorial defence and they equally suddenly stopped trespassing. The urge and ability to mate seemed to coincide with their recognition of pack territory and their graduation as active members of the pack.

It is much the same with the average pet dog. Sexual maturity brings about several behavioural changes. A bitch matures almost overnight, and sometimes as young as six months old (depending on breed, climate and other factors). One day she is just another young dog, and the next she is a female in oestrus for the first time and finds that her relationships suddenly change. Males who accepted her as just one of the pack yesterday now find her irresistible and she, too, begins to become interested in them. For a young male, the change into puberty is more gradual. He may have begun to take a very active interest in oestral bitches from the age of perhaps four months old but he is not at that stage physically capable of satisfying his instincts. At the same age he begins to cock his leg a little, every now and then. He begins to sniff the air for bitches and may start wandering in search of them during the next few months. He becomes more possessive about his home territory and more positive in his relationship with other dogs and people. Gradually he becomes more sure of himself: his leg-lift gets more emphatic and by perhaps eight months old he is probably capable of a fertile mating, though he has not yet acquired the social maturity to be a successful suitor. He is like an adolescent entering a new and uncertain world where there is much to be challenged. His voice 'breaks' and his bark deepens.

Barking is a very doggish means of communication. No other canid has developed barking so extensively. Wolves, jackals and coyotes may yap now and then, or give an occasional gruff and monosyllabic bark. Basenjis never bark and dingoes do so infrequently but none of them practise the stringing together of a sequence of barking sounds in the manner of dogs. Wolves, jackals and dingoes can, however, learn to bark continually in the presence of dogs. The main point of the reiterated barking of dogs is to alert the dog's pack, to let other members (usually human) know that something unidentified or strange needs investigating by somebody. It is also used to advertise a dog's loneliness or general disquiet, and to proclaim its territory and dissuade intruders from entry. A bark is very much a signal of presence – here I am, come and join me if you are my pack but keep away if you are not – and it locates the barker precisely, whereas some other canine sounds can be quite elusive and almost ventriloquial. The baying of hounds is more akin to yelping and howling, and generally serves as a means of communication during the hunt, enabling members to keep in contact with each other and with the development of the chase. Many sight-hunting dog breeds, however, hunt silently.

Barking has probably been encouraged in dogs for centuries in their important role as vigilantes. It is also a sign of timidity and in a wolf pack it would be the most timid member who would be the most alert to potential danger, real or imaginary, and would let the rest of the pack know about it. Barking is a reversion to puppylike behaviour and in wild species barking is more common in the cubs than in adults.

There are many ways in which the domestic dog seems to have been bred selectively for characteristics which would ensure its early death in the wild. Basically dogs can be considered as puppies which have never really grown up. For humans, they are indeed perpetual children and you can often see the parental mistakes which have affected the behaviour of a family's children reflected in the behaviour of the family dog.

SIX

Only Human

'He's almost human!' Many a dog owner has made such a claim and many do indeed regard their dogs as human companions, perhaps as substitutes for children who have grown up and moved away, or were never born. Many treat their dogs as equals in the home, sharing food, sleeping accommodation and conversation. Others recognize 'human' emotions and behaviour in their dogs and marvel at the similarities.

Sir William Beach Thomas was prompted by 'a life-time bettered by the companionship of dogs' to write a perceptive and good-natured book called *The Way of a Dog* in the final chapter of which he draws astute parallels between the development of children and of puppies. He found striking similarities in the way the minds of both species work. For example, a dog accumulates knowledge by association of ideas, in much the same way as a child learns about language. Puppies learn entirely by trial and error and if the trial leads to a rewarding or pleasurable result, the experience is remembered and the method will be repeated for similar situations or problems. Like people, whatever a dog learns when it is young, whether positive or negative, it will remember.

Dog-training is really a series of problem-solving but the dog, like the child, does not let the problem interfere with the situation. As Beach Thomas puts it, 'The inferences are instinctive – that is, immediate – and the end is reached without distracting thoughts about the means. Neither the child nor the dog . . . knows why or how it knows.' The minds of young children and dogs are not cluttered up with the human adult's overwhelming attic rubbish of reasoning, logic, pessimistic anticipation and other intellectual boobytraps which somehow get between man and his goals. There is a classic cartoon by

Murray Ball whose Great Palaeolithic Hero, Stanley, is confronted by an obstacle, a substantial rock. He pauses to 'apply man's powers of logic to the problem!' and while he is considering whether to push it aside, hack his way through it or tunnel under it, his dog walks past him in a straight line, makes a minor detour around the rock and continues on his purposeful way. 'We do not progress by side-stepping the problem' yells Stanley. 'What problem?' wonders the dog.

For a dog, a problem is solved within a context: it is strongly associated with place. Many people are only too familiar with the frustration of a dog which is perfectly obedient at the training school, or retrieves without a flaw in back-garden sessions, but becomes a total failure when asked to show off its skills in another setting (which is sometimes due more to the dog's sense of humour than to stupidity). Animal psychologist Dr Roger Mugford, a specialist in helping people with 'problem' dogs, was brought two terriers which insisted on chasing people in the park and were quite uncontrollable if they spotted a jogger in the distance. In a field behind Mugford's consulting rooms, he and several helpers play-acted the part of innocent park strollers and joggers but they carried plastic bags full of water. As soon as the dogs pursued them, the actors dropped their harmless water bombs and the dogs received a wet surprise. After three experiences the dogs could not even be cajoled into investigating strangers across the field. However, they had only learned a lesson that within that particular field they would get soaked if they chased people; the lesson was not relevant to the park until they received similar experiences in that more familiar environment.

Learning is a clear process of stimulus/response/reinforcement. The trained dog receives a command (stimulus); if it reacts appropriately (response), it is praised (reinforcement). The aim of a trainer is to try to shape a dog's responses by encouraging something which approaches the desired response. If he understands dogs, he will anticipate the animal's likely natural reactions and behaviour and will seek to manipulate that behaviour. The art of education, after all, is to nurture and direct natural abilities rather than to impose alien behaviour. It is noticeable that a very dominant trainer gets earlier results but a more co-operative attitude brings results which actually last. It is also true that dogs respond much better to training which is fun, and their owners get a great deal more pleasure from working with a relaxed trainer than with an authoritarian martinet who yanks at the choke-chain at every opportunity. A few dogs do need to be dominated but, bearing in mind that the human is usually seen as the dog's pack leader, personality is more important than physical chastisement.

It is very rarely necessary, or beneficial, to punish a dog physically: best results come from an unexpectedly firm vocal reprimand accompanied by a glare. No dog needs hitting but sometimes, if there has been intentional disobedience and you are sure it is not simply a misunderstanding, the best reprimand is to assume a severe face (and mean it – no play-acting) and, taking the dog by the loose skin on either side of his neck, give him a brief shake that lifts his forefeet off the ground. That will make him feel like a guilty puppy. However, a dog does have a sense of personal pride and dignity, and it is unfair to make him lose face in front of others unless it is absolutely necessary. Respect the dog.

The problem is that too many people simply do not understand the true nature of their dogs, however well meaning both parties might be. It is, as Gerald Hammond wrote in *The Abominable Dog*, a problem of 'communications between two minds of vastly different wavelength but arguably comparable intellect'. Hammond's parents had an Airedale which (typical wolf) was always protective with children and had rescued several from drowning. He could not resist helping a child but, as soon as any human being reached adolescence, however well the dog knew them as children, he saw them as instant adults, a species which he hated with a venom and frequently bit. Hammond, cherished by the dog when he was a child, very suddenly found himself its enemy simply because he grew up. There came a time when a judge had to decide whether the dog's child-rescuing record was enough to outweigh its adult-biting record.

Another Airedale, Muggs, which belonged to James Thurber's mother, was equally famous for biting people. According to Thurber, every Christmas his mother would send boxes of chocolates to the dog's victims and the list grew to forty names during Muggs's eleven years of life. However, he was terrified of thunderstorms and could be distracted from attacking people by the rattle of a tin sheet which Thurber's mother kept behind the sofa.

Young children, dogs and most other creatures have senses which are far more acute and finely tuned than those of adult humans, who have come to depend more on their powers of thought and use of verbal language than on their instincts. As Sir William Beach Thomas so charmingly puts it, some children 'can hear a fly walk along a window pane, can smell a bee's sting, and see stars by daylight'. Children's senses are more acute not only because age has not yet caused physical deterioration but also because the senses are fully exercised – they have not yet been dulled by the preference for relying on the mind.

So it is with the dog. Most of the dog's senses are more acute than a human's and it makes full use of them. In the wild, those senses are vital to survival. The ears of the wolf are large, upright and mobile, and all the canids can hear frequencies that are beyond the range of the human ear. For example, most humans cannot perceive sounds at more than 20,000 cycles per second whereas dogs can certainly hear a sound at 35,000 cps and possibly as high as 70,000 or even 100,000 cps. Dogs are also very adept at locating the exact source of a sound; their ears move independently and can be adjusted to focus on the source and pinpoint it by a sort of triangulation technique. (A human has to turn the head from side to side because human ears are resolutely immobile and we therefore only vaguely know where a sound is coming from.) As well as this precise pinpointing, a dog can hear more than a quarter of a mile away a sound which a human could only hear within a hundred yards or so.

An aging springer spaniel, which had become deaf in one ear, partially deaf in the other, and was losing his sight, was quite capable of following any rabbit that crossed his path by using his nose, as he always had for game. However, he had difficulty in finding his master again, and in response to shouting and whistling tended to head off in the wrong direction because he was no longer able to pinpoint the source of what had become a rather faint sound. From the habit of a lifetime, he still tried to see and hear his master rather than drop his nose to the ground and make a cast until he found his trail. Once he had learned to accept his failing hearing and sight, he was able to trust his nose instead.

The dog's sense of smell is almost unimaginably more powerful than a human's – something like forty times better. Dogs have perhaps two hundred million olfactory cells, compared with a human's five million, and on top of that their sensitivity to smells is hugely better developed. Tracker dogs often follow the smell of human sweat (and a frightened or tense man exudes more sweat and also spices it with the smell of adrenalin, which even the most pampered family pet would recognize immediately) and an average dog would be able to detect the smell of just one gram of sweat even if it had evaporated into three hundred feet of airspace spread above the full extent of a sizeable city. A hungry dog has an even sharper sense of smell.

A dog's eyesight is also different to a human's in some major respects. There are general similarities in that both species have eyes typically placed for a predator, facing forwards, which gives a better sense of depth. The eyes of prey species are placed to the sides of the head, giving better all-round vision. However, some breeds of dog have a quite wide field of vision; for example in greyhounds it approaches something like 270 degrees (70 more than in a human), although a greyhound's field of *binocular* vision is about half that of a human (around 70 degrees compared with 140 in humans). A blunt-nosed breed like a Pekingese or bulldog is a little better, at about 80 degrees for binocular vision. Thus dogs are generally better at catching a glimpse of something out of the corner of their eye than we are but not so good at determining how far away it is.

Judgement of distance is a skill that depends on the efficiency of an animal's stereoscopic vision and mental interpretation of what it sees, which determines the degree to which an object is perceived as three-dimensional. The world looks generally flatter to a dog than it does to a human.

Nor is a dog as capable of quick re-focusing. The human eye can adjust its focus so quickly that we do not notice the difference when looking up from a close object to scan a distant horizon. It seems that in ground-living mammals this ability is linked with the animal's dexterity in using its paws (hands) to grasp objects. The focusing characteristic is measured in diopters and a capacity of one diopter means that the animal can see clearly up to one metre. Dogs have a capacity of one diopter; rabbits, which do not use their forepaws as adroitly as clumsy dogs, register nil on the diopter scale, whereas cats range from 3.5 to 11.5 diopters. Expert manipulators and builders like beavers and otters are top of the scale, excluding primates and man.

The majority of wild animals, including wolves, are generally far-sighted but domestication literally narrows their horizons and domesticated animals and birds are often near-sighted, especially if they are confined in hutches or pens. They have lost the need, and therefore the ability, to focus their eyes on distant horizons.

In general, dogs are good at identifying basic shapes but are not very good on detail within the form. Nocturnal creatures rely on movement for visual identification and detail is not important to them; but if an object moves very quickly against a static background a nocturnal creature would not be able to see it.

Something like sixty per cent of all carnivorous species are active at night and have adequate night vision. Eyes which are well developed for seeing in minimal light are less capable (or incapable) of discerning colour and this conflict of needs is apparent in crepuscular creatures, i.e. those which are most active during the twilight hours at dawn and dusk. Feral dogs and wolves tend to be crepuscular in their habits, but domestic dogs have adjusted to human ways of life. You can still see evidence of the dog's crepuscular ancestry if its eyes are caught in the light of a torch or car headlights at night, when they usually give a luminous greenish-yellow reflection. The eyes of nocturnal animals have a layer of mirror-like cells (to increase light-gathering capacities) and this layer glows in the dark. The colour of the reflection varies in different species and sometimes in different subspecies.

Dogs are thought to be dichromat, that is, partially colour-blind. Researches continue but it is probable that a dog can distinguish colours in the blue (short) wavelengths very well and also to some extent yellows, but is quite unable to recognize greens, which appear to a dog as colourless or white, or reds which generally look dark brown. Many other mammals share this colour limitation and it is also the most common form of colour-blindness in humans.

In humans and in dogs the perception of colour deteriorates as the amount of light decreases. At night, vision depends on contrasts of brightness and a nocturnal animal has a different perception of brightness from coloured sources. For example, to the normal human eye a yellow flower petal seems to be brighter and lighter than the green stem and leaves, but to a creature that is only active after dark the flower looks less bright than the leaves, and a red flower is virtually invisible.

In general, then, the dog has less visual range than humans. Its colour vision is probably limited, as is its perception of depth and detail, but it is good at perceiving form and shape, and has better night vision than we do. By day or by night, a sight-hunting dog is chasing the movement of the bobbing white scut of a rabbit or a deer and does not perceive a detailed image of its prey.

Some years ago an article in *The Field* tried to convey how a human might appear to a young puppy and the accompanying pictures showed how alarming such an apparition could be. The basic argument was that the eye of the dog acted like a fish-eye lens on a camera so that an approaching hand rapidly grew very large as it came near (a fly has the same sensation). A standing man towering above a puppy seems to have enormous feet and the rest of his elongated body tapers away to a small, distant head which suddenly looms large as the man leans forward or crouches down to talk to the pup. If this theory is right, no wonder some puppies retreat from human beings!

With so many differences between the senses of dogs and humans, perhaps it is little wonder that we often fail to understand dogs. They live in a different sensory world. We tend to forget that a dog's view of life is very different from our own and we also forget that dogs rely to different degrees on their various senses.

It is for the similarities between dogs and humans that we choose to share our lives with dogs, regardless of the differences. Domestication has encouraged those similarities, especially in physical appearance: dogs have been 'humanized'. For companions many people choose dogs with long, floppy ears hanging down the side of the head like tresses of hair, or dogs with short muzzles and rounded faces, which are far more human than wolfish. The King Charles spaniel with its soft, wavy ears, blunted muzzle and large, adoring eyes is the perfect lapdog, made more so by its small size. A wolf is definitely not cuddly and would never stoop to being a lapdog; like the dingo, it has far too much sense of its own worth and equality to fawn like a dog. As Lois Crisler puts it in her book *Captive Wild*: 'Dogs are no substitute for wolves. Wolves are clear, uncomplicated; they're your *equals*. They have no doggish cuteness but great sweetness. They're not depending, seeking, asking, needing. They're free, clear, intelligent – strong and on their own inside. Friends.'

Dogs, especially today, are encouraged to be 'cute' and dependent. Humans have made sure that they are so; they have reduced their size and vigour, they have dwarfed them in every dimension, they have crippled their legs into bandy, stumpy, babylike props, they have squashed their faces so that some are forced to snuffle and puff, they have even chopped off their tails so that dogs are more like tailless human beings. We have not yet managed to turn dogs into two-legged animals like ourselves but we do teach them to beg, reared up uncomfortably on their hind legs and deprived of their dignity, looking like toddlers taking their first faltering steps.

These developments of the dog are all quite recent. Selective breeding has altered the physical features of dogs so that it is often hard to believe that they have anything at all in common with their lupine ancestors. Fortunately we have not yet totally destroyed their heritage and there is much that is genuinely human-like in the original, basic, wild dog, the recognition of which has made the relationship between the species potentially so good.

Dogs live naturally in packs, which are extended families, just like human tribes. Within the pack, even within a single litter, dogs come in a wide variety of characters, skills and physical abilities, as humans do. Diversity is an outstanding feature of both species.

The pack is a subtle and sophisticated social organization, full of inhibitions against violence, living within very strict codes of behaviour, depending on co-operation (not coercion) in everything from hunting to rearing the young and providing for the mothers. The pack defends its homeland against invaders and looks to leaders, as we do (whether head of family, head of tribe, head of state or god). Leaders are, on the whole, respected, sometimes feared, sometimes loved, and often copied and humoured, and the success and harmony of the pack, with its endless permutations of personalities, depends on a combination of good leadership, wise delegation of duties, recognition of interpersonal relationships and individuality, and the ability of every member to communicate with and understand every other member. Like humans, dogs use an enormous variety of gestures, attitudes, looks and vocalizations to express their feelings and wishes, and every animal needs to have the sensitivity to understand this complex code which makes social living possible and desirable. As social species, humans and dogs are well matched and can recognize each other's social organizations.

Because of their communicative adroitness, dogs are eager to understand the humans around them and do so a great deal better than we understand them. They watch our body language closely and put more reliance on it than on other verbal or overt communications. Like children, dogs are alert to every undercurrent, every nuance, every mood, however veiled. They watch our faces; they watch our eyes and our mouths. A famous turn-of-the-century dog, Jock of the Bushveld, would watch Sir Percy Fitzpatrick's face constantly and, should the man roll over, the dog would reposition itself so that it could still see his face. The huge silver wolf which accepted the Indian Gregory

Tah-Kloma (described in *Queen Wolf* by Robert Franklin Leslie) communicated with him to a large extent through eye contact and would look for long moments into his face in times of greatest emotion and mutual understanding.

Many animals will not look a person in the eye but dogs have learned all the tricks of the soulful gaze, although they, like any other animal including humans, can be greatly discomfited by a steady stare. A stare is too close to a glare, and a glare is a threat. The cat almost hypnotizes its prey with unblinking eyes; a sheepdog holds the flock with its steady 'eye'; a wolf stares aggressively at a rival or subdues a subordinate with a steady stare. British postmen, who must be the most bitten sector of human society, receive very little advice on how to handle aggressive dogs other than: 'Don't look the dog in the eye; look at the ground, stand very still, and then retreat, very slowly, backwards.' A dog which gives the postman a silent stare means business more seriously than the one which barks itself into a frenzy; trained police and army dogs, knowing they are winners, attack without any warning sound at all, silent and deadly. A human stare accompanied by vocal reprimand (like an emphatic 'Ach!') is all that most dogs need by way of reproach.

Aggressors and protectors apart, most dogs take pleasure in human company if the humans take the trouble to be on an appropriate wavelength and learn to read the dog as well as the dog can read them. The artist D.V. Cowen often kept bull terriers which, as a breed, can be a little untrustworthy with strangers, whom they fear. She tells of a particularly nervous dog which always disappeared behind a sofa if a stranger came to the house. A woman arrived one day and, before she could be warned of the dog's liability to bite, had swept it into her arms and made such an immediate fuss of it that the dog forgot to be alarmed and thought it had known her all its life. Its owner then realized that, despite its history of taking nips at guests, it was probably preferable not to warn newcomers because their own apprehension would be sensed by the dog, which would instantly flee or attack. Most dogs attack through fear, just like humans.

Dogs are capable of sharing many other human emotions.

They have a greater sense of humour than most animals and a tremendous sense of fun. Play is the essence of dog life and it is also the essence of a good relationship between dogs and humans. The owner who cannot remember how to play is depriving the dog of a vital element in the relationship. Play includes uninhibited physical romping (for those who are physically able) and also a stimulating variation in voice tone.

Dogs are quite capable of enjoying a good laugh at their own instigation. Some sixty years ago, at a frontier post in southern Sudan, there was a long-tailed, leggy mongrel known as Tiger because of his black-striped, olive brown coat. Tiger was popular with everyone on the station but, like many soldiering dogs, he belonged to no one in particular. He appointed himself certain duties such as supervising the mounting of the guards, checking that the sentries were at their posts, keeping a sergeant-majorly eye on the men at drill, and generally helping any fatigue party he could find. His most important duty, however, took place every morning as the bugler of the Sudanese detachment sounded the reveille. The mongrel would seat himself a yard or two away, throw back his head, and give tongue to a prolonged, discordant howl. Once the bugler had finished his performance, the dog would cease his howl, have a brief scratch and head for the kitchens.

A new station commander, H. Channer, soon grew exasperated at the hideous morning duet and ordered that steps should be taken to prevent it. Dutifully, the men hurled a few sticks, boots and anything else to hand if their commander happened to be in sight, but the dog knew well enough that it was only a game and he did not falter a single note of his howl until the day that Channer himself hurled a heavy marching boot with more serious aim. Tiger yelped with indignation and scrambled off on three legs into the long grass, more offended than physically hurt. He disappeared for several days, to the dismay of the entire detachment, including its commander. But he then returned accompanied by a podgy little bitch who was of a local breed much esteemed by the Nyam Nyam tribesmen as a table delicacy.

The very next morning both dogs assembled with the bugler and both lifted their voices in a full-hearted howl. Tiger, enjoying his double revenge, cast a mischievous look at the commander out of the corner of his eye while he howled and the bugler, in mid-reveille, collapsed with laughter. The joke was shared with relish by every Sudanese on the station. Tiger was a born actor. He savoured his moment of glory and then, with great dignity and at a leisurely pace, escorted his lady to the kitchens for an extra large bone. He had won, conclusively.

Otto was another army dog, a dachshund who belonged to an English brigadier in command of a Ghurka regiment in northern India. The dog had lost one eye (a golfer had inadvertently scored a direct hit when Otto was chasing a jackal across the course) but this never deterred him from pursuing the family cats. He always turned his blind eye to them so that they had nothing to scratch. Otto accompanied the brigadier every morning on his inspection duty, taking it upon himself to march well in advance of his master. One day the brigadier was ill but Otto was not a dog to neglect his duty. He set off self-confidently and fooled every man on the post into lining up and jumping smartly to attention, with not a brigadier in sight to warrant their respect. Otto thoroughly enjoyed himself.

A small Jack Russell developed a passion for lettuce and would bark himself into a frenzy of excitement when someone prepared a salad for lunch. He knew what he was doing: lettuce, eaten in any quantity, is in fact a soporofic – a drug! The terrier showed his playful side when his master went down to the allotment and worked methodically down a row dibbing in his lettuce seedlings, while the little dog equally methodically worked along the row behind him, digging them up again.

In another case, a couple of British expatriates were farming on Vancouver Island, where they had a white Welsh terrier as a house dog and a brown spaniel which was kept outside. Every evening, just after the family had finished its meat course at dinner, they would hear the spaniel barking at the front gate, followed immediately by the house terrier. One day they asked their Chinese servant what it was all about. 'Ah,' he said, 'that brown dog heap smart dog. You see, every night when you finish your meat I put two plates outside the kitchen door with scraps on them for the dogs. That brown dog he eat his dinner very quick – he look see small dog not finish yet – he run front gate bark – small dog think someone come and he run front gate and bark too – brown dog he come round other side of house and eat little dog's dinner!'

W.H. Hudson tells a similar tale of artful deception in London at the turn of the century. The hero was one of those little red dogs that Hudson had seen in so many parts of the world, the poor man's cur. One winter morning in Regent Street a skinny, scruffy lurcher was gnawing a large, stolen bone on the pavement, just by Peter Robinson's store. A small red dog, trotting busily along the pavement from Piccadilly Circus, caught sight of the lurcher and froze in a low, bristling crouch, watching for several moments. Then he suddenly rushed back towards the Circus, barking excitedly. The lurcher leaped to its feet to investigate, barking wildly as well as he chased after the little dog and passing him by in his hurry to discover the cause of the excitement. The small red liar immediately doubled back, picked up the bone and disappeared, grinning all over his face.

The nineteenth-century writer C.J. Cornish, who liked to study the ways and emotions of all vertebrates, decided that 'humour in its most developed form is possessed by dogs alone among the animals; and that they have acquired the faculty partly from man'. He was careful to point out that, as with humans, not all dogs have a sense of humour and he told with relish a few stories of serious, down-to-earth working dogs which had to be persuaded to relax their dignity and join their masters in various improper escapades. Such dogs were quite bemused at the antics of their humans; not understanding this uncharacteristically playful behaviour, they strongly suspected they were being ridiculed. Many dogs take offence if they are laughed at; they dislike being made to look foolish. Indeed Edward Mayhew, in his book *Dogs: Their Management* (published in 1854), said that dogs were not only far more intelligent than most people gave them credit for but that they also had enormous pride; they could not endure laughter against themselves and 'rather than have their dignity offended, dogs will quickly become honest, especially when deceit is experienced to be of no avail'.

Life is not all laughter and dogs are equally capable of feeling and sharing sadness, depression and grief. They are highly attuned to their owners' moods and will be very sensitive and sympathetic to hidden sadness, giving comfort with the gentle touch of a friendly nose or paw. They can also experience deep sadness, despair and grief themselves. The famous tale of Greyfriars Bobby is a classic example of a faithful dog grieving for a dead master. The original story was published in the *Ayrshire Express* in 1865:

Nearly six years ago a terrier dog was found lying under a horizontal grave-stone in Old Greyfriars' grave-yard in Edinburgh. The poor brute had evidently been there some days, and, although exhausted with hunger and thirst, viciously refused to be removed. It was coaxed with milk and other canine luxuries, and through the kindness and attention of the gravediggers was soon in a position to run about; but it resolutely refused to leave the kirkyard. There had been a number of funerals from the country for some days prior to that on which the dog was observed, and it was believed that the dog's master had been among the number laid under the sod; but whither it came no one could tell. From that day to this 'Bob', for such is the name he gets, has remained in Greyfriars' Kirkyard. He sleeps in it every night, and spends most of his time in it during the day. During the inclement winter the year before last, Sergeant Scott, of the Royal Engineers, one of Bob's best friends, got him coaxed into his house for a night or two; but the dog was evidently unhappy, and soon returned to his quiet quarters under the tombstone. Bob got to know the Sergeant's dinner hours to a minute. With military precision he would meet him at George IV Bridge at a certain hour each day, go home with him, and share his dinner. In the afternoon, when Sergeant Scott prepared to return to the office, Bob would give him a 'Scotch convoy' a short distance past Greyfriars, give a farewell wag or two with his tail, and trot away back to the graveyard . . .

Forty years later there was a letter in *The Field* entitled 'Grief in Dogs' in which two examples were related. The first story was of a black Newfoundland bitch, very much a household pet and so docile with children that 'she would lie on the hearth rug, and allow the infant to amuse itself by punching her with the prongs of an old table fork without so much as a growl'. For some reason, the dog was sold to a new owner, who decided it was best to chain her up for a while to prevent her from returning to the old beloved home. The combination of this treatment and what seemed like rejection by her previous owners had a disastrous effect. When her original mistress visited her a few weeks later the bitch had turned quite grey and seemed to have completely lost her senses.

The second story was about a toy black-and-tan terrier which was 'foolishly petted, even to the extent of being allowed to sleep with his master and mistress'. The little dog became ill and, much against the wife's advice, was sent away to a local dog doctor for treatment. Within the week the broken-hearted terrier died, waiting only for a visit by its owner who was given 'a last sad look' from the betrayed pet. The writer continued: 'He was taken away for stuffing, when it was discovered that the hair of the head in that short time turned partially grey.' (It was then the fashion to stuff a favourite pet, just as today in California people have been known to freeze-dry their dead lapdogs and instal them on cushions in the living room.)

The correspondent goes on to remark that he had often seen dejected dog patients in veterinary infirmaries and that he considered it cruel to send household pets away from home for treatment. A cure was more likely to be effected, he suggested, if the dog remained at home surrounded by familiar faces and routines, with the vet paying occasional visits. 'This would be much more successful than constant attention in hospital by strangers, who, as well, occasionally find it desirable to apply the whip to stop their howling.' Many human patients today also feel that home treatment is preferable to the most elaborate and sophisticated hospital ward – yet another parallel between people and dogs. The writer of that letter back in 1898 concluded: 'Perhaps none of what we call the lower animals except the dog absolutely suffers from grief, as the word applies to man. That the dog does so grieve, I do not think anyone who understands him can well doubt.'

C.J. Cornish, writing about the same time, said that a grieving dog was in one way superior to a grieving human. The dog would keep its sense of proportion, would never make sorrow cheap by wasting it on trifles, and, when it did show grief, would be 'respectable, never morbid'. Dr Caius of Cambridge, a sixteenth-century writer on British dogs, was a level-headed intellectual, a skilful physician and an active administrator of the university college which he founded – hardly a twee 'doggy' man. Yet when he produced an 'epitome' on dogs for the Swiss naturalist, Conrad Gesner, he wrote a great deal more about the moral and mental qualities of dogs than about their physiology. He described the emotion of grief in dogs as 'love' and illustrated this quality with verbal sketches of what he called 'defending dogges . . . that love their masters liberally, and hate strangers despightfully', to such an extent that they always championed their master's cause, protected him from all comers whatever the odds, and continued to 'forsaketh not his master, no, not when he is starcke dead; but induring the force of famishment, and the outrageous tempests of the weather, most vigilantly watcheth, and carefully keepeth the dead carkasse many dayes, endeavouring, furthermore, to kill the murtherer of his master, if he may get any advantage. Or else by barcking, by howling, by furious jarring and snarring, and suchlike means, betrayeth the malefactour, as desirous to have the death of his aforesaid master rigorously revenged.' How human, to seek revenge for such a grievous loss.

Caius gave several examples of such grief and faithfulness, and there have been countless others. Wordsworth's verses tell the story of the Dog of Helvellyn, which accompanied its master, a Manchester man, on a hike in the Lake District. The man slipped in the dusk, fell over the rocks and was killed. His body was not discovered for three months, when a shepherd found it still being guarded by the mourning dog.

Another famous loyal pet, The Dog of Montargis, probably served as a model for Caius's original thesis. The story dates to 1371 and the court of King Charles V, where chevalier Macaire was jealous of fellow courtier Aubry de Montdidier. Macaire chanced upon his rival in the forest of Montargis, alone except for his dog, and he murdered and buried the man. The dog lay on his master's grave, howling, for many days and nights but eventually, driven by hunger and perhaps a desire to communicate the story, paid a fleeting visit to a friend of his master in Paris, who gave him food. The dog then returned immediately to the forest grave. This became a regular habit and always the dog's manner was sober; he seemed to be oppressed with care and uttered doleful barks. He was finally followed to his retreat and at a mound of freshly turned earth in the forest he resumed his heart-rending lamentations. The body was discovered but no one knew or even suspected by whose hand Montdidier had died.

The dog stayed with relatives. One day he happened to spot Macaire in a group of people and flew straight for the man's throat; he had to be beaten off by bystanders. Still no one suspected Macaire but the dog, though gentle and good-natured to all others, flew into a violent rage whenever it saw the murderer. The king heard of this behaviour and arranged a confrontation between man and dog at which the dog again sprang furiously at Macaire and had to be forcibly dragged off. Macaire, however, strongly maintained his innocence and in the manner of the time the king decided that the case should be settled by mortal combat and the judgement of God. If innocent, the man on trial would survive.

In front of a large audience, the man faced the dog. He was given a heavy stick but the dog had only its natural weapons and an old cask in which it could take refuge. It had no thoughts of self-protection or defeat, however, and, skilfully evading the wielded stick, it managed to grab Macaire by the throat and force him to the ground. The murderer promptly confessed; the dog was pulled away and Macaire was subsequently hanged for the crime.

Dogs seem to react much more emotionally in a human relationship, expressing grief, affection and jealousy in respect of people, than they do with their own kind. However, there are many instances of lifelong mates who grieve for and remain faithful to a dead partner, in true wolf fashion. If a wolf's mate is killed, it will howl over the body for hours, and it will continue to pine long afterwards. It is unlikely ever to seek another mate.

If a wolf pack should lose its leader through sudden death the entire pack will be unsettled, nervous, confused. The leader

1a. *above left* Berenice Walters with Emma, a single-coated 'tropical' dingo, and Error, a thick-coated alpine type.
1b. *above right* Julie, a dingo with an exceptionally gentle and caring nature. She was particularly sensitive towards blind people, whom she would adopt.

1c. Ken Walters with Napoleon – a classic example of the living dog-blanket. Napoleon, a tropical dingo, loved human company and was frequently seen on Australian television. He achieved very high levels at his obedience classes.

2a. Black-backed jackals (*Canis mesomelas*) in the Kalahari.

2b. European wolves setting off in single file.
The pack leader is second in line, with its tail raised.

3a. Aggression between two sledge dogs. The Eskimo dog on the left is dominant,
showing the typical 'small-mouth' threat seen in wolves and in domesticated dogs.
The tongue protrusion of the other animal is probably ambivalent:
he is not sure whether to be aggressive or to offer appeasement
with puppyish licking gestures.

3b. Sledge dogs, English-style.
Simon Daly's six-dog team of Siberian huskies training in Sherwood Forest.

4a. A Springer spaniel with her new puppies.
4b. Racing greyhounds in action at Hackney
– a close-up which the punters rarely see.

5. A working Jack Russell terrier:
a. sensibly respectful of its ferret partner
b. proud of its catch   **c.** homeward bound

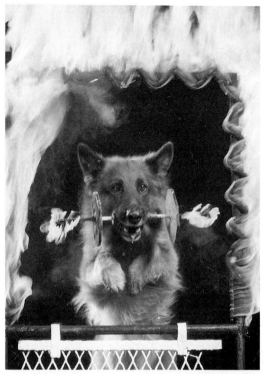

6a. A German shepherd jumping fearlessly through
flames – a highly trained member of the
Royal Air Force Police Dog Demonstration Team.

6b. A German shepherd being tested at the
Royal Army Veterinary Corps training school at
Melton Mowbray. The bold stare and lack of hackling
show that the dog is confident in its attack.

7a. Arun District Council dog warden George Moore with a starving lurcher found in a shed.

7b. Battersea joy. An armful of some of the hundred abandoned dogs accepted at Battersea Dogs' Home in Christmas week – Claire Oram makes them welcome.

8a. A good working collie,
more interested in sheep than in the gossiping men.

8b. Blind boat enthusiast Malcolm Cannell
finds freedom with his sea-loving guide dog Andy.

is vital to the success of the pack and its death is, in a way, mourned but perhaps it is fear of the future that plays most on the pack's emotions at such a time, rather than grief as we understand it. Or do we understand grief? Grief in humans is entangled with anger – anger at the betrayal of loss – and with fear of a future without the loved one.

Humour and grief – what other 'human' emotions and qualities does the dog share? There are those who, in very persuasive language, argue that no animal other than man is capable of emotions and that to credit such feelings to animals is at best ridiculous and at worst evil. The term 'anthropomorphic' is used as an insult, implying that the scientist or the intellectual, as dispassionate observers, are superior to the rest of us who feel more equality with other living creatures. There is no reason to be so presumptuous: animals' emotions may be set in different contexts to our own but that is not to say they are inferior or to deny they are real. Less narrow minds are at last having their say and James Serpell, in his soundly reasoned and thoroughly researched book *In the Company of Animals*, should go some way to redress the balance and cast doubt on many centuries of prejudice.

Time and time again, people who know dogs really well and have taken the trouble to understand something of their ways have concluded that dogs are moral animals, with strong consciences. This should surprise no one. In the wild pack such qualities are vital for pack unity and survival, as indeed they are in human society.

But does anyone 'know dogs really well'? In reviewing Mayhew's book in the nineteenth century, *The Field* said: 'Everybody keeps a dog, and nobody knows how to treat him. Though there is possessed of no other animal such opportunities for knowledge, of none does more ignorance prevail.' Mayhew himself made some fairly extraordinary statements in his book, for example, speaking of the temperament of the dog, he declared:

Any one who will observe the animal will soon be made aware of its excessive irritability. The nervous system in this creature is largely developed, and, exerting an influence over all its actions, gives character to the beast. The brain of the dog is seldom in repose, for even when asleep the twitching of the legs and the suppressed sounds which it emits informs us that it is dreaming. No animal is more actuated by imagination. Who is there that has not seen the dog mistake objects during the dusk of the evening? Delirium usually precedes its death, and nervous excitability is the common accompaniment of most of its disorders. To diseases of a cerebral or spinal character it is more liable than is any other domestic animal. Its very bark is symbolical of its temperament, and its mode of attack energetically declares the excitability of its nature.

Mayhew concludes that the only way of handling such a nervous species is with gentle firmness and confidence. As a vet, he speaks with feeling of the problems of handling an unknown dog in its own home, especially if it is over-indulged by its owners, to whom it will ham it up shamelessly. 'Dogs are great imposters,' says the long-suffering vet, 'and he who has had much to do with them soon learns how cunningly the pampered "toy" of the drawing-room can "sham".' Yet even Mayhew admits that dogs are honourable creatures, and it can only be to our benefit to trust in their better qualities. Although he describes himself as 'slow and infirm', he had never been bitten by a dog and he puts this down to his practice of working upon the sympathetic nature of the dog rather than trying to compete with it in strength or 'outvie it in agility'. 'Mental supremacy appealing to the source of action ensures safety, by subduing, not the resistance, but the desire to resist.' (He gives a practical hint too: an unfailing sign of an irritated dog, he says, is a dilation of its pupils.)

It is that 'sympathetic nature' of the dog that has given it such a bond with mankind. How did man first recognize its human qualities and how did he set about confirming the special alliance and sympathy between man and dog?

SEVEN

Taming the Wolf

It is often pointed out that man has domesticated only a limited number of species among the wide variety of creatures with which he shares this earth, and that of those few domesticants only two share his home willingly and are greeted kindly there: the cat and the dog.

William Watson, in his poem 'A Study of Contrasts', compared cat and dog – and likened the differences between them to the differences between the East and the West. The cat, 'throned in monumental calm . . . immobile, imperturbable, like one whose vision seeks the Immanent', surveyed with considerable disdain 'his Collieship . . . his effervescence, volatility, clamour on small occasions, fussiness'. She, 'the face within this transitory mask . . . Viewed his upbubblings of ebullient life, / She seemed the Orient Spirit incarnate, lost / In contemplation of the Western Soul!'

The cat uses man but is not his servant. The dog, on the other hand, serves man in a wider variety of roles than any other species. A dog can be all things to all men. Other species fulfil some of the roles but no other species has such a potential for variation as the dog, except, perhaps, the pig, whose potential is as yet underdeveloped. Pigs make good plough-pullers (better drawers than oxen, some say); they have excellent noses and have been trained to find truffles and drugs and to track scent-trails; they have even been used by gamekeepers to locate and retrieve game, and a feral pig can be almost as dangerous to unshepherded flocks as more commonly recognized predators. Recently a farmer found his pigs helping the collie round up his sheep; some people have pet pigs in the house and many a peasant knows the value of pig body-warmth in shared quarters. Pigs are intelligent and quick to learn all kinds of tricks but their main role in a human world is as pork or bacon. As companions they really cannot compare with a dog in two major respects: their bodies are stiff, unwieldy and bristly rather than agile, lithe and furry, and they are far more interested in pleasing themselves than their human companions. A dog essentially wants to please and is skilled at knowing how to do so.

Cats share many of the canine characteristics. They are anthropomorphically pleasing with their round, flat faces, soft fur, large eyes, manipulative paws, agility and elegance. They are good hunters. What if man had chosen to develop the cat more fully as his universal aid? Would he have been able to breed cats which helped his hunting by showing him where the prey was, running down selected victims and (very important) bringing a killed animal back to him? Perhaps, but most members of the cat family hunt alone (lions are an exception); they are not naturally co-operative. A cat's kill remains its own: it is not shared.

Yet in India cheetahs were used as hunting aids. They were very docile and were taken to the hunt in flat carts, wearing hoods (which made them that much more amenable). When the herd was found, the cheetahs were unhooded and released. They crept up on the herd and at the last moment would bound towards a chosen victim. Immediately, horsemen galloped up and gave chase. Sometimes the cart was a nuisance and the cheetah was walked on a chain towards the herd but it would get so excited at every smell that its keeper would have with him an empty coconut shell at the end of a handle. Salt was sprinkled inside the shell, which was then dangled in front of the cheetah by the handle, and the animal became so interested in licking the salt that it forgot all the excitement and walked quietly.

Cheetahs are not long-distance runners: they usually catch their prey within a dozen bounds once they have stalked it, and these tame cats were easily dissuaded from spoiling the horsemen's chase. How about cats and livestock, then? Could any of the cat family have been trained to round up sheep, to separate out certain ewes the way the cheetah selected a victim from the herd, or to encourage cattle to move in the right direction?

Perhaps the lion family were the most likely candidates but man never tried it out and the big cats never offered to help.

That is perhaps one of the crucial factors. In the first place, the dog chose to be chosen by man: it made itself available and amenable. The second factor was that innate variety found within every litter of pups. Whatever wild canid formed the basic ancestral stock of the domestic dog, it handed us on a plate a choice of individuals – a tracker, a herder, a selector, a killer, a watcher, a softy, a protector. They were all there, just waiting to have their particular qualities developed into the many different skills that man needed in his allies, and the potential for different sizes, shapes and colours was there too.

There will always be speculation about the first 'dog' – the first animal tame enough not to run from man or attack him and determined enough to come back every time it was chased off. E.H. Baynes, in an article written in 1919, imagined a pleasant scenario. As the intellectual gulf began to widen between man and all the other animals, only the dog longed to leap across and join him again. The dog yelped and danced on the edge of the chasm; the man heard it, understood, and called 'Come!' And the dog leaped but only managed to clutch at the far edge with its front paws. It hung there, looking steadily into the eyes of the man, and the man reached out and helped it to his side.

There are many imaginative stories and allegories along these lines: different cultures have different ideas. What *was* that first dog? The term 'dog' is used to describe the domesticated animal we know today, and like any other creature, there had to be a wild species before there could be a domesticated version. The question has been puzzling leading scientists for the last hundred years at least but despite all kinds of theories, studies and investigations there is still doubt in some minds about the origins of the dog.

The most widely held opinion is that the dog – in all its amazing modern variety of shape, size, colour and tempera-ment – is a tamed wolf. That is only a majority view. In the 1850s Mayhew argued with emphatic vindication that the dog was and always had been a distinct canine race. He absolutely denied 'the dogmas put forth by some naturalists' that the dog was descended from the wolf or the jackal. He stated: 'Beyond the circumstances of the habitats of the animals being distinct, is the well-known fact that all domesticated animals have a disposition to return to their original formation; but who ever heard of a dog, however neglected, or however wild, becoming either a wolf or a jackal?'

At that time, and indeed even today, most people could see no virtues in wolves, jackals, coyotes or any other wild canid. They were considered sneaky, cringing, immoral, verminous, treacherous creatures and they generated general loathing and contempt. It was not until people began to study these wild animals in their natural environments that they began to realize that there was a great deal to admire in them and that they could be considered worthy ancestors of man's closest ally.

Whole books have been written about why the wolf – or the jackal, coyote, dingo, or even the crab-eating fox – should be considered the true ancestral dog. Learned papers argue about matters like cranial dimensions, jaw structure and other physiological factors. Maybe the true story will never be known. Certainly there are many behavioural patterns in dogs which reflect those of wild wolves, and some which are more like other wild canids. Some people believe that dogs are so diverse they must have had more than one root: some are wolves, some are jackals and so on. Animal behaviourist Konrad Lorenz proposed in his 1950s' book *Man Meets Dog* that there were definitely two very different strains of dog, a wolf type like the northern dogs (huskies, chows, Samoyeds, etc.) and a jackal type, with plenty of intermingling along the way. However, Lorenz later retracted this theory and in his foreword to *The Wild Canids* (1975) he said that he was 'guilty of writing a popular book on domestic dogs and also of having propounded an erroneous hypothesis . . . that the bulk of domestic dog races are descended from the golden jackal.' But he still believed that what he originally described as 'lupus dogs' (the northern ones) had a different wild ancestor to most other breeds and he settled for a timber wolf for the former and the smaller Indian wolf, a born scavenger, for the rest. Notice that both are species of the wolf, *Canis lupus*, an animal which, before man took a hand in the matter, was spread throughout the northern hemisphere and Asia.

Dr Juliet Clutton-Brock of the British Museum, perhaps Britain's best known writer on the domestication of animals, goes entirely for wolf ancestors and suggests that, although there is as yet no conclusive morphological or behavioural evidence proving all our breeds of dog can be traced back to a single common wild ancestor, it might be that the smaller wolf of western Asia gave rise to most of the European dogs and to those of southern Asia (including the dingo) but that there may have been occasional inbreeding with Lorenz's golden jackal. She also suggests that the early Chinese dogs may have descended from a small Chinese wolf and that the northern husky-type dogs owe their origins to the local North American wolf.

Domestication did not happen suddenly, nor did it happen all over the world at the same time. In different regions, different races may have domesticated different canid species. For example, there were no wolves in South America and the Indians may have tamed the Dusicyon foxes, while the Indians of North America probably befriended the coyote: they certainly worshipped it in some tribes. The Egyptians worshipped Anubis, who looked more like a jackal than a dog, and there is plenty of evidence that the ancient Egyptians did keep captive jackals, even if they were not truly domesticated. Jackals are basically an African species; coyotes occupy the jackal's typical niche in North America, a niche which is quite separate from that of the wolf.

Given that early man was surrounded by all sorts of canids, which would he choose (if that is the appropriate word)? First of all, the potential dog had to tolerate, or even seek, the proximity of man. It is reasonable to suggest that a species which already lived in a social group of its own was more likely to tolerate man than was a species which tended to be solitary or live in pairs. Co-operation is the essence of society and a naturally co-operative (as opposed to independent) species is more likely to extend its clan to include another species.

The two most social wild canids are the wolf and the African hunting dog, with the jackal probably rather more social than has usually been recognized. Hunting dogs do not have such a highly developed system of social dominance as wolves and man, and their bonds tend to be forged more by mutual acceptance of regurgitated food than by a complicated language of body postures and facial expressions. Would man be prepared to accept such offerings? And return them? The wolf's methods of communication and organization were much like man's which would therefore make it easier for both species to interpret and understand each other. There could be reciprocity. It must again be stressed, however, that so far the evidence is not absolute in favour of one ancestor or another for the dog, be it wolf, jackal or whatever. Let the experts keep on arguing.

Assuming that a wild species of some kind or of several kinds had some similarities with man and was prepared to tolerate his presence – what then? There are several ideas as to how the ancient alliance might have begun and how it developed. Many of the theories rely on the dog's scavenging instincts: wild canids followed man to eat what he did not, trailing him after the hunt and hanging around the camp knowing that bones and scraps would be going begging. Perhaps such scavengers were at first driven off but persisted until they were tolerated, and then accepted, and finally encouraged. Prisoners, alone in their dungeons, have often befriended animals that normally they would crush; rats, for example, are offered food because they provide living company. Perhaps dogs, at first a nuisance to be repelled, were occasionally thrown scraps on purpose; their persistence paid off and they had placed their paws on the first step of the ladder to domestication (whether that ladder led upwards or downwards). Like pariahs today, these camp scavengers would have performed a useful role as waste-disposal units cleaning up the general rubbish of human settlements. The Zoroastrians, incidentally, regarded the dog as a sacred animal and human corpses were purposely left unburied so that the dogs could clean them of flesh. These canid scavengers sound more like jackals and coyotes than wolves, though all the canids are happy enough to share someone else's kill given the chance.

A more constructive and equal relationship has often been suggested which gives weight to the wolf-ancestor hypothesis.

Pack wolves are expert hunters; men, too, were pack hunters, often pursuing the same prey as the wolves. Both types of predator used cunning in the hunt, driving herds into ambushes. It could be that the wolves were the more skilful and that man copied some of their techniques – imitation based on respect for a fellow craftsman. Or perhaps the wolves realized that men were often more successful and began to follow them on the hunt. It is difficult to imagine co-operation between the two species at this stage but who knows?

Others believe that man always saw the wolf as an arch rival to be driven away or killed at every opportunity, but that sometimes a litter of orphaned cubs would be found, perhaps by children, brought back to the camp and raised as pets, or fattened for food. If the cubs had been young enough when captured – say three weeks old – they would have accepted humans as their own pack quite readily.

There is also the reverse theory of the wolf-children, in which wolves adopt lost children and rear them in much the same way that humans rear pet animals. The most famous of the tales of wolf-children are probably those of Romulus and Remus, who were suckled by a she-wolf (so Rome owes its foundation to the wolf), and Rudyard Kipling's Mowgli. There are reports of such children even at the turn of this century. It was said that they had been carried off by wolves and kept by them for several years, in which time they became 'relapsed humans', extremely ferocious and nervous, entirely carnivorous, with the voice of a wild creature and a tendency to move on all fours so that their knuckles, feet and knees became toughened like pads. They could run fast in this posture. They would drink in the manner of a horse, sucking up and swallowing liquid in eager draughts rather than drinking like men or lapping like wolves. Of course they went naked and they often developed body hair.

These children are not to be confused with lycanthropists, those tragically sick people who believed themselves to be wolves and who even around 1900 were not uncommon in the Ardennes and other European regions where wolves still existed. Patients were brought to be touched by the holy stole of St Hubert, which was supposed to 'drive the latent poison of hydrophobia from the tainted blood'. Hydrophobia, of course, is one of the classic symptoms of rabies.

A Colonel Sleeman, who had taken a leading part in the suppression of the Thugs in India in 1826–35, was particularly interested in the phenomenon of children found living in wolves' dens in the Province of Oude. His first find was in an area near the Goomtee River, where wolves were abundant and were never killed by the natives for fear of bringing bad luck to the village. A native trooper saw a she-wolf leaving her den followed by three whelping cubs and a small boy, all apparently part of one family and all guarded with equal care and attention by the mother. They went down to the river for a drink; the trooper chased them to catch the child but they all fled back to the den, the boy on all fours running with as much speed and agility as his wolf brethren. Later a squad of men dug them out and, though they bolted, the boy was captured, tied to a rope and brought to the village. His behaviour was wholly wolf: he growled and snarled, he tried to bolt into every hole they passed on the way. For a while he lived under the kindly care of a Captain Nicholetts but the boy never spoke, smiled or laughed, always ran from adults and tried to attack children, destroyed any clothes he was given and approached his food on all fours. He sucked up whole pitcherfuls of buttermilk without drawing breath. The only friendship he showed was towards a pariah dog, which he allowed to share his food. He died within two and a half years of his capture.

Another child captured in similar circumstances in the same area would only eat raw flesh, which he held down with his hands as a dog might use its forepaws. He drank in the manner of the first boy; he always ran on all fours and his knuckles and knees were quite hardened. He was completely savage, although reclaimed by his natural mother, and finally he lived like a pariah dog, roaming the streets by day and taking cover in the jungle at night. His life was not long.

A third child was caught near Hasaupur. He, too, though capable of walking upright, preferred to run on all fours and could outstrip any man running after him on two legs. For the first three nights wolves came and played with him, licking him and cavorting with him. Like the other wolf-children he did not survive to reach maturity. Another account is given by a Reverend Singh who in the 1920s found two children in a wolf-den in India. He took them to an orphanage where he tried, not very successfully, to educate them and he wrote a full account of their story in 1939.

But were these children actually *raised* by the wolves or did they just happen to have befriended them? It hardly seems likely that a human baby could survive on wolf's milk (which usually only lasts for seven weeks) and an early diet of regurgitated raw meat. There is little doubt that wolves would accept an abandoned child and look after it, but it would have to be well past the baby stage to survive the feeding.

Farley Mowat claimed that it was once quite common practice for Eskimo parents to place a boy-child in a wolf's den for a day or two. The wolves accepted the child, often with affection, and he would play with the cubs. Thereafter he would be able to understand and communicate with wolves in their own language and would learn many valuable matters by means of a kind of lupine telegraph – that a group of his Eskimo friends were on their way to meet him, or that the caribou had gathered at a certain place, for example.

There are so many wolf-children stories, from many parts of the world and within many very different cultures, that there must be at least a grain of truth in them. Above all the stories highlight the generous, caring nature of wolves where young are concerned. Eskimo folklore emphasizes the ability of wolves and men to communicate with each other and this is the vital basis of the domestication of the dog. As James Serpell points out, dogs are very skilled at conveying their feelings of friendship and affection for humans and they do not need words to do so. Whatever the dog's wild ancestors might have been, surely it was the canid that chose the human in the first place and offered friendship. Nor was it necessarily cupboard love.

In 1984, C. Manwell and C.M. Ann Baker, of Adelaide University's Department of Zoology, published a paper entitled 'Domestication of the Dog: hunter, food, bedwarmer or emotional object?' in which they explored some of the more popular domestication theories with special reference to the dingo of Australia. The paper was reproduced in the December 1986 issue of *Merigal*, the official newspaper of the Australian Native Dog Training Society of New South Wales, run by Berenice Walters. The question they considered was why man had domesticated the dog in the first place – for what purpose?

Was the dog exploited originally to help with the hunting? Well, later perhaps. Dingoes and coyotes, canids of arid or semi-arid areas, do not usually hunt in packs because they habitually tackle only small game, and depend to some extent on carrion. They are good scavengers but not necessarily good hunting partners for man. Nor do the tribes of Australia, Africa and South America use their various dogs as essential hunting aids. The Aborigines may take their dingoes along on a hunt, either involuntarily or for a bit of light sport, but never for serious meat-gathering. The Siriono of Bolivia never hunt with dogs. The Yanomama of Venezuela 'love dogs, all dogs' but admit they are quite useless for hunting. The much-studied !Kung bushmen of southern Africa do sometimes use hunting dogs but not with enormous success. On the other hand, wolves are the cream of pack hunters and it does seem possible that, as they are so co-operative by nature, tamed wolves raised by humans from cubhood might well have been taken along on hunting sorties: their sense of smell and fleetness of foot would have been great assets to their human pack. But it is unlikely that this assistance was the original *reason* for taming them, merely a useful bonus later.

Manwell and Baker next look at dogs as guards. Dogs are naturally territorial and alert to intruders but for humans a good watchdog is one that barks. Wild canids rarely bark so, although suitably vociferous animals were eventually selectively bred, this was probably not their initial role in the human camp. Guard dogs, on the other hand, do not need to be barkers so much as attackers. Their aggression must, however, be discriminating: they should not bite their owners' families and friends or attack livestock. Humans did not have domesticated livestock until well after the domestication of dogs and it seems very possible that, without herd dogs of some kind, domestication of cattle, goats, sheep, etc., would have been more difficult.

Even after centuries of breeding it takes plenty of training to ensure that guard dogs do make such discriminations, whether they are employed to look after property, people or stock, and, again, it is unlikely that this was the dog's original use.

Then there is the edible dog, especially important in eastern and south-eastern Asia and the Pacific islands, and with evidence of similar value in southern and central America and several African cultures. However, the custom was by no means the norm. The Indians of Tierra del Fuego, for example, had enormous respect and affection for their small, fox-like native dogs, which were expert at catching fish and guanacos for their masters. The little dogs swam out to sea as soon as a shoal of fish was sighted near land and, by dint of much splashing and diving, they drove the fish into the men's nets or channelled them into shallow creeks. They were also adept at catching sleeping birds, slipping the captives back to their masters and returning for more; so quiet were their raids that other birds slept on undisturbed, not aware of the danger. These bushy-brushed, sharp-nosed animals, with their large, erect, pointed ears and dark, rough coats, were utterly faithful to their masters and made very good watchdogs, barking furiously at strangers. Although the Fuegians rarely fed their dogs, which had to forage for themselves by catching their own fish after they had fulfilled the fishermen's requirements, they valued them for their abilities and it was said that they would eat one of their old women before they would eat one of their dogs!

The Patagonians, who also had guanaco-catching dogs, similarly abhorred dog flesh, but the Sandwich Islanders regularly ate their dogs, although they loved them passionately and treated them like children; they would carry the dogs when the going got muddy or rough, and resented an injury or insult to a dog more strongly than injury to their own children.

The Chinese also ate dogs and China is probably the only country where dogmeat has ever been a major source of protein for humans. Even there, however, it was more likely to be an occasional delicacy than staple fare and the common practice was to breed dogs specifically for eating, feeding them on an entirely vegetarian diet to make their flesh more tasty. Only a hundred years ago the practice still continued in China, though

apparently only among the poorer classes. In Vero Shaw's
Illustrated Book of the Dog, published in 1879, Archdeacon Gray
reported that the flesh of black dogs (and cats) was always
advertised outside Cantonese restaurants 'patronised by
mechanics and others' and he reproduced a bill of fare which
included 'black dog's grease' and 'black cat's eyes (one pair)'.
For most of its history, China has regarded dogs as practical
assets, either to be eaten or used as watchdogs but never as
pets – unless the dogs were those bred for the palaces.

Dog-eating was not unknown in Europe and it was certainly
practised in ancient Rome. On the whole, however, humans
tend not to eat other carnivores so, although there is a case to
be made that the occasional wild canid puppy was taken back
to prehistoric camps and fattened as food, it seems likely to
have been only on a minor scale.

A much more common role for dogs was, and still is, as a
provider of warmth to humans. The Aborigines, though they
often drive scavenging dingoes away from the camp during the
day, welcome them at night. Initially the dogs were probably
attracted to the warmth of camp-fires and possibly tried to insert
their own bodies closer to the fire than the humans, but a
compromise was reached and in cold weather the dogs became
living blankets for their human companions, the two species
sharing each other's warmth in what Manwell and Baker
describe as 'reciprocal altruism' – mutual generosity for mutual
benefit. The practice was such a common one that every
Australian today is familiar with colloquial expressions like 'It's
a six-dog night!' How much more convenient, in a nomadic
existence, to have a walking, warm-blooded blanket following
you everywhere voluntarily rather than a dead pelt which has
to be carried.

Other races, primitive and modern, use dogs for warmth.
The hairless dogs of Mexico, for example, have a particularly
high body temperature and act as living and very portable hot-
water bottles. Chihuahuas probably had the same role, although
in their past under the Aztecs they were bred for rather shorter
lives. Cortes, in his letters to his Emperor, Charles V, told of
Montezuma's amazing zoological garden, a private palace zoo
full of animals, birds and fish of all kinds. The system of

management was as sophisticated (or more so) than that of any modern zoo and there were three hundred keepers in attendance. Some of the inmates were big cats, probably jaguars and pumas, and there were also (apparently) wolves. The little dogs bred by the Mexicans made excellent fresh meat for the wolves and the big cats and snakes. To be fair, the carnivores were also fed on human flesh.

As living blankets, dogs are naturally fitted for the role. They are used to sleeping in close contact with the rest of the pack. Kennel hounds sleep in ever-shifting, flopping heaps, all of a tangle. Many other warm-blooded mammals huddle together but it is not common between two different species. To do so requires absolute trust on both sides, a certainty that neither has aggressive intentions or will take advantage of sleep. Such certainty can only come through experience and through good communications, such as men and dogs are able to share.

So far, most of these possible reasons for man's domestication of the dog have been based on practical exploitation. However, throughout history dogs have also been valued for emotional reasons. They have played their part in religion, they have been developed for aesthetic pleasure as well as practical work, and they have been very willingly accepted as companions, whatever they look like and regardless of their usefulness or lack of it. Girls of the Damara tribe living on the west coast of Africa adored their pet dogs and treated them like children, carrying them everywhere in back-slings like babies.

The emotional value of dogs, whether or not it is recognized or admitted, is on the whole a far greater influence in their relationship with humans than their utility value, however varied their potential roles might be. Modern or 'civilized' man is not so far removed from his primitive ancestors as he may like to think and it could well be that, when the wild canids first sought out humans and made it clear they were willing to befriend them, those humans, perhaps already beginning to notice the gulf between man and the rest of the living world which would grow to such awesome and unbridgeable proportions as civilization progressed, welcomed the gesture with relief and reached out to accept the friendship and seal the voluntary covenant of the special alliance which, later, man would often betray.

It is still the dog that makes the first approach. Watch someone choosing a puppy from a litter or a dog from a crowded refuge. The choice does not really lie with the human. It is the way the dog plays on their sentiment that swings the balance – the puppy that seems to gravitate towards them, or the abandoned collie that looks them in the eye and says, 'Choose me'. My mother, as a girl, was chosen by a bedraggled, mud-plastered Afghan hound named Lutchi which came across the Khyber Pass with a camel driver en route for India. Lutchi made the choice – though my mother had to pay for her – and after a good bath she turned out to be a beauty. She would happily accompany my mother on walks with the donkey, Veronica, but the hound loved nothing better than chasing jackals across the golf course (just like my grandfather's dachshund, Otto). She once fell into a ditch in mid-chase and broke a leg but, nothing daunted, she could run just as fast with her leg in plaster and always lived up to her name – Lutchi, Swift As The Wind.

EIGHT

The Working Partnership

Domestication is not sudden; it takes place very gradually, imperceptibly, over many generations. Wolf cubs taken from their wild mother's den are never domesticated animals, however long they live with man and however friendly they become. They are *tamed* animals which have learned, from personal experience, that the humans they live with do not intend them any harm and will provide them with food, shelter and company.

Among such a litter of cubs there are bound to be individuals that never seem to fit comfortably in their human pack. Perhaps one is naturally dominant and will not submit to human strictures, or another is nervous and keeps running off or hiding. Yet another might be generally bad-tempered and untrustworthy, or physically deformed in some way. Since humans prefer more amenable or attractive animals around them, the unmanageable ones are killed or driven off. The quality that saves the remainder is their ability to understand what is wanted of them and willingness to submit to the demands made on them. They are tame, and they are tractable: they accept close contact with man and live with him on his terms.

Selection by man, rather than by nature, is thus the first step towards domestication. A domesticated animal is essentially one whose breeding is controlled by man for man's benefit. Man shapes the animal to his needs, choosing its colour, its size, its character and its productivity. In exchange, the domesticant is fed, protected from predators and given shelter, and this often means that its numbers greatly increase, probably at the expense of its wild relatives. For most species, domestication also means confinement (except in the case of those willing allies of man, cats and dogs) and dependence on the continuing beneficence of man.

As time passes, selective breeding changes the species so much that the animal would find it more and more difficult to survive without human assistance, direct or indirect. In terms of survival in the wild, the domesticant is a degenerate animal. The dog, for example, now has a smaller brain than its ancestors; its body is smaller in all proportions (unless it has been bred deliberately for size), which means that it is more manageable and eats less; its teeth and jaws are nothing like as efficient as a wolf's; it is prone to all sorts of genetic defects like distorted joints and limbs, hampered breathing, eyes that bulge or are constantly worried by facial hair; its skull has changed shape, in some breeds to an almost lethal extent.

In encouraging dependence, man has effectively debased and retarded his domesticated animals so that they are in a state of perpetual juvenility. In dogs, this tendency has been emphasized by selectively breeding them to be more puppylike. For example, wild canid cubs have drooping ears that become upright with adulthood but many breeds of dog have floppy, puppyish ears. Cub fur is softer than an adult pelage and many dogs have soft, caressable, puppylike coats. Large, appealing 'baby' eyes are favoured in many breeds of dog and so are soft shapes, dwarfed legs and general babyishness.

Another change brought about by domestication is in the carriage of the tail. The tails of all wild canids hang straight when they are relaxed but dogs' tails always have at least the suggestion of a curve, like a sickle. Certainly no wild canid curls its tail over its back in the manner of spitzes, chows, huskies, Nordic dogs and many pariahs. Only a deformed wild canid would be born bobtailed like some sheepdogs: tails are essential to balance in fast-moving, quick-turning, agile predators.

Then there is coat colour. In the wild canids there is some variation in coat colour, especially between subspecies of jackals and wolves, but nothing like as extreme as with the domestic dog. The possible exception is the 'painted wolf' – the literal translation of the latinized species name for the Cape hunting dog – individuals of which have a unique pattern of yellow and white splodges on their dark coats, although the species as a whole has a uniformity to its coat colour.

Domestic dogs, however, come in all sorts of colours and patterns, though there is a remarkable uniformity all over the world in feral dog populations. Dingoes, pariahs, New Guinea Singing Dogs and many mongrels tend to have a generally tan-coloured coat, varying from foxy red to sandy yellow, with a touch of white at the tip of the tail and on the muzzle and socks and perhaps chest and underside. The same colouring can be seen in ancient breeds like the pharaoh hound, the North African sloughi, the Ibizan hound and the basenji from the Congo.

It may all be to do with early selection for tameness, though this is not proven. Studies of the dog's cousin, the fox, have shown an interesting correlation between coat colour mutations (those which differ from the wild colour) and the mutants' behaviour. An amber fox, selectively bred by fur farmers for its unusual colour, has a reduced body odour, a less bushy tail and considerably less aggressive instincts than a normal red-col-oured fox, for example. The amber eats more quietly, lives more quietly and, not surprisingly, grows plumper; its pituitary and adrenal glands, which govern so many facets of behaviour, are smaller than those of red foxes. Perhaps, therefore, colour mutants in the wild canids were carefully chosen for breeding during domestication not only because an unusual colour lends distinction but also because colour mutants were that much more amenable. But that is all speculation.

The increase in barking in dogs was also presumably 'selected for'. If barking was desirable in a camp watchdog, it would of course be encouraged – it is very easy to 'teach' a puppy to bark by setting it an example – and good barkers would be used to produce new litters of barking watchdogs. In the same way other traits were encouraged for the many different roles that man soon found for dogs. Those with the best noses helped to locate prey and gradually developed into hunting hounds, mantrackers, truffle hounds, rescue workers and sniffer dogs. Dogs inclined to use their eyes more than their noses, usually those that came from the plains and open spaces (noses are more useful when trees and undergrowth obstruct the view), became 'gaze-hounds', coursers and racing dogs. Pack members which specialized in setting up the hunt by getting prey on the move, spotting the weaker animals and separating them out, became herding dogs, while more possessive, aggressive and strongly built animals became shepherd (as opposed to sheep) dogs guarding the flock from predators and were also developed as fighting dogs, war dogs, guard dogs and attackers.

Sturdy animals with stamina became draught dogs; barkers became watchdogs; cunning underdogs joined circuses and theatres; small dogs with cunning, tenacity and courage became vermin destroyers; good-looking dogs took to parading with troops and pageants or appearing in exhibition rings, stately homes and royal courts. Very special dogs with the combined qualities of steadiness, kindness, humour, sympathy, the ability to communicate and the desire to help became guides for the blind, aids for the disabled, friends to those in institutions and companions to men, women and children all over the world.

Quite apart from huge numbers of mongrels, there are probably up to four hundred different 'pure' breeds of dog in the modern world, many of which are hunting dogs. In a typical encyclopaedia of world breeds, perhaps a third are listed in the hunting and gun-dog section. They include pack chasers like foxhounds, beagles and harriers, gun-dogs like pointers, setters, retrievers and spaniels, water dogs like poodles, barbets and otter-hounds, methodical trackers like bloodhounds and bassets, and specialist prey dogs like dachshunds, elk-hounds, puffin-hounds, coon-hounds and wolf hunters. There are also the sight-hounds or gaze-hounds like greyhounds and salukis.

Many cultures use less-than-pedigree dogs to help with the hunting: who cares about looks or parentage as long as the dog is good at the job? The Kaffirs used to use quite small dogs to divert charging elephants, which are very unsettled by small animals, especially dogs – and mice. The Samoans had highly trained dogs for hunting boar; they were 'very ugly and most unpromising to the eye', according to *Wood's Natural History of Man* published in 1868, but most courageous and skilful. Their job was to catch smaller pigs by the ear, shoulder and tail to check their flight so that the hunters could complete the kill with a stick pressed across the victim's windpipe.

Several of the sporting breeds have found new roles in which their marvellous noses are exploited against enemies and criminals. The bloodhound's man-tracking skills are legendary; once on the trail this very dogged dog will keep at it through thick and thin. Like a pet dog chasing a rabbit, bloodhounds are not really interested in the end result: it is the actual tracking they love, and the 'prey' is almost irrelevant. In the old days, however, a tracked miscreant was quite likely to be attacked by the hound and possibly killed.

In the seventeenth century people used to rub bloodhounds' noses in vinegar to quicken their sense of smell, although it was hardly necessary. The hounds were often used for tracking down criminals and some of their feats seemed to be almost supernaturally brilliant though in fact they simply followed their noses. One famous hound called Nick Carter in Kentucky was responsible for the conviction of more than six hundred criminals; he could pick up a trail four days old and would follow a man whether on foot or on horseback, for mile after relentless mile.

Today very few police forces use bloodhounds but German shepherd dogs find all sorts of roles. Dox, a famous German shepherd living in Italy during the 1950s, was a highly successful investigator who, it was claimed, not only tracked criminals but could untie complicated knots, unload a pistol, and solve many crimes on his own without the help of his handler. By the time he was fourteen he had seven scars from bullet wounds and a string of awards for bravery. His exploits included keeping twelve men at bay with their arms raised, saving a child from an oncoming car, catching a burglar after a three-mile chase despite running on three legs because the fourth had been smashed by a bullet, and recognizing and 'arresting' a criminal who had eluded him in a chase six years earlier.

One of the newest roles for nose-dogs is as sniffers, searching for contraband drugs or hidden explosives or anything else that someone with questionable motives is trying to conceal. Police, customs officials, prison officers and the armed forces train dogs as specialists whose lives are devoted to the discovery of specific smells. However, it takes much more than just a good nose to make a good sniffer.

In an untidy outbuilding at a police dog-training centre in Surrey, three or four grown men have dropped their inhibitions and are behaving like children. One of them crouches beside a young flat-coated retriever, holding it by the collar. He converses animatedly with the dog: 'Look over there, Bob – what's he doing? What's that man got? Where's he putting it? Did you see? Where *is* it, Bob? Where's he put it?' A colleague is running around the place, ducking down now and again, waving a tied bundle of rags, pretending to hide it here under a bench, there behind an old plank, up here on top of a table, in there between some empty boxes and paint-cans. The dog is agog, watching every move, eyes bright, ears alert, tail wagging furiously, little barks of excitement escaping him, straining to join the game, never actually seeing where the bundle has been hidden but aware of all the possibilities.

At last his handler releases him, still talking non-stop: 'On you go, Bob – find it, find it! Is it over there? Where is it, Bob? Where is it?' The dog relies on his nose, pushing it into every crevice, under every projection, round every corner, tail working, rushing from one place to the next, working his way around the room and, joyfully, finding the bundle, pulling it from its hiding place, bearing it aloft with his head high, his tail high, prancing, glancing at the men out of the corner of his bright, laughing eyes, showing off the trophy, taking it teasingly to each one but not as a gift, only as a display. Everyone is exclaiming, 'Well done, Bob, well *done*! *Good* boy! What a clever guy!', responding to his pleasure and pride, acclaiming his success, and his handler persuades him to part with his prize under a welter of hugs, friendly body slaps and verbal praise. The dog does a quick tour of all the men to receive more enthusiastic praise and hearty pats from each one in turn and then he is taken back to his kennel. A new dog is brought in, a springer spaniel with an even more expressive tail, and the whole performance begins again and is repeated with just as much energy and enthusiasm for a couple of Labradors later.

The Labradors are brothers from the same litter. The first is as enthusiastic and merry as the retriever but his brother is very different. He is hesitant, wary, expecting a box to drop on him, not keen to go under a table or on top of a chest, but he is intelligent and methodical. He does not rely on hit-and-miss: he does not rush around the room knowing that some time, somewhere, he will happen to find that bundle. He has watched the hider carefully and only checks out the places where a hiding gesture had been made. He locates successfully and quickly, with much less fuss and much less enthusiasm than his brother. He has to be encouraged to draw the bundle out of its hiding place.

Although it is a cold December day, all the men are sweating freely by the end of the session. The dogs were having their first assessment to see whether they had the potential for further training as sniffers. They had each come from private homes the previous day, from families who, for whatever reason, had decided they could no longer keep them and had donated them to the training centre. The police rarely need to buy or breed dogs: there are more than enough being given to them because the owners do not know how to handle them, or find them too boisterous, or have unwillingly had to change lifestyles because of money problems, unemployment, divorce, bereavement, or a new job in a new area. If the trainers find that the dog is not suitable for their purposes, then a new home has to be found.

These four dogs, then, had come from the friendly environment of a family home and had just spent their first night in alien surroundings, in individual outdoor kennels rather than in the family kitchen, and with strange dogs and strange people all around them. It must have been a traumatic night: dogs suffer considerably when they are suddenly transferred from a familiar environment, however friendly their new 'pack' might be. Now they were being judged to see which of them might make a sniffer. They had to show enthusiasm and courage as well as sniffing power and they needed to 'click' with the man who would become their handler for the duration of a working lifetime. The handler had already formed an attachment with Bob the retriever: he liked the dog on sight and communication between them was immediate. During the hiding games he found that he also admired the way the spaniel worked. The first Labrador had potential, too, but the brother was no good to him at all: it had the brains but was too sensitive for the work. A sniffer dog must not shrink from its task. It must be bold enough to go straight to its target, no matter what real or imaginary obstacles there might be. It must enjoy its work, as if it was all one tremendous game, and it must really *want* the object it is searching for. It must have a sense of play and, sadly, some dogs are so restricted by their owners that they never learn how to play, or they have all their natural sense of fun suppressed.

Each of the dogs had been given a few minutes to become familiar with the bundle of rags. They had been encouraged to play with it, retrieve it, possess it, *own* it. Having owned it, they wanted to keep on owning it – that was part of the incentive. Even the best-controlled, fiercest-looking police dog probably has a favourite rubber ball or other toy which travels with it in the van wherever it goes.

This possessiveness is essential in training a specialized sniffer. Television viewers may remember a little news report a couple of years ago when a sniffer dog was showing off its skills in front of the Princess of Wales. It located its target in a piece of hand-luggage and nothing would induce it to loosen its grip on that bag, not even the friendly approaches of a princess.

There are many methods of training sniffers to concentrate on their speciality. A room is emptied completely – no furniture or curtains or carpet – nothing, except for a sample packet of whatever it is the dog is being trained to find. The dog is sent in and told to search. Naturally it retrieves the only object in the room, and it is lavishly praised for doing so. Next time, the packet is placed on, say, a lone chair in the empty room. No dog is going to retrieve a chair, so it selects the packet and, again, is enthusiatically praised. Thus it continues, with more items being added to the room and always, somewhere, that packet. Dogs learn by association. Thinks: 'I get praised whenever I pick up that packet, so obviously it's worth finding.' Simple deduction, simple technique – and successful. Every trainer has his own methods of getting a dog to associate a particular smell with reward but every successful trainer makes sure that the whole exercise is a game, and that trainer, handler and dog are just friends having a good time.

Therein lies the secret of training at that Surrey police dog centre. Work must be fun, never routine, never boring, and the dog must always succeed at its task. Dogs, like children, quickly lose interest if they fail and should never be asked to undertake a task in which they are likely to fail. Failure automatically brings reproof, disappointment and lack of confidence.

The same techniques of childish enthusiasm are used by trainers and handlers for every type of working dog – drug sniffer, explosives detector, crowd controller, street patroller, criminal catcher or guard dog. The second rule is that every handler must know his dog inside out, understand every nuance of its behaviour and trust the dog's instincts absolutely. During the earliest days of training, handlers are encouraged to set aside at least half an hour every day to spend with the dog in its kennels, or in a quiet private room, and literally just chat with it, give it lots of affection, and generally get to know each other. Some handlers may feel foolish at first and they tend to be the least successful.

A handler told me many stories of his dog's miraculous achievements; not least a hair-raising rooftop escapade in which the dog saved his handler's life when he lost his footing and slithered down the tiles by bracing itself on the other end of the lead and holding him steady. On another occasion he warned a trigger-happy gunman by the softest of growls which was yet so utterly menacing that the man immediately yielded his weapon and his freedom. The same handler tells of the day he had to borrow another man's dog, a dog whose method of communication was so subtle that it was easily misread or overlooked. They were tracking a thief at night through the suburbs, going along towpaths, down alleys and sidestreets, a long track but the dog did not give up. It hesitated for a split second by a back-garden gate and the handler, tired with the painstaking trail, urged the dog on down the towpath. A man came out of the house, watching them, and called out in a friendly way: 'Evening, guv. Nice dog, that. Need a cuppa?' His offer was accepted; they had a little chat and then the handler went back to the station. Later he discovered that the tea-maker was the very thief he had been tracking. The dog had been right; the handler had failed to understand the animal and had ignored its message.

The Royal Air Force patrol dogs are trained at Newton, Nottinghamshire, and, as with the police forces, they are all now acquired through public donations. The trainers found that the German shepherd dog was ideal for the work, and donations of such dogs were not lacking. German shepherds are superb dogs, fine to look at and highly intelligent, but many people acquire them without knowing enough about them and then find that the dog outgrows the house, or is too much of a handful or, being misunderstood, has turned nasty. In most cases it is the people who are at fault rather than the dog. Such dogs have been bred for work and they need to be well occupied and well exercised, physically and mentally. Their talents are wasted if they are treated only as household pets and that leads to frustration. Other people acquire German shepherds and other police-dog types like Rottweilers or Dobermann pinschers for self-protection, or more often to boost their own images of themselves as tough characters, and they can ruin a very good dog by encouraging it to be unnecessarily aggressive. There are many more bad owners than intrinsically bad dogs.

The RAF dogs operate as specialists within a team, like all self-respecting wolves. Their main task is to detect the presence of intruders and to convey the fact to their handlers, and for this part of the job the dog needs to be exceptionally alert and intelligent. The very presence of a German shepherd is often enough to deter intruders and, like many police dogs, the RAF animals are usually well built. All but the most determined would think twice about an encounter with a shaggy, 120-pound, wolf-like dog, though there is a pleasant tale about a police dog of just such proportions which was charmed by a friendly burglar who understood dogs well (and German shepherds in particular): the dog, to his handler's perpetual embarrassment, disappeared into the wood in pursuit of the burglar but more like a happy family pet on a walk than a highly trained patroller. It was found a few miles away the next morning, a Sunday, shut up in a small country church. The vicar had quite a surprise.

It often happens that a patrol dog is required to chase and detain an intruder but only on the instructions of its handler. This work requires absolute control by the handler to direct and moderate the dog's aggression. It is essential, of course, that the handler is recognized by the dog as its pack leader. During training, dogs are taught specific methods of attack which they practise on voluntary 'runners' who wear protective padding; the 'bundle of rag' technique comes in useful here, though the bundle is transformed into padding for, say, a man's forearm. The dog is encouraged to feel possessive about the pad and in due course, when it chases a runner, its aim is to repossess the pad on his arm. It is trained to attack by seizing the arm (or, in the dog's mind, the pad) and, if necessary, pulling the man to the ground and either retaining its grip or maintaining a threatening stance until the handler calls the dog off.

The best dogs for this kind of work are not only intelligent but also highly courageous, agile and adaptable. There must be absolute trust and confidence between dog and handler, mutual respect and complete understanding, qualities which are shown at the public demonstrations given by teams of RAF dogs all over the country. The crowds marvel at the disciplined team-work and the agility of the dogs as they scramble up sheer obstacles, fly over barriers, retrieve batons, twist through rings of fire. These results would be impossible if fear played any part in the training.

The balance of aggression in a patrol dog, whether in the RAF or the police force, is a delicate one and the dog needs to learn a lot about human psychology. It is innately adept at reading people – any dog, from a pariah to a highly trained pure-bred, instinctively knows what a person's real emotions are, whatever front is put up. A police dog can sense human fear instantly, probably as much by the smell of adrenalin as by posture or facial expression, and it must then learn whether the fear will lead to flight, freezing or self-protective aggression. It already knows the symptoms for all these reactions in other dogs, especially in one-to-one situations.

Crowds can be more difficult, both for the handler and for the dog, and the early days of training are crucial. Dogs are basically trained in the familiar surroundings of the centre, where they are 'mobbed' by groups of play-acting policemen. However, any dog knows that this is not for real and the day comes when the dog must face a genuine crowd, perhaps at a football match or a street demo. It is important that the dog should first learn to handle friendly crowds, for it must retain its confidence in the face of considerable odds and an initial confrontation with a hostile crowd can destroy months of training. People in a crowd tend to remain wary of a dog, especially if dog and handler exude confidence, but there are always likely to be a few clever Dicks who begin to taunt and perhaps edge forward. Such a potentially explosive moment is the crucial test of the dog, which must remain dominant and bold, quelling with its presence and its eye, exactly like a sheepdog controlling the flock.

Flock dogs have two completely different roles. The larger, stronger breeds are shepherd dogs, whose jobs it is to protect the flock – originally from wolves and rustlers. The German shepherd dog is a typical shepherd dog but, as a breed, it has only been recognized since the late nineteenth century. Many similar dogs have been used for centuries as herd guards; they have developed from various local types in different regions and often have the large, erect ears, weatherproof coats and feathered brushes of the German shepherd. They are essentially hardy, healthy, bold, courageous animals with quick reactions and excellent hearing, eyesight and scenting powers, and something of the look of a wolf about them.

As wolves and predators became less of a threat, many of the shepherd dogs found roles in wartime or in keeping the peace as police dogs. Their war exploits are truly inspiring: they carried messages over territory no man could traverse, they located and rescued wounded soldiers, they carried explosives and ammunition on their backs. In ancient times mastiff-type dogs were trained to attack; Roman attack-dogs even wore armour. War dogs were still used in this aggressive role in the times of Henry VIII and Elizabeth I.

In World War I several armies made extensive use of dogs for reconnaissance and Red Cross work, and as sentries and patrols. Germany had six thousand shepherd dogs fully trained at the outbreak of war in 1914 and twenty thousand were sent into battle over the next four years. Seven thousand British dogs, many from Battersea Dogs' Home, were killed in action during that war, and the French sent ten thousand dogs to the front and also used eight thousand sledge dogs in the Vosges mountains. During World War II Germany used two hundred thousand dogs, mostly to guard concentration camps; Britain had a War Dog School; the Americans sent dogs into the jungle to find their wounded and flush out snipers, and the Norwegian Defence Minister had power to mobilize all privately owned elkhounds as sledge dogs for the war effort. There were many, many stories of canine heroes, and many more untold tales of faithful companions who gave their lives for their soldiers.

In World War I an entire British battalion was saved by Airedale Jack, a trained messenger dog from Battersea Dogs' Home. His Sherwood Foresters were in dire straits in France, on the verge of being annihilated under a ferocious barrage which had cut off all their communications. Desperate for reinforcements, they sent Jack off to the headquarters with a message. He kept close to the ground, as he had been taught, slipping like a shadow through an unending rain of bursting shells and flying debris. His destination was four miles behind the lines and within the first devastating mile his lower jaw was smashed by shrapnel, his body was gashed along its length and his front paw was shattered. Yet he dragged himself to his goal, delivered his message in its leather pouch on his collar, and died at the commander's feet. The battalion was saved.

At Verdun in 1918 an American marine was adopted by a mongrel, Belle. The two became accidentally separated when the regiment was moved to Chateau-Thierry but Belle found her own way and turned up at the field hospital just as her marine was being hurried in on a stretcher, badly wounded and unconscious. Her compassionate licks on his face brought him round and she never again left his side.

The 1914 yearbook of the National Canine Defence League cites the story of Lassie, a bearded collie, who saved the life of a sailor. John Cowan had been carried to a house from the wrecked HMS *Formidable*, which had been sunk in the Channel by a submarine, and been laid on the kitchen floor believed dead, as all efforts to revive him had failed. Lassie, the household dog, knew better. She lay beside him, licking his face for about half an hour, and then gave a joyful bark: he was showing signs of life. The sailor eventually recovered fully, and he and the dog became inseparable.

Then there was Bobs, a fox terrier who was ship's pet on HMS *Tornado*, another vessel attacked by German submarines. Ten men owed their lives to Bobs, whose persistent barking attracted the attention of the crew of HMS *Radiant* to the exhausted survivors lying frozen and unconscious in a life raft.

In the next world war, a shepherd/collie/husky cross called Chips went to Sicily as part of the K-9 Corps in 1943. He and his handler, Private John R. Rowell, were with the 3rd Division Infantry Regiment of General George S. Patton's 7th Army when it was pinned down by an Italian machine-gun post. Chips was set loose and attacked the post alone, flying at the throats of the gunners, who promptly surrendered. In the same war, across the sea in Tunis, a mongrel aptly named Flak was the grounded mascot of a bomber crew. He always came on to the airfield just before 'his' crew's plane returned – he had unerring timing. One day he came on to the field and set up a mighty howling; he knew, before anyone else did, that the crew had just been shot down over Italy. The tales are numerous of dogs aware of the death of their soldiers, sailors and airmen hundreds or thousands of miles from home. But inspiring as these tales are, the use of dogs in war is the nadir of exploitation: war is not practised between dogs, wolves or any species other than man. They have better ways of working things out.

To return to more peaceful matters: the sheepdog. A true sheepdog is not quite the same as a shepherd dog, although shepherd dogs have been seen quite often in German sheepdog trials. A sheepdog is a herder more than a guard and its herding instincts are naturally strong. The most typical sheepdog – and the supreme one – is the border collie, whose work is now familiar to millions of British television viewers. Collie and master are the perfect team, of one mind, with an absolute understanding of each other and a superb system of communication over great distance. The working collie is perhaps the epitome of the special alliance.

John Holmes, in his classic book *The Farmer's Dog*, points out that a dog's herding instinct, which has been carefully cultivated by generations of farmers, is in fact a facet of the hunting instinct, and Dr Gail Vines, an ethologist at Bristol University, has shown just how wolf-like a sheepdog really is. In her article of 10 September 1981 in the *New Scientist* she described the behaviour of a wolf pack hunting caribou, an animal which a wolf would find difficult to bring down alone. As has already been explained, co-operation and individual versatility are essential to successful pack-hunting and in the caribou wolf-hunts the potential sheepdogs are easily spotted: the ones that head off, single out and drive the prey. It is not their job to kill; that is reserved for more powerful and aggressive wolves. The herders' qualities are great agility, speed, instant responses, considerable intelligence and foresight, the ability to concentrate, endurance and, above all, the willingness to co-operate and work in a team.

Even among the herders there are individual traits: most react to a straying animal by 'guarding' it until pack reinforcements arrive but some prefer to gather, others to follow or drive, and farmers often use different dogs for different jobs. Some dogs have tremendous 'presence' and can hold a flock not necessarily by the famous collie 'eye' but simply by their absolute self-confidence and sheer power of personality. They know and understand their sheep; they have learned to anticipate the flock's behaviour and to work *with* the sheep. They know when the sheep are feeling edgy and then they ease off the pressure, relaxing the flock until it calms down again. The sheep quickly recognize that respect is due to such a dog. You could call it charisma. The confidence of the dog reassures the sheep, yet it is the potential threat of the dog, especially in the typical hunting stance of a predator, which keeps the flock bunched together and under control.

The sheepdog, behaving naturally by exercising its herding/hunting instincts, is only a member of the pack and not its leader. The shepherd fulfils that role and this is vital to the success of the partnership, especially in the early stages of training when the young dog must accept that the dominant human is directing the tactics of the 'hunt'. More experienced dogs, who understand their shepherd and his ways and who have learned to predict the responses of the sheep, are able to work with him by what almost seems to be telepathy. In fact they are making full use of the knowledge they have gained from experience, and they respond immediately to the behaviour of the flock and of their pack leader almost by second nature. They know precisely what effect their own actions and attitudes will have on the sheep and on the shepherd. A carefully trained sheepdog, like a carefully trained police dog, will at all stages have been given problems it can solve successfully, so that its self-confidence is reinforced and it feels in complete control of its sheep. Its own behaviour determines the behaviour of the flock.

Shepherd and dog are in constant communication with each other, in the same way that the members of the wolf pack are at every moment fully aware of every other member's position, activity and intent. Wolves literally keep an eye on each other and often seem to space themselves quite deliberately when first stalking the prey. They tend to maintain an equal distance between themselves and like to know that there are other wolves on either side of them to plug the gaps. The sheepdog, often working alone with the shepherd, may feel disconcerted by the lack of pack reinforcements and has to operate at speed trying to take the place of all those absent colleagues which, in the wild, would be part of the circle around the prey herd. The shepherd is the dog's only support and point of reference.

The shepherd conveys his directions with a combination of vocal signals, physical gestures and stance, and the dog is alert to every one of them. Basically a young dog is probably taught to respond to perhaps ten or a dozen signals, which tell it where to go, when to stop, whether or not to remain static (dropped or standing), and when to ease off or increase the pressure. Shepherds are very close to their dogs: the animals are essential to the work and each relies on the other, so that the relationship is a particularly special one. Over the centuries sheepmen have acquired an astute understanding of the mind of the dog and they exploit their knowledge of canine tendencies to the full.

The art of working any dog is to use its natural behaviour patterns to your own advantage, working with its instincts rather than attempting to eradicate them. For example, a shepherd has trained his young collie to lie down once she has the flock between them. (Many shepherds prefer female collies, considering them more steady and intelligent.) He then moves a few paces to his left; the sheep automatically move in the opposite direction and the dog automatically moves to her own left to re-establish a 'north/south' axis with the shepherd, who anticipates her move by giving a signal for 'Come by', the instruction for the dog to move to the shepherd's right. The dog soon learns to associate the signal with her own move and the shepherd no longer has to shift position himself: he has taught the dog to move clockwise around the flock on command. There are many similar training tricks, each attaching a signal to something the dog hardly realizes it is already doing.

Whether the signals are gestures, calls or whistles is a matter of tradition, choice and circumstance. Vocal communications are used by wolves to keep in contact during a hunt and from the dog's point of view a shepherd's whistles and verbal commands are just a variation on canid vocalizations. Actual words are not as important as inflexion, tone and pitch of voice. Some people claim that every household pet dog has a vocabulary of maybe a hundred words, but more often than not the dog is reacting to an association of ideas. If its owner speaks in a flat, robotic monotone the dog will probably fail to react even to trigger words like 'dinner' and 'walk', especially if there is no unconscious, give-away body language. It is the mood of the speaker which needs to be communicated rather than the formal words.

There is also a farm dog which speaks back: the Huntaway, a New Zealand dog, which 'speaks' to the sheep. He can simply stand in the field barking and the sheep take note of what he tells them to do. 'Speak' is one of the commands in his repertoire, and he controls sheep with a mixture of voice, vigour and size. 'Shut up' is another of this dog's commands which no collie would recognize, and so is 'Get up' which sends the Huntaway into a pen of sheep where he walks on their backs. Huntaways, it is claimed, are easily trained, friendly, untemperamental dogs with 'a great understanding of some of the daft things their owners expect', as Clive Dalton, the New Zealand animal behaviourist and author, puts it.

The author Dr John Brown told the story of his dainty, graceful collie bitch called Wylie who had a passion for rounding up sheep. She began to disappear once a week, always on Tuesdays at 9 p.m., returning late on Wednesday plastered with mud, tired but happy. One day the doctor was walking across the market-place with Wylie at his heels when two shepherds recognized her, although they did not know the doctor. 'That's her,' said one, 'that's the wonderfu' wee bitch that naebody kens.' Apparently she had been turning up at dawn on market day for months and working like a true professional, entirely of her own accord (the doctor was no shepherd), helping the men get their sheep and lambs into the market place. 'She's a perfect meeracle,' they said. 'Never gangs wrang; wears but never grups. A perfect meeracle, and as soople as a maukin.'

The story highlights several interesting points. First of all, Wylie was a born sheepdog, a descendant of generations of working dogs bred for the shepherd, and she adored working with sheep. It came so naturally to her that she did not need training, nor did she seem to need any instructions from a pack leader. She would work for any shepherd, using her own intelligence to sort out any problems. Many sheepdogs are so finely tuned to their own shepherds that they find it difficult to work with anyone else, even if exactly the same words and inflexions are used. When good dogs do change hands, the first act of a wise shepherd is to shut the dog in its new kennel with an old jacket of his or a pair of shoes so that by morning the new master's smell is thoroughly familiar to the dog and the serious business of learning about each other can begin. Wylie apparently needed no such education. And how did she know the day of the week?

Farms also use quite different dogs for cattle work. Cattle are big and do not behave like sheep. They are often more easily led than driven: they follow out of curiosity, as any dog-walker in a field of bullocks will quickly appreciate. It is quite easy to persuade a herd of cattle to go through a gate by letting a confident dog wander ahead of them in the right direction. Most cattle dogs, however, are drovers by tradition. They run behind the herd, depending on the predator/prey relationship, and they have perfected the art of nipping a cow's heel to keep her moving and then jumping smartly out of the way before the kick-back comes. Another technique, which farm collies tend to use, is hanging on to the cows' tails, a sure way of hastening their leisurely pace. The herd soon knows how far it can trust a dog and again it is not the size or the strength of the dog that counts so much as its self-confidence. Many of the traditional cattle dogs are small and short-legged, like the corgi and the Lancashire heeler. An interesting worker is the Australian cattle dog or Queensland heeler, purpose-bred in the 1840s by crossing Scottish blue merle collies with local dingoes. This combination produced a dog of exceptional resilience, strength and agility which would work flat out all day and control Australian-sized herds of cattle without a qualm. Like all the best working dogs, it needs the stimulation of training and work.

Another, recent, role for dogs on the farm is as spotters: they use their noses to identify cows on heat so that they can be put to the bull or given artificial insemination.

Farm dogs interrelate with a wide variety of domesticated animals. Bitches have been known to save the lives of newborn lambs by licking them vigorously to restore circulation and have fostered all kinds of youngsters, even kittens. Early in the eighteenth century, spaniels regularly suckled 'sow babbies', so that the pork would 'eat as fine as any Puppy Dog'. In the 1980s a Newfoundland living in Sussex adopted a duckling and the two became inseparable companions. A hen in Somerset decided to take over a litter of seven pups while she was nursing her only surviving chick; she would gather them all under her wings and brood with great contentment, to the mild concern of the displaced spaniel mother who was only allowed in to suckle the puppies.

The father of Landseer, the famous painter of dogs, had a bitch which fostered a lion cub in the 1820s and another which looked after some tiger cubs. A great fosterer of today is Meg, a whippet living in Dorset who, when one of the bantams rejected her clutch of eggs, was given them to keep warm overnight in her basket. Meg hatched one of them, and Rover the chick firmly believed Meg to be his real mum. Meg is slightly confused by it all but they are an inseparable pair. The question is, did the chick think he was a puppy or Meg think she was a hen?

The northern dogs, which look so much like wolves apart from their jaunty tails and which are sometimes mated out to wolves to increase their qualities, have been used since time immemorial by the tribes of the lands of ice and snow. Eskimo hunters trained their dogs to detect seals' breathing-holes and to attack bears from behind, disabling them so that the hunter could make use of his harpoon. These dogs were highly intelligent, and strangely generous to their masters. A dog called Barbekark, belonging to the mid-nineteenth-century explorer Captain Hall, once killed a deer of its own accord, ate a single mouthful from its neck and then went and fetched his master to the carcase. Barbekark's brother was an expert seal-catcher; he was also the lead dog in the sledge team and on one occasion he spotted a seal on the ice, dashed forward at full speed dragging the team and sledge with him, caught the seal by its hind flippers just as it was plunging back into the water, and hung on while it struggled until, aided by colleagues, he managed to drag the seal back on to the ice for his master to kill.

Sledge drawing is the role in which most people envisage the handsome dogs of the north, pulling their loads in teams across a bare, bleak, sub-polar landscape. Eskimos used to use a team of seven to ten dogs, harnessed together very simply with strong seal-hide cords or traces. The dogs were accustomed to sledge work almost as soon as they could walk and a team of seven could draw a heavy sledge, laden with men, a mile in four and a half minutes. Early in the nineteenth century Captain Lyons said that three dogs took him on a hundred-pound sledge over the same distance in six minutes flat; his dogs used to keep their noses to the ground and gallop at full speed even on the darkest nights or in blinding blizzards, and never set a foot wrong. They were guided by a whip with a lash anything from eighteen- to thirty-feet long but skilful drivers rarely touched their dogs with the whip. They used their voices, aided by a flick of the whiplash to one side or the other near the leader who knew exactly what the signals meant. To stop, the driver cried out a loud sound very like the 'Woah!' we use for horses. Then, when the sledge had come to rest, he would throw the lash gently over the dogs' backs and they would all lie down, and remain thus for hours even if their master was absent.

The dogs were very quarrelsome amongst themselves and there was plenty of snapping and snarling as they galloped across the snow. Every now and again someone's temper would go and a general fight begin, with dogs tumbling over each other and the traces becoming totally entangled. The whip was then used in earnest but it only served to make the dog which was lashed think its neighbour was responsible for the stinging pain and he would give him a sound bite around the ears. If a dog was really unruly, the driver would take the more drastic remedy of pressing the dog's nose into a hole he had made in the snow with his boot-toe and then clouting the animal with the ivory handle of the whip. The dog never howled or tried to escape but simply gave a low whine. The treatment always worked and the punishment never needed repeating.

Despite the work demanded of them, those nineteenth-century dogs were ill fed and lived on fish bones, seal bones, scraps of hide and whatever other meagre scraps the men could not eat themselves. They were often so hungry that they would eat anything and Captain Lyons reported that one night they ate a thirty-foot whiplash and on another occasion a single dog ate a six-foot-long piece of walrus hide and blubber, an inch and a half square, in all of seven seconds. Yet their endurance was remarkable; they seemed to be able to work over seventy miles with nothing to eat for forty-eight hours and still come home as fresh as when they left.

The Dutch naturalist Niko Tinbergen, who studied for many years with Konrad Lorenz, noted in his book *Curious Naturalists* that in Greenland there is rarely deep and at the same time soft snow, and therefore the Canadian single-track sledging system is not used. Greenland dogs fan out, so that the weight of the team is widely spread over treacherous areas of sea ice. Even in Tinbergen's time in Greenland, the 1930s, the Eskimos were still whipping their dogs furiously if there was a fight, which only exacerbated the situation because they lashed at the aggressor, who was normally socially higher up the scale and whose position of dominance was thus threatened by loss of face. It would be better, unfair as it may seem, to hit the lower dog so that it more quickly appreciated its place in the scheme of things and remembered not to irritate its neighbour in future.

That was in eastern Greenland. In the west there seemed to be a tradition of skilful training and very little actual whipping, the technique being similar to the one described by Lyons, with the lash being used lightly but accurately. Some hunters were rougher and less skilled than others and Tinbergen once saw the tip of a dog's ear flicked off and others had lost an eye to the lash. In spite of it all, the adult dogs would go wild with joy when their master came out with their harness for the first time in the autumn and they all seemed eager to push their heads into the harnesses while they danced around him wagging their tails enthusiastically.

'Mushers' are now being seen in Britain, when conditions permit. As a sport, sled-racing is on the increase and the dogs used here tend to be Siberian huskies rather than the bigger dogs of Greenland. These dogs, which tend to be less bad-tempered than some of the dogs Tinbergen knew, had a better life in the old days than their Greenland cousins: like the dingoes, they served as living blankets for their human families. They are trained with wheeled rigs when there is a lack of snow and in early 1987 there were two hundred Siberian huskies competing in the fifth annual Spillers-Bonio Snow Rally at Aviemore. The number of these dogs in Britain has trebled in three or four years. It is not quite like Alaska, though, where mushers drive their teams on routes of 1,100 miles. In 1985 the Alaskan Initarod trail sled-dog race was won by Libby Riddles in just over eighteen days (twenty minutes over) in weather so bad that the race had to be halted twice so that dog food could be flown in and dropped at checkpoints. Fifteen of the sixty-one entrants gave up and a sixteenth was disqualified for killing one of his dogs. Eight other dogs died accidentally in the course of the race.

Sledge racing apart, draught dogs are no longer seen in

Britain but they were once common, pulling their carts laden with milk, meat, fish and other goods for butchers, bakers, milkmen, knife-grinders and hawkers of various kinds. Newfoundlands often carried fish from the coast up to the London markets and a team of four could draw a load weighing three or four hundredweight. Long teams of dogs drew travelling shows from one country fair to another and were a familiar sight. In Sussex there was a team of postal dogs which carried the mail between Steyning and Storrington.

The matter of draught dogs was debated in the House of Lords in 1854, during the reading of the Prevention of Cruelty to Animals Bill, which proposed to extend the prohibition of driving dogs with carts to all parts of the country (there was already trial prohibition in certain areas). It seems there was a fairly heated debate, with several noble lords appearing as friends of dogs and others decidedly hostile to them. On the day before the Bill's second reading in July 1854, a case was heard in Portsmouth which caused the bench to draw attention of the noble lords to 'what constantly took place' in the Portsmouth area, especially concerning dog carts used for carrying fish along the coastal roads: 'half-rabid dogs, driven by reckless men at a speed exceeding that of the fastest horse.' The case involved one John White, a rag-and-bone collector whom the RSPCA (founded thirty years earlier) accused of cruelty. He was seen driving two dogs pulling a dog cart at their topmost speed, 'notwithstanding which the defendant continued to beat them most unmercifully, at the same time jumping up and down in the cart, and swaying the whole weight of his body to and fro, so that the dog attached to the shaft was nearly crushed to the ground every time he did so.' White was found guilty and was sentenced to a month in the House of Correction, with hard labour. The Bill was eventually passed in 1856 and it is an indictment of the British that its passing was due more to the fact that people were annoyed by the noise of the draught dogs and the barking they always generated in the neighbourhoods through which they passed than any repulsion for the cruelty involved.

Another form of work was the labour of the treadmill. Turnspit dogs paddled for hours to turn roasting meat or mill wheels or prayer wheels. One eighteenth-century tale relates that William Warburton, Bishop of Gloucester, officiating at a service in Bath, began reading from Ezekiel – 'As if a wheel had been in the midst of the wheel . . .' whereupon with one accord, all sorts of little bandy-legged dogs leaped off their masters' feet (which they had been keeping warm in the manner of the time) and left the church in haste, tails clapped between their legs. They were turnspits, and the word 'wheel' meant work.

Some dogs had more pleasurable work. The truffle-dogs, for example, were prized for their scenting powers in locating the site of truffles, the edible underground fungi considered a great delicacy. A human expert can guess where they might be hidden but a dog can confirm it with its nose before the digging starts. In Britain truffles can be found on chalk downland, especially beneath beech trees and also among the roots of parkland cedars, limes, oaks, hazel and Scotch fir. Several stately homes boasted truffle troves in the nineteenth century, among them Longleat, Kingston Lacey, and the homes of Lord Winchelsea, Lord Jersey, the Countess of Bridgewater and the Earl of Abingdon.

The fungi vary in size from minuscule to a medium-sized potato and are found here and there individually, or sometimes in clusters of twenty, thirty or more. On the continent pigs are traditionally used to hunt truffles, although the pigs tend to eat them. The French used a rare breed of dog, specifically known as a truffle-dog, which weighed about fifteen pounds and was almost pure poodle – white, black, or black-and-white – with a homing instinct so acute that if it was sold it would immediately find its way home. Such dogs often travelled as much as sixty miles home, covering most of the journey by night.

Truffle-dogs were used to working at night, in absolute silence, and truffle hunters preferred black dogs so that suspicious keepers and groundsmen could be avoided. A good dog was worth a small fortune: one old, blue, grizzled truffle-hound in France in the 1860s supported a man and his family of ten children without him needing any other work or income.

Such dogs were born with excellent noses and were carefully trained from about three months old. The training was fairly straightforward: the dog was first taught to retrieve a truffle laid on the ground and then, once he was doing so properly and cheerfully, a particularly fragrant truffle was covered with a little earth. As the dog became more involved and amused by this game, the truffles were buried more deeply until he was ready to find one for real in a spot where an experienced dog had already indicated truffles were growing. The luckiest dogs became attached to one of the mansions, or even to royal palaces.

Unlike the French, who would use no substitutes, the English believed that any dog with a good nose could be a good truffle hunter and they trained them by giving puppies truffle ome-lettes to accustom their palates (and of course their noses) to the special aroma of the truffles. It was said that during the seventeenth century a Spaniard brought two genuine truffle-dogs with him to Wiltshire, where he made quite a fortune selling truffles, and when he died he bequeathed his money and his dogs to a farmer who had been good to him. The descendants of those two valuable dogs were still hunting for truffles on the same land two centuries later.

Truffle-dogs use their noses to please the gourmet but other dogs use their noses for more active hunting. The popularity of dogs in Britain owes a great deal to the gun-dogs that work in partnership with shooting men. In this relationship the dog is working fairly naturally and, as with police dogs and sheep-dogs, the best trainers make sure that the dog finds that its work is fun. There are, of course, sober-natured dogs who take it all very seriously, just like their owners, but training should still be enjoyable and stimulating. Some may marvel that a retriever willingly brings a bird back to its master, unmarked by its own teeth, and delivers it to him gladly, but the wild canid frequently brings food back to the den to feed the family.

A correspondent writing to a sporting magazine in 1887 had a useful tip for those whose retrievers were 'hard-mouthed'. He suggested that the dog could be taught to pick up its birds quickly and return at full gallop by the simple ruse of its master turning his back on the dog and running away from it, whistling as he did so. The dog would be in such a hurry to catch up and see what was going on that it would have no time to chew its bird. Another correspondent, writing in *The Field* in 1953, was rather more thoughtful. He had a young German pointer which within three months of training was the kind of dog he had always dreamed of: it was perfect with dead and cold objects. However, the first warm bird it retrieved was a disaster – the dog tore it to shreds and proudly brought back the tattered remnants. One day the dog, Rommel, chased the household cat and the owner, knowing it would be certain death for the cat if caught, intervened smartly. He picked up the cat and made a great fuss of it in front of the dog. Rommel wagged his tail. Then the owner had an idea. He went straight to the larder, brought out a dead pheasant and spent an hour showing Rommel how much he loved that pheasant – plenty of stroking and talking. After a few sessions of this, the dog was cured of its hard mouth. He realized that pheasants were precious and he would take the greatest care not to spoil them for his master.

The nose-dog has performed many other roles, some trivial, some literally vital. Countless people owe their lives to dogs which have found them wounded on the battlefield, crushed under quake-shaken masonry, or buried and half-frozen in the snow. The rescue dogs need a lot more than a good nose. An acute sense of hearing is just as important, together with strength, tenacity and intelligence.

In Britain the Search and Dog Rescue Association (SDRA) uses collies (and Alsatians and Labradors) to find hikers and climbers who get lost in the mountains or on moors, especially in winter. Collies are well suited to the work: they have the necessary intelligence, curiosity, speed, agility and endurance to run the hillsides for several hours in the desperate search for people who may be injured or suffering severly from cold as well as from panic. The dog works in partnership with its handler, usually a voluntary part-timer, and they train together for two years before they are ready to work for real after a series of trials with the SDRA.

Training begins with basic obedience work for the young dog, which must learn to listen to its handler and react to his every command despite any distractions. A youngster living perhaps with other farm or rescue collies must learn in their company to resist running with the pack and heed the human command instead – quite a test, as the dog must watch its pack race off light-heartedly across the fields. Next, the dog must become absolutely stock-proof: rescue work in this country often involves ranging widely over upland areas grazed by sheep and there must not be the slightest chance that the dog, frequently out of sight of its handler, will worry livestock. In its final trial with the SDRA, the potential rescue dog is left on its own in a field, with no support at all from its handler, while a trained sheepdog drives a flock towards it and past it. If the dog so much as looks at the sheep, its two years of training are wasted: it will not be accepted. To achieve such a miracle of self-control, the handler takes every opportunity to work the dog in the vicinity of sheep, verbally chastising it with great severity if it even glances in their direction, until eventually the dog is not just familiar with sheep but is thoroughly bored by them.

The next stage is to encourage the dog in games of hide-and-seek, using very similar methods to those of police sniffer-dog trainers. The handler restrains the dog, at the same time exciting it, while someone runs off across the hillside and hides in a dip in the ground or behind a rock or among shrubbery. The dog is then released and encouraged to find the hider. The whole business is treated as a huge game, exploiting the dog's instinctive curiosity and sense of fun.

Unlike police tracker-dogs, rescue dogs do not put their nose to the ground for a scent. They are cast at right angles to the wind and, working at speed, they range an area under shepherd-like instructions from their handler until they catch a human scent on the air. They then follow the scent to its source. To alert their handler to a find, they are encouraged to be vociferous (they are often quite a long way from the handler) and they run back, with great excitement, to persuade the handler to come and see what they have found. It is all part of the hide-and-seek 'game'. A good dog can cover a far greater area in much less time than a whole team of people, and can scent a human body under twenty feet of snow. The risk is that a bad handler may not believe the dog can possibly be right, but it will be, and it must be trusted.

The stamina and skill of these trained search-and-rescue dogs is considerable. They may have to work all night, with a phosphorescent tube attached to their bright orange identification coats so that the handlers can see where they are. They will keep ranging regardless of the terrain, plunging without hesitation through gorse and thorn, over sharp scree and boulders, up steep slopes and down sheer precipices, often in the harshest weather conditions, but they never give up even if they have to run almost blinded by swirling mountain mists or struggle through deep snowdrifts that test their strength to the limit.

Rescue-dog work is still in its infancy in Britain, but in the snowy ranges of Europe it is an ancient tradition. The St Bernard dogs are usually pictured as mountain rescue dogs but in fact their original role was to guide travellers through the mountain passes. With a good dog, no traveller should have become lost or buried in an avalanche in the first place. The search-and-rescue role came later.

Tradition has it that St Bernard de Meuthon built his Hospice du Grand Saint Bernard as a refuge for pilgrim travellers. It was on the site of an ancient temple to Jupiter and is one of the highest human habitations in Europe. The monks of the Hospice developed their massive, benign guide dogs over the years but there is no certainty about the basic breeds which went into it. There is a picture of the Saint himself accompanied by a dog very like a bloodhound but there is also a story that six hundred years ago a Danish bulldog bitch was crossed with a Pyrenean mastiff or shepherd dog and that this formed the basic stock of the St Bernard.

In 1867 the huge dogs were still being used as guides, as they had been for five centuries. Generally only the males worked in this role. The daily winter routine was for two dogs (an older and a younger) to travel every morning the route on the Italian side of the mountain, towards Aosta, while two others travelled on the Swiss side towards Martigny, about nine miles from the Hospice. Each pair went as far as the last refuge cabins which had been built for travellers, their large paws leaving a clear trail in the snow which the pilgrims could follow to the Hospice. At the cabins the dogs entered to see if anyone had taken shelter there and, if so, they induced them to follow them. If they found someone suffering from the cold, they licked their hands and faces to try to restore circulation, which usually succeeded in warming up the victim. If not, they would return with haste to the Hospice and come back with well-equipped human help.

In 1812 during a devastating snowstorm in which every dog at the Hospice was pressed into service, including females, the majority of the dogs perished. Only a few males survived and the monks experimented with other breeds to keep the line going. They tried crossing the few remaining heroes with Pyreneans and Newfoundlands but the young dogs had long coats which in winter became so clogged with snow and ice that they became exhausted and often died on the mountains. However, a back-cross of the first generation St Bernard/Newfoundland was more successful and thereafter puppies were selected for their similarity to the old breed. Long hair was still rejected by the monks but outsiders appreciated the luxuriously coated dogs, gave them good homes in less extreme climates, and started a new fashion in the dog-breeding world. One of them, named Barry because he bore a striking resemblance to one of the original pure St Bernards, was particularly splendid, so much so that he was killed and stuffed for display in Berne Museum – no way to treat a loyal, hard-working breed which would brave any weather for the sake of a human being in distress.

NINE

The Special Relationship

Working dogs, especially in the past, were only cherished as long as they could earn their living – as long, that is, as they served man's purpose. In several ages, cultures and parts of the world they were not cherished even then. James Serpell has written about the way in which people distance themselves from animals in order to be able to exploit them, and has looked at the reasons behind this. When people's lives are hard and their survival is constantly at risk, there is no room for animals except as food or tools. Nature has no place except to supply the needs of the people. As Serpell puts it, a dog which kills a rabbit has no need for self-justification; a cat has no scruples about playing with a battered mouse; a starving man has no qualms about devouring meat if he is lucky enough to obtain it.

In many cultures people feel guilt about exploiting nature and they rationalize their acts by distancing themselves from the rest of creation, claiming that humans are on a higher plane from other animals, which are incapable of suffering or whose suffering is irrelevant and which exist purely to serve man's needs. The more civilized man became, the greater was that gulf he created between himself and the rest. Primitive man respected the animals he killed; he killed only when he needed food and even then he apologized to his victims. Animals were seen as man's equals, mentally and spiritually, or even as his superiors. Kinship with animals was admirable and sought after. The hunter had respect not only for his prey but also for the predators that competed with him.

In Britain today, those who treat animals as equals are often ridiculed as being anthropomorphic or sentimental, or are berated for 'preferring' animals to humans, as if it was not possible to love both. Religion has had a strong influence in the matter and produces many contradictions. Despite the Christian belief that man is a superior being and that other animals have no souls, in the West the dog is seen to possess such good qualities (like fidelity and selflessness) that it is not only almost human but is often more admirable than a human. The Islamic religions taught that dogs are quite the opposite – base, unclean, defiled and defiling – yet the richest lords and princes of Arabia bred elegant coursing hounds like the saluki and kept them in the lap of luxury, while the pariahs that roamed bonily in the streets, accused of depravity, were never likely to be befriended. Yet dogs, along with other animals, were idolized in ancient Egypt; they were legally protected from being killed, they were guardians of temples, they were mourned by the whole human family when they died, and they were never considered to be subordinate to man. The bodies of dogs were sometimes embalmed and every town had a graveyard especially for dogs. The Egyptians were great breeders, domesticating or taming as many wild creatures as they could find. It is quite possible that they tried crossing the pariah dogs with local jackals and their elegant god, Anubis, was probably a jackal.

The Koran frequently refers to prohibitions against cruelty to any animal, unlike the Bible, in which there is hardly a kind word for a dog throughout the Old and New Testaments and one has to go to the Apocrypha to find the only polite reference to a dog. Tobias's dog was a loyal companion and friend which accompanied its master on a journey, and even to heaven, but not in Aramaic or Hebrew versions of the text because such a concept of canine affiliation would be quite alien.

Despite the biblical condemnation (understandable given the starving pariah dogs plaguing the streets and countryside, as Jezebel's relatives soon found out), not all types of dog were abominated. The Jews favoured Maltese dogs even while they despised the ubiquitous pariahs which devoured the bodies of the dead and the faeces of the living. Dogs could be useful; Abel probably had shepherd dogs. Again the pariah found itself in a vicious circle: it had to scavenge to live, and by its scavenging it became despised, and because it was despised none would feed or care for it so that it had to continue to scavenge, with all the consequences of ill health, rabidity and a mean appearance which increased human antipathy towards it. All over the world, in every culture, there has been discrimation against the semi-feral mongrels of the streets in favour of the select band of pure-breds whose breeding is controlled by man. There is, in the minds of many people, a difference between the pedigree dog and the cur.

Miles Kington, in his 'Moreover' column in *The Times* of February 1986, could not resist a gentle dig at the somewhat distorted world of the dog-breeders. February is the month of Crufts Dog Show and Kington's article promised that a totally new breed of dog would be unveiled: the Cruft. 'Bred in secret as the ultimate in show dogs, the Cruft will have all the features that make a pedigree prize-winner: long legs, a short body, hair which sweeps down over the eyes to the ground, powerful fore-quarters, spacious hind-quarters, a small kitchen and planning permission for an extension behind.' The article inspired a 'prize-winning dog of many years standing' to comment on 'the present state of the British dog-breeder . . . It strikes me that there are far too few breeds of breeder for comfort's sake . . . Frankly, I shudder at some of the examples I see around me.' Perhaps the dog has a point.

Crufts worships the dog, in its own peculiar way. The Javan Kalays worshipped a Red Dog; in Nepal, dogs were worshipped at the Festival of Khich Puja; in the Mithraic religion the dog was the constant and venerated companion of the God of Light; in ancient Rome only the upper classes were allowed to keep dogs (but as that great civilization crumbled, so did dogs become scavenging outcasts). The wolf has been worshipped too, and has been associated with powerful deities like Zeus, Apollo and Odin. Coyotes were heroes to several North American Indian tribes and the coyote was seen as a supreme supernatural being and creative force by many Californian tribes. Some Greenlanders believed that the dog was the ancient father of the human family, but the Siberian Yakuts, like the Hindus, believed in reincarnation and thought that the souls of the most worthless would end up in dogs. Pythagoras, conversely, said that the dog was the best possible animal for a dying man's soul to enter so that his virtues would be perpetuated.

In classical mythology, there were admirable dogs like Argos, the only member of the family who recognised Odysseus when he came home after twenty years' absence, and the dog of Xanthippus which was so faithful that it swam alongside its master's ship when the Athenians fled to Salamis. There were also fearsome dogs like the monsters Gargittios and Orthos, slain by Hercules, and Cerberus, the fifty-headed watchdog which guarded Hades. The Molossian dogs were real, aggressive and fierce, but they were devoted to their owners, who wept when a dog died.

Dogs have accompanied and served man for more than ten thousand years, and without them man's conquest of his environment would have been much less comprehensive. Over those millennia man has changed, developed, become civilized (one might say domesticated) and the dog, too, has changed enormously – more so than man, perhaps, because with their shorter lifespan and greater fecundity dogs reproduce themselves on a much shorter time-scale than man, allowing much greater opportunity for selective development and rate of change. At a rough estimate there have been something like four thousand generations of dogs in domestication, compared with a mere four hundred human generations over the same period.

A lot can happen to the descendants of a wild wolf cub in a man's lifetime. Even within one or two generations the changes begin, partly because of a drastic alteration in the animals' way of life and partly because the runtier and perhaps more docile littermates which would not survive in the wilds are encouraged to survive in a domesticated state. It takes only a few generations for the typical morphological changes of domestication to become noticeable: the reduction in size, amelioration of attitude, differences in coat colour, the upright carriage of the tail, the development of dew-claws, the disappearance of dorsal glands by the root of the tail, altered seasonal behaviour enabling bitches to have two litters a year regardless of whether it is spring, summer, autumn or winter, and that useful but aggravating habit of barking repeatedly and intensely.

Very soon, the differences develop into specialities in particular families and you have the beginnings of the breeds. Breeds, however, except in the case of a few of the ancient lines, did not develop to such extremes as we see today until the last few hundred years, particularly as recently as the eighteenth and nineteenth centuries when many of today's breeds were created. Now breeds vary so enormously from each other in appearance and temperament that it is difficult to believe they all originally sprung from a similar source. Sadly we do not seem to notice that some dog-breeders are apparently determined to preserve and spread injurious genes and generally to weaken the species, producing animals that would disgust the ancestral wolf. In humanizing dogs, we run the risk of destroying them.

That plasticity of the ancestral wild canid which enabled man to develop so many breeds can be attributed largely to the wolf's monogamous instincts (many different sires, rather than one sire covering a large number of females as in herd animals) and to the relatively short breeding life of any canid, which has led to bigger litters as the natural way to ensure survival of the species. There is also the crucial characteristic that dogs (and tamed wolves) have transferred their allegiance from canid pack leaders to mankind: they accept man as pack leader and the distinctions between the two species are blurred.

It is one of life's injustices that a man can outlive so many of the dogs that have been his companions. As E.V. Lucas wrote in *The More I See of Men*, 'In any properly organised world the span of man and dog would coincide . . . A dog's life is so short.' In return for the loss of so many friends in our own lifetimes, we gain an insight into several succeeding characters with whom we have been privileged to share our lives. Even then, though, most of us fail to look really closely at dogs and we miss much of what they can teach us about themselves and about us. We are familar with their ways but often misunderstand their motives or misread the signals they give us, though those who truly share their lives with dogs know better. Sir Percy Fitzpatrick wrote in *Jock of the Bushveld*: 'He was standing slightly in front of me and I happened to notice his tail. It was not moving. It was drooping slightly and perfectly still. Evidently there was something out there, but he did not know what, and he wanted to find out. He stood stock still with his ears cocked and his tail motionless – then his ears dropped and his tail wagged gently from side to side. Instinctively I understood. He sees something he knows: he is pleased.'

Jock and Sir Percy lived a hard life in the bush; they shared many a life-and-death encounter and Jock was an expert working partner, finely attuned to his master, as his master usually was to him. Sir Percy raised Jock from puppyhood, when he was the runt of the litter, and observed his behaviour with a close, sensible and humorous eye. He could read Jock's every signal, however subtle, and rarely misjudged him. This working dog was almost an extension of his master and they shared everything, good and bad. They were the closest of companions and their friendship was based on mutual respect and affection.

A road in the Transvaal is named after Jock of the Bushveld, and many other dogs have earned memorials, grand and simple, as evidence of their owners' admiration. Some were heroes, like Balto the malamute who made an epic journey to deliver life-saving serum to a settlement in Nome, Alaska. Others were examples of incredible loyalty, like Greyfriars Bobby. Others were simply devoted friends mourned by those who had loved them, like Lord Byron's Boatswain and Sir Walter Scott's famous Maida, both large dogs. The big dogs, especially wolfhounds, have often caught the human imagination and many of them feature in literature and mythology. In a Bestiary produced in 1431 there is a graphic picture of a wolfhound dragging a rather startled, naked man by a chain around his waist; apparently he represents a mandrake, and the only way to tear this precious root from the ground was with a wolfhound!

Perhaps one of the most famous wolfhounds, and one of the clearest examples of a tragic breaking of the unwritten contract between man and dog, was Gelert, the faithful dog of the Welsh prince, Llewelyn. The prince returned to his castle in the middle of a hunting trip because Gelert had not joined him. The hound bounded out to greet him, blood dripping from his jaws. Inside the castle, Llewelyn found that his baby son's room was in chaos, the cot overturned and no sign of the child. Jumping to the inevitable conclusion, he immediately slaughtered the dog with his sword. Gelert's dying cry of despair woke the child, which was in fact lying unharmed under a pile of bedclothes, and beneath the bed was the battered, torn body of a huge wolf Gelert had attacked and slain. A stone marks Gelert's grave near Snowdon, and the story itself marks human failure to understand even the best loved of dogs.

A wolfhound called Aibe so caught the eye of a twelfth-century king of Ulster that he offered the staggering sum of six thousand cows for it and fought a battle when his offer was refused. In a different part of the world, the nineteenth-century Matabele chief, King Lobengula, fell for an Italian greyhound and paid two hundred head of cattle for it. Dogs have royal connections in other African tribes too: the Waganda people of Uganda, for example, say that they owe their ancestry to a hunter called Uganda who, early in the seventeenth century, came from Unyoro with a spear, a shield, a woman and a pack of dogs. Thereafter all Waganda were expected to keep at least two spears, a shield and a dog (no mention of women) and the chief was always accompanied by the trappings of royalty: a spear, a shield, a woman and a white dog.

Dogs have even been crowned. Rakkae was a small dog which was crowned king of the Danes, and Saur was a dog which 'ruled' Norway for three years after the dethronement of a loathed despot, giving judgement by wagging its tail in favour or growling in disfavour. Saur was killed protecting a lamb from a hungry wolf.

The imperial dogs of China were especially bred for the palace by eunuchs whose whole life was devoted to their care. Early nineteenth-century writers knew nothing of these imperial pets but in 1860, when Western troops entered Peking, they found in the Summer Palace five small, imperious Pekingese dogs. Two were kept by Admiral Lord John Hay, two were sent to the Duchess of Richmond, and the fifth was formally presented to that well-known dog-lover, Queen Victoria. It was not until the turn of the century, however, that Pekes suddenly became all the rage. E.V. Lucas quotes a translation of 'Pearls Dropped from the Lips of Her Imperial Majesty, Tzu Hui, Dowager Empress of the Flowery Land' in which the breed characteristics of the palace dogs are lavishly described. Her Majesty even included details of such a fine dog's diet: shark fin, curlews' livers and breast of quail, washed down with tea brewed from the spring buds of Hankow tea-bushes and the milk of antelopes grazing the imperial parks; in case of illness, the patient should be anointed with clarified fat from the leg of the sacred leopard, and given a drink from a throstle's eggshell full of custard-apple juice containing a dash of shredded rhinoceros-horn.

Dogs can mean a great deal to their owners and can inspire thousands of people who never knew them but were heartened by stories of their courage, fidelity and apparent love for mankind. Many a book has told of the bravery and loyalty of dogs, and many a film has played on the emotional strings of people who might never have had a dog themselves and who may well resent their neighbours' dogs. Film dogs are always admirable, either for their cheekiness or for their heroism. Think of Asta in the *Third Man* series (a schnauzer in the original book but a wire-haired terrier called Skippy in the films), or that shaggy mongrel Benji (also masquerading as Higgins in a television series), or Daisy, the comic-strip mongrel in the *Blondie* films, or Lady and the Tramp. Mongrels come into their own in the film world but none has been as famous as the pure-breds like the rough collie, Lassie, and 'her' descendants (the original Lassie was actually a male called Pal, and later Lassies were also male). The supreme dog stars, however, are the German shepherd dogs like the white Chinook of the Yukon, the outstanding Strongheart and the immortal Rin Tin Tin.

The original Rin Tin Tin had been found as a puppy in an abandoned German dug-out in France during World War I. He was a superb actor and stunt dog, loving every moment of his work and always the centre of attention. He had his own private staff, including a chef, a valet and a chauffeur for his personal limousine. In his films he was always saving people's lives in the nick of time, bursting dramatically through window panes, leaping through fire, scrambling up twenty-foot walls. Lee Duncan, the corporal who had rescued the tiny puppy from the trenches and who managed his film career, never 'trained' the dog for film work. He claimed that all he had done was to know the dog so well that he could teach him anything in moments. He never lost his temper with Rinty, certainly never hit him, and often the dog seemed to know what was wanted even before Duncan had explained it to him.

However, he was a one-man dog and immediately he stepped out of his acting role he was more than likely to take a nip at the star with whom he had just been acting out a tender, affectionate scene for the camera. Stuntman Charles Hargan did many fight scenes with the dog and one day he was bitten hard on his padded leg. Hargan immediately bit Rinty back, on the ear, and the startled celebrity never bit him again. A similar story is told about the painter, Landseer, who had a way with dogs and was asked to deal with a ferocious creature tied up in a yard which no one dared approach. Landseer entered the yard on all fours, growling and snarling fiercely, and the terrified dog snapped its chain, leaped over the wall and was never seen again.

Strongheart's story was very different. He was a German police dog trained from puppyhood to kill. He had never known the fun of playing or the pleasure of being petted, and his one aim in life was to obey the command to attack, in absolute cold blood, without anger, but as an automatic response and without fear. Undaunted by his past, film director Larry Trimble looked deep into the huge three-year-old's cold, military eyes one day at an audition. The dog looked back and there was an immediate bond and trust between them. Trimble once said: 'When you are with an animal, never be surprised when he does what you ask. Always expect the impossible to happen. If there is no response, that is always a sign that *you* need more education yourself, not the animal.'

There was something very special indeed about Strongheart. His very presence on set seemed to dwarf even the most famous and experienced human actors. J. Allan Boone, in his perceptive book *Letters to Strongheart*, wrote: 'What counted most was not his outward appearance, impressive as that was. Nor his unusual intelligence and the remarkable things he was able to do with it, although these were contributing facts. It was his character. His integrity. His attitude towards life. The fine things he stood for inwardly and outwardly . . . He was making better use, more consistent use of his qualities in both public and private life . . . He was always looking for opportunities to share himself. When he found them he let go with everything he had. Like all dogs, he never gave less than his best, never gave less than his all.'

So many dogs have moved men to eulogy that there must be a lot more to the relationship than shallow sentimentality. Those extra dimensions are for each individual to discover personally. Relationships between dogs and humans vary considerably in depth and character, like relationships between humans or between dogs. Apathy and antipathy towards dogs are as common as sympathy and empathy: in mythology and folklore there are as many evil dogs as honourable ones, and every region has its satanic or ghostly Black Dogs which terrify lone walkers on dark nights. As late as the nineteenth century a ghostly black dog, in the area of Long Compton in Warwickshire, was said to foretell of doom. Barghest, a monstrous, horned goblin-dog, is one of Yorkshire's versions. Winchester has its Black Dog, Wakefield and Leeds their Padfoot, Tedworth its Demon, Lincolnshire its Hairy Jack, and Lancashire has its Trash, or Striker or Skriker. In Norfolk and Cambridge they call it the Black Shuck or Black Shock, said to have fiery eyes and to be as big as a calf; 'shuck' is dialect for devil or fiend, and Black (or Owd) Shuck is a phantom dog or dog fiend with a coarse, shaggy coat – last recorded as being seen on 22 September 1893 by one F.A. Paley but there is no subsequent report of a death, which was the usual consequence of a sighting.

In Wales, Gwyllgi is the huge Dog of Darkness, and on the Isle of Man there is Moddey Doo, the black Mauthe dog, which haunts a castle on the island and (apparently) somehow deters soldiers from swearing! The blood-spattered Scandinavian monster, Garmr, was chained at the gates of Hell and when the world ended he had mortal combat with Tyr, the god of war.

There are other ghosts as well as the black spaniel of Mauthe. A small dog is one of several hauntings at Sandford Orcas, a manor house in Dorset, and it appears every year on the anniversary of its own death in 1900. A much more unpleasant ghost used to haunt Ballechin House, near Logierait in Scotland, until it was exorcised (the house itself has since been demolished). Its story goes back more than a century, to an owner who declared that he would return after his death and would enter the body of his favourite spaniel. When he died in 1874, his unnerved relatives shot all his fourteen dogs, including the spaniel; the house was sold and one day the wife of the new owner (had she heard the story?) caught a whiff of a doggy smell and felt something brushing against her. That was the start of it. All sorts of bangs and crashes and voices began to plague the house for the next twenty years or so. In 1897 the Marquis of Bute, who was fascinated by psychic occurrences, rented the house and sent in a team of researchers, who were instantly rewarded with all kinds of happenings and visions. One night one of their own dogs, a Pomeranian, woke its owner with its desperate yelps of sheer terror. It was staring, trans-fixed, at two disembodied black paws pressed on top of the bedside table. All the dogs of darkness are black!

Terrifying dogs come in packs, too. Woden (or Odin), the father of the Scandinavian gods, would ride his eight-legged horse across stormy skies with a pack of hunting dogs which looked like wolves, and at Wistman's Wood on Dartmoor the headless, phosphorescent Yeth or Wish hounds race across the moon with their demonic, one-eyed huntsman Dewer – Woden in English disguise. Christianity transformed the pagan god into the Devil and his hounds were said to hunt for the souls of unbaptized babies. All over Britain there were such 'wild' or 'phantom' hunts and many were the tales of men who had died after witnessing their outings. The Yeth hounds probably inspired Conan Doyle's *Hound of the Baskervilles*; and Wistman's Wood (north of Two Bridges) has a decidedly spine-chilling atmosphere to it, an ideal setting in which black imaginations can run riot along with the hounds of darkness.

Enough of such phenomena! Somehow dogs, to those who know them, are not ideal material for apparitions: they are much too down to earth. Yet I have to admit a personal experience which was quite the reverse of terrifying. It was no more than a sense of presence and the lingering whiff of the familiar, honey smell of my own dog who had died two years earlier; it happened in a house he had never known and, strangely comforting and friendly though so momentary, it gave me the final impetus to write this book.

*   *   *

What sort of people own dogs, and why?

In 1985 the Pet Food Manufacturers Association published one of its annual profiles of pet ownership in Britain, a country which has a population of about fifty-six million people living in more than twenty million households. There were also more than six million dogs living in five million of those households, eighty-three per cent of which had only one dog. The canine population was densest in the midlands and north, and the highest level of ownership was in the 35–54 age group. Cats apparently tend to settle for the south and Wales and appeal to the 35–44 age group; they also prefer to live in owner-occupied houses.

A third of dog-owning households were classified as what is termed socio-economic group C2 and just under a third as DE. The more people there are in the household, especially children, the more likely that there is also a dog in the family. Unemployment does not seem to have made much of a dent in the dog-owning population. German shepherds were the most popular breed again in 1985, then Yorkshire terriers and Jack Russells. More than half the country's six million dogs are registered as pure-bred animals.

In 1985 more than twenty thousand dogs found themselves in Battersea Dogs' Home; more than fifteen thousand of them were mongrels and nearly a thousand were German shepherds. Other breeds and types registered mere hundreds at the most. The Royal Society for the Prevention of Cruelty to Animals (RSPCA) finds homes for more than fifty thousand dogs a year and has to destroy about as many again – and here, too, the vast majority are mongrels, with significant numbers of German shepherds and quite a few greyhounds (difficult dogs to place in new homes). The People's Dispensary for Sick Animals (PDSA) also found that the majority of their clinic patients all over the country were mongrels, especially collie/Labrador or collie/German shepherd crosses, with Alsatians, Dobermanns, assorted Jack Russell types and Yorkies also at the top of the lists.

A survey of veterinary clinics in the London area showed a significant breed difference between north and south London: in the south they went for larger dogs, about half of them mongrels, but in the north they preferred pure-breds and smaller dogs, and their dogs paid more visits to the vet than the southern ones – though whether this was because in north London the dogs generally lived longer or because south London owners had less disposable income is unclear. In both areas the majority of dogs were vaccinated and about ten per cent were known to be neutered. A large number of the dogs died before they were a year old, more so in the south than in the north, and it seemed that thereafter larger dogs tended to die at a younger age than smaller dogs.

But what do statistics show and what do they hide? Why is it that mongrels seem to have such a disproportionate tendency to get lost or abandoned? Why do people seem to be more attentive to pure-bred dogs? Does the price of the puppy make such a difference to its real value? Are dogs merely the Jones's living consumer durables? Why *do* people choose the breeds they choose? Why do people have dogs anyway?

In an article in the *Sunday Times* of 15 December 1985 Lewis Chester made the wry comment: 'If a nation grows to resemble its dogs, then the British are getting bigger, stronger and more savage-looking than at any other time in their history. Whereas once the corgi frisked with the poodle as our top dogs, now they have been supplanted by more grim-visaged breeds.'

At the beginning of this century the fox terrier was the most popular dog in the country, and in the streets and at the shows, with the rough collie running a close second and other terriers like the Irish and the Airedale not far behind – all thoroughly home-bred sorts of dog. In the 1880s there was no mention at all of even the existence of German shepherd dogs or Alsatians: they were not recognized by the Kennel Club until after 1920 and a good one had been bought by auction at Crufts for exactly £1 just before World War I. Then a small group of men took the matter into their own hands, set up the 'Alsatian Wolf Dog Club' and in a few short years over eight thousand Alsatians were registered with the Kennel Club – more than any other breed in the country in the 1930s. Their fortunes waned during World War II but since 1948 they have rarely been out of the top three and headed the popularity table from 1965 to 1973 and 1980 to 1985, coming second in the intervening years when the breed name was officially changed to German shepherd dogs.

In 1903 the Labrador was described as 'never popular' but that was the year in which it was first exhibited by the Hon. A. Holland Hibbert, who soon established the breed as popular gun-dogs, though it was not until 1966 that Labradors entered the Kennel Club top three, where they have been ever since.

It was the friendly, wagging, barking, anthropomorphic cocker spaniel that really trotted away with the prizes for popularity, topping the polls for a quarter of a century until the mid-1950s, with Scotties putting in a brave appearance as third best until the Second World War. The British flirted for a while with foreigners like the Pekingese in the early fifties and the smaller poodles in the fifties and sixties, but remembered their national pride in the late fifties by favouring the Pembroke corgi. However, once the Labrador entered the top three in the late sixties along with the Yorkie, no breed except the German shepherd dog was going to get a look-in, and the same three breeds are still top today.

This gives a very confusing picture of the British, with the vogue over these last twenty years going for a highly intelligent and powerful working police dog, a friendly and biddable gun-dog and a spunky, beribboned miniature terrier. Recently the more aggressive breeds are on the increase, particularly and alarmingly Rottweilers and Dobermanns, both of which were originally bred to attack. Does that mean British dog-owners are becoming more violent, or that they feel the need for more self-protection against other people's violence?

Many of these larger dogs are bought by people with little or no experience not only of the breed but of any kind of dog at all, people who live in terraced or semi-detached urban or suburban properties quite unsuited to big, active, working dogs, and the consequences could be disastrous, especially as so many owners treat their dogs as status symbols or incidental artefacts and never really try to know or understand them. Many Alsatians already end up with the RSPCA or are given to police forces and the services because their unwitting owners have, so to speak, bitten off considerably more than they can chew. Why do they do it? It would be presumptuous to guess (though quite often the more aggressive bigger breeds seem to be chosen by people who are in subordinate positions at work) but the net result is that those who are already apathetic about dogs are beginning to become antipathetic, and exaggerated diatribes are written in the press or aired on television about evil dogs biting postmen and attacking children, roaming the streets, fouling the pavements and the parks, and spreading disease.

The diatribes have the facts on their side. Dogs do occasionally bite people. In Scotland, for example, it is estimated that about twelve thousand people are bitten by dogs in a year, the bites ranging from negligible bruising and a slight affront to a person's dignity, to something more serious requiring hospital treatment. In the London postal region, about six or seven hundred cases of bitten postmen are reported annually. A claim was made in an American journal in 1984 that each year more than ten children out of every thousand aged under fourteen receive dog bites on the face that need hospital treatment, which sounds alarming, but the article went on to point out that as few as five per cent of those bites were caused by dogs reacting in anger or fear, i.e. with aggression. The rest came about quite accidentally when the child had instigated a voluntary rough-and-tumble with the family pet. Children all too often forget that dogs are *not* humans, nor do they necessarily behave like the anthropomorphized doggies in children's literature, and the pet dog in its excitement momentarily forgets, too, that a child is not another dog and that its face is much more vulnerable than a dog's to playful, friendly snaps. There is no vicious intent. Even in cases where the dog does seem to be vicious, it is more often than not the fault of a human (its owner, or the victim, who fail to understand dog ways) rather than the dog itself. If man's intellect is supposed to be so much greater than the dog's, then man has a duty to understand and make allowances for the behaviour of the 'lesser' animal.

Bernard Levin wrote a long piece in *The Times* of 29 January 1986 about an Alsatian which had bitten a child who had appeared on its doorstep in fancy dress demanding 'trick or treat' at Hallowe'en. The child needed twenty stitches; a judge ordered that the dog should be destroyed and many people protested at his judgement. The owner claimed that the dog was normally gentle and placid but had been frightened by the child's strange appearance. Levin was deeply shocked, wrote at great length about the evils of 'odious anthropomorphism' and the attribution of human feelings and qualities to a mere dog, and voiced a general loathing of all Alsatians because, he claimed, they were 'literally untamable'. Perhaps one can see his point, but perhaps equally one can agree with the owner. Certainly one can sympathize with the dog, which was in its own home and no doubt believed it had a duty to protect its family from threatening apparitions like witches and hobgoblins that tried to blackmail people into giving them sweets.

It is also true that dogs do spread certain diseases, but scaremongering in the press exaggerates the true picture. In 1985 dramatic figures were cited of sixteen thousand cases of toxocariasis and thirteen thousand cases of entiritis and a list of more than sixty other diseases 'associated with dogs'. A number of these diseases are known to occur in both man and dog, but that is not the same as saying they are transmitted from dog to man. Only about a dozen infections on this alarming list were relevant to Britain in the first place. One of them was rabies, which is at present excluded from Britain thanks to stringent precautions. Others included pasteurellosis (less than a hundred cases a year, usually associated with dog bites); hydatid disease (no more than half a dozen cases in Scotland where there is a close association between man, dogs and sheep – both the latter can pass on the tapeworm that causes this disease); various mites and fleas which cause minor irritations which are simply treated; leptospirosis (of which there are several types, and only rarely recorded in dogs, most of whom are vaccinated anyway); ringworm (which can be caught from any animal and is much more common in cats and cattle than dogs); salmonellosis and campylobacter infections (both of which are mainly carried by food which might happen to infect a human and an animal coincidentally – in ten years only two incidents of salmonellosis associated with infected dogs were confirmed and even then there was no proof that the dog infected the humans directly); and finally toxocariasis, from a common roundworm in dogs.

Perhaps two per cent of Britain's population is exposed to

this roundworm at some time and just about every litter of puppies in the country is infected, normally while still in womb. The worms can be passed to humans, usually to children who play in places fouled by dogs, and very occasionally infection can have serious results involving lesions in the eyes, but in Scotland, for example, only a couple of eye cases are reported annually. If dogs are wormed regularly from the age of two or three weeks, and if they are prevented from fouling public areas where children play, the problem would virtually disappear. Incidentally, a French study of how dogs react to each other in the presence or absence of their owners revealed the strange fact that the majority of dogs on leashes 'deposit their scent-marking products on areas with a mineral or non-porous substrate', i.e. pavements and roads, whereas dogs with their owners but not on the lead go for earth and grass for scent-marking and definitely prefer vertical surfaces like trees, walls and 'council urban equipment'.

There has always been an anti-dog lobby, particularly in towns and cities. In 1919 a correspondent using the pseudonym Cave Canem ('witty' pseudonyms were always used by such correspondents) started a gentlemanly war of words in *The Field* between dog-lovers – in the majority – and those who saw the animals' faults only too clearly. One of the main contentions just after the First World War was that dogs deprived people of food; the logic of the argument was irrational, on both sides, but it seemed to be heartfelt. More sensibly, Cave Canem wrote about hygiene. He was no dog-hater himself; he had always had dogs about him and had been 'shipmates with many'. He said that on board ship dogs were generally clean and well looked after and were 'improved by having no dust-bins to scour, neither is there any filth for them to roll about in . . . It is very noticeable now when one comes ashore from a ship how disgusting our pavements are with the filth of dogs . . . In Venice one is surprised at the wonderful cleanliness of the streets, till one realises there are practically no dogs. Why? Well, the authorities have realised that they are not suitable inhabitants for a town, and only the rich can pay the licence. Venice is wonderfully free from disease, and everyone appears quite contented without needing the companionship of a dog. Children are numerous!'

Like Levin, he has a point but how presumptuous of him to conclude that only the rich should be allowed dogs, and how wrong to claim that everyone was quite content without the companionship of a dog. One wonders whom he asked.

Some nine or ten years after this correspondence, a National Dog Week was organized with the object of telling people how to manage their dogs properly and bringing home to them the responsibilities involved in keeping a dog. From this movement sprang the famous Tail-Waggers' Club, the membership of which was restricted to dogs whose owners were prepared to feed and tend them properly. Eighteen months after the Club's opening, more than quarter of a million members had been enrolled.

The aims of the Club were absolutely right. It is not the dogs which are at fault but their owners. Today some of those owners are once again beginning to give all dogs and dog-owners a bad name in this country, creating an anti-dog media hysteria that would have been unimaginable to the dog-loving British twenty or thirty years ago. How sad, and how dangerous. Philip Howard wrote in *The Times* on 16 August 1986 that 'we are letting the jungle back into our cities. The anti-dog environmentalist fanatics quote some horrifying statistics about a thousand tons of canine excrement and a million gallons of canine urine deposited on the streets of London every day, or some such figures.' He goes on to castigate the 'idiots who have just discovered that pet animals are almost as difficult to live with as the human sort' and who dump unwanted Christmas puppies on motorways. Some, he says, would argue that humans living in cities should be deterred from keeping household pets but he then writes quite passionately about how humans have always, always liked having animal companions and that it is natural and healthy to have an animal around the house. Although basically a cat person himself, he 'by the little accidents of life, lives with dogs' and he sums up his article (entitled 'Down, Doggie Doubters'): 'One ought to have another animal about the house, in addition to humans.'

Maybe that is why people have dogs – as a link with the rest of the animal world to which we so often forget we, too, belong. Zeuner, the highly respected writer on domestication of animals, calls it the 'solidarity of life, especially related life [which] is characteristic of most higher animals which have developed a social medium of some sort and which are not enemies'. This linking role is one which dogs, above all, fill so well: they are human enough in their ways and morals to act as the missing link between man and all other life. They relieve the loneliness of our species.

Dr Aaron Katcher of the University of Pennsylvania has a theory that the presence of undisturbed living organisms exerts a calming effect on other organisms. The sight and sound of undisturbed animals (and plants) has throughout man's existence indicated to him that all is well, and safe. Thus the household dog can be a sensor: if the dog is unperturbed, there is no danger lurking unseen and the family can relax.

Various studies, often reported at symposia about the relationships between humans and animals, show that people frequently refer to the feeling of security their dogs bring them, not just as guard dogs or watchdogs but as companions. A study carried out in Cambridge by James Serpell, interviewing children aged from eight to twelve, found that eighty-nine per cent of the children 'felt safer' with a dog. Professor Giselher Guttman of Vienna has noted that pet-owning children are better at reading non-verbal communications from other people and are more popular among their classroom peers. Stuart Hutton, a social worker in Hertfordshire, found that the foster parents he talked to were well aware of the value of a family dog as an aid to communication between themselves and foster children and to bring harmony in the family.

Serpell's Cambridge survey also highlighted some other reasons why people enjoy the companionship of dogs: 86 per cent of the children said that their dogs acted sympathetically when they were in trouble and 75 per cent said they felt better for that sympathy; 46 per cent confided in their dogs (one might expect that figure to be considerably higher) and 35 per cent said a dog was their best friend. Moreover, 86 per cent stated that they loved their dog more than their brothers or sisters – but then most children claim to dislike their siblings. In another survey

Serpell found that dog-owning women considered themselves physically more attractive, more competitive and more critical than non-owners but it was hard to say whether these characteristics were the result of owning a dog or whether those who were predisposed to own a dog already had such personality traits. Among the children, Serpell found that dogs seemed to act as mediators between children and other members of their families and were frequently able to ameliorate a situation.

This has been noticed in other relationships. How often do a husband and wife seem to communicate through the family dog? It may sound like the basis of a farce but in real life the dog can play an important role as a catalyst in relieving pent-up human emotions and a channel through which people can communicate when they cannot bring themselves to speak directly. Dogs can have a marked effect in reducing marital stress between unhappy couples, though it can be to the dog's disadvantage.

The lonely converse with their dogs; the despairing confide in them and are consoled; the misunderstood find it easier to explain their feelings through the dog, while the misunderstander is listening; the man seething with frustrated anger swears at or kicks the dog just like the wolves and huskies take out their embarrassment, frustration or loss of face on the pack scapegoat; the nervous or those with high blood pressure find peace in the simply physical act of stroking a responsive dog (physiological tests have proved this); the suicidal often find it easier to tell the dog than the Samaritans. Dogs are so understanding and accepting. Rosemary Ross Skinner, who had the courage to write a book about her own alcoholism (*Horizon House: The True Story of an Alcoholic*), said in an interview with Sally Brompton that her dog Sapphire used to lead her home when she was really drunk, gently taking her hand in her mouth. 'I'm sure she kept me alive, because not only was there always Sapphire to try and look after, but I would wake up and find her lying beside me on the kitchen floor. Without her, I'd have died of cold.' Here was a dog which, more than most humans, was able to accept the worst in her owner and still love and cherish her – *and* do something thoroughly practical about the situation, as best she could.

In Serpell's Cambridge survey, more than half the children said that their dog helped them to make friends and a French survey revealed that a valued bonus of owning a dog was that it acted as a catalyst in meeting new people. It also encouraged owners to go for walks and hence acquire 'greater personal space' – that is, they broadened their horizons. In streets, parks and countryside, strangers who would otherwise pass by without a flicker of interest will talk happily to someone's dog and then, the ice having been broken, they will converse with the dog's owner. Dogs are responsible for many new acquaintanceships, made willingly or otherwise. The jogger drubbing his lonely way across the common deliberately avoids any social contact but a boisterous dog ignores his social armour and joins his run. The dog probably gets booted, if the jogger dares to break his rhythm, and the owner may remonstrate, but human contact has been made even if it is tinged with belligerence. (Dog jogging is a serious occupation in the United States. Someone in Texas has written a guide book for jogging dogs and in places like Los Angeles a daily session with a jogging owner may be the only fresh air and exercise a city-dwelling dog ever gets.)

Jilly Cooper tells many a story of encounters created by her uncontrollable dogs, and her circle of acquaintants (desirable or otherwise) has been hugely widened because of the dogs' escapades. Dogs give people an excuse to meet. In a roomful of strangers, it is a relief to meet a dog, chat with it, stroke it, and in no time at all other people join the nuclear group of dog and newcomer. The ice is broken.

Rabbi Lionel Blue, never averse to telling stories against himself, had a big black bitch called Re'ach, a 'manipulative animal, who got worse as she got older'. If she had decided a walk was too long or boring, she sat down, and if her ebullient master tried to encourage her to continue their stroll she hammed it up, cowering and trembling as if he was the cruellest man who had ever evaded the RSPCA. The act was even more grossly exaggerated if she glimpsed a potential audience in a passer-by. One damp and dreary day, Re'ach took up her customary heel-digging cower in a doorway near Marble Arch and the rabbi, shamed by passing tourists, opened the door in desperation. He found himself in a chapel, an oasis of absolute peace in contrast to the bustling, wet crowds and roaring traffic of the Bayswater Road outside. Re'ach approved of this shelter and it became a regular refuge where man and dog were quietly accepted by the unobtrusive nuns of Tyburn convent, whose chapel it was. Over the years Blue came to know them – although they seemed more aware of Re'ach than of the rabbi – and he found much to admire. But for the dog, he would never have come across these good women who remembered to pray for those the world forgot in the darkest hours of the night.

TEN

Amazing Dogs

Rabbi Lionel Blue finished his *Evening Standard* article about Re'ach and the nuns by saying that someone had written to him asking if he had been led by a spirit guide. Re'ach was hardly a 'see-through spirit' he said, but 'one shouldn't be snobbish about the messengers of God'.

Spiritual guides or not, dogs have often been credited with psychic powers. No doubt most of the many stories have perfectly rational explanations and the 'sixth sense' so often attributed to dogs is often simply a more acute use of the basic five we share with them, aided by the gift for reading our body language and sensing our emotions. People believe what they want or need to believe. Strongheart, the film dog mentioned earlier, was an expert communicator and was said to be able to 'converse' with producer J. Allen Boone by acting out little pantomimes. He was a particularly intelligent and sensitive dog and there is no reason why eyebrows should be raised at descriptions of Boone and Strongheart succeeding in telling each other what they wanted in this way. Apparently it all began one day when Boone took the dog aside and conveyed his displeasure about some aspect of their relationship. Most dogs would submissively accept the criticism but Strongheart answered back and acted out a little routine which showed that he, too, was dissatisfied – from *his* point of view – and that there were specific steps which might be taken by Boone to make everything more acceptable to Strongheart so that they could continue to work in harmony. Why should the dog always have to concede to the demands of the man?

There are more elaborate claims for dogs' abilities to converse – literally. Some dogs are said to sing with their owners, which again is perfectly natural: a howl is a howl, and it was always a joint effort in the pack. Discounting such musical dogs as Fudge the boxer (who made the mistake of swallowing a musical watch and kept repeating the strains of 'American Patrol' at precisely 6.45 a.m. and p.m.), there was a Californian chihuahua called Pepe who was said to 'sing' actual words and who used to appear on television. Then there was Mr Lucky, a Boston terrier living in Utah, who was supposed to speak in a high, thin voice like a talking doll, and Blitz, a big German shepherd dog living in the Bronx in the 1940s who could apparently give his owner important messages in so many words, like 'Want out' or 'I want a hamburger'.

A more common dog trick is to respond to verbal questions by barking an appropriate code or making pawing gestures, but there has to be a strong suspicion that the questioner betrays the answer with quite unconscious and almost imperceptible body language, especially in counting sequences. Missie was a 'clairvoyant' Boston terrier living in Denver in the 1960s whose speciality was to tell people's ages by barking the appropriate number of times, or barking their telephone numbers (she had a little muffled sound for zero), or adding up sums, or saying how many letters there were in a word or a name, how many coins hidden in a purse and so on. She also predicted election dates and winners (scoring a notable hit with November 1964 and Lyndon Johnson for President), or the results of sporting contests months in advance, or the date of birth and birthweight of unborn babies. She had a large cardboard clock and would adjust its hands for time questions and predictions, and as a finale she accurately predicted the date and time of her own death: 8 p.m. on a day in May 1966.

All dogs have an inbuilt personal clock (as humans do). They know to the minute when it should be time for dinner, of course, and often seem to know the day of the week simply by associating regular events with it, like Americans touring Europe in a week ('if this is Tuesday, it must be London . . .'). Some seem to recognize annual events, like Gup the German shepherd dog from Tennessee who left home in a huff when the second baby was born (a traumatic event for any dog) but came back for Christmas Day every year without fail for ten years. No one knew where he lived for the rest of the year but no doubt his new owners prepared for Christmas just like anyone else and it was not difficult for the dog to recognize the imminent date. Any wolf could do that, without human aid of any kind: wolves tend to migrate with the season and their winter hunting ground is often hundreds of miles from their summer one.

Dogs are also good navigators and there are plenty of tales of journeys covering great distances over unknown territory, returning to previous owners, or, more unusually, finding their owners' new homes although they had never been there before. In the 1890s a Mr W. Atchison acquired a fox terrier from Bourne, in Lincolnshire, and took it by train to Louth, in the same county but a journey of about sixty miles as the crow flies. Within the week the dog had found its own way back to Bourne. A hundred years earlier, in 1793, Miss Emily and Miss Marion Tayler [sic] left their two springer spaniels in the care of their groom in Newcastle-upon-Tyne and took a ship to Woodbridge, Suffolk, where they disembarked and headed for Bredfield to settle into their new home in East Anglia. The dogs and horses were to join them later but the dogs set off of their own accord and turned up at Bredfield three weeks after their mistresses' departure from Newcastle. They were very thin and their feet were sore and inflamed. Neither the owners nor the dogs had ever been to Suffolk before in their lives, let alone to Bredfield.

Ted Patrick, in his book *The Thinking Dog's Man*, relates the famous story of Shep, a collie whose job it was to tend sheep in New York's Central Park in the early years of this century. The sheep kept the grass mown but in due course power mowers were introduced instead and the aging Shep was forcibly retired to an indolent life in the country. He was put into one of the park trucks and driven to his new farm home thirty or forty miles upstate, a round trip which in those days took all day. Three days later, a very grumpy and footsore Shep reported for duty back at Central Park, having found the country life dull and empty and knowing that he had a responsibility for his city sheep. The journey had involved foot-slogging down the road on the west side of the Hudson, hitching a sneaky lift on the Weehawken ferry, and footing it again from the dock at 42nd

Street to the Park. The newspapers turned it all into front-page news and everybody marvelled at his amazing instincts and skill. How did he *know* about the ferry?

Ted Patrick dismissed all the hullabaloo and looked at it from a sensible dog's point of view. Shep was well aware that something was up the moment he was put in the truck: people were being a bit sneaky about it all. So he registered the directions in which they drove and of course he could easily recognize the smell, noise and motion of the ferry. He used all his senses to take note of the route, especially his nose and his sense of direction. It was really very simple: it just required a little care to keep off the roads at first (hard on the paws and he would be too easily seen and picked up) but he always kept the tarmac within smelling and hearing distance. Once he got to the river he could recognize the distant smell of his city on the other side and with a little bit of cunning he was able to tag on behind a vehicle as if he belonged to it when it drove on to the ferry . . .

There was a spaniel in the 1920s called Sam who lived in the heart of London but occasionally had the pleasure of a country weekend with a friend of his owner, who had a country house and a residence in town. Those weekends were heaven for the dog – ratting, rabbiting, country smells and freedom – and he naturally associated the good things of life with his owner's friend, who was awakened in his London home one morning by the sound of barking outside his window. There was Sam. The dog had only visited his London residence once, coming with his master in a taxi and remaining in the taxi all the while, never setting foot on the pavement or lifting his leg against the railings. Yet he had found his own way right across London, from Portland Place to Queensgate, and must have crossed many a stream of traffic to do so. He was not the kind of dog who was allowed to wander the streets and he was not street-wise. He made the same pilgrimage twice more but on the third attempt he was run over on the way.

Bobbie was a young collie bitch living in Ohio. Her owners were moving to a new home in Oregon and on the long drive there they stopped for a while in Indiana, where Bobbie wandered off. Three months later she turned up at the new home, battered and very thin. She had never been to Oregon before in her life.

Another epic journey was even more remarkable because it involved a trip of considerably more than a hundred miles each way as the crow flies and it also entailed the relaying of detailed information from one dog to another. A small West Highland terrier lived near Petersfield, in Hampshire, and was the devoted friend of a large mongrel belonging to the neighbours. The mongrel would visit the terrier every morning for a romp in the garden. One day the terrier was taken down to Devon for a three-week holiday with its owner and while there it was attacked by a local Alsatian. It needed several stitches and it was some time before the little dog was well enough to return to Petersfield.

As soon as they reached home the mongrel came to pay his customary visit. He was visibly distressed when he met his small friend, sniffing the wounds and obviously full of sympathy, but he did not stay long. The next morning he failed to turn up and the little terrier seemed quite unconcerned. The mongrel's owner apologized for his absence: he had disappeared.

Two weeks later the mongrel came home, very footsore, very tired and with a torn ear. He went straight to his friend, whose greeting was ecstatic. The owners later learned that he had found his way to Devon and had given the attacking Alsatian a thorough bashing.

How did he know where to go? How did he find his way there and back? How did he know which dog was guilty? How had the terrier conveyed all that information? You tell me. His behaviour was exactly what one would expect of a wolf pack leader: judge, jury and executioner.

Many animals and birds have excellent 'homing' instincts and can find their way to an attractive destination, given time. There have been several pleasant little reports of 'homing drakes', for example. Writer John Burroughs, in his book *Ways of Nature*, had a chapter entitled 'The Wit of a Duck' in which a drake was brought in a sack from a farm two miles away to mate with Burroughs' two ducks. The drake had no intention of coupling in such an enforced marriage and repeatedly tried to escape.

Eventually Burroughs released it and followed at a discreet distance. The drake did not attempt to fly but walked 'as if an invisible cord was attached to him, and he was being pulled down the road'. He never wavered in his direction, which was absolutely accurate from the first waddle, and when he at last began to recognize local landmarks he positively raced home (still at a waddle). He had never ventured over the interlying area before and until that last dash he was guided entirely by an acute sense of orientation rather than familiarity.

Experiments with homing pigeons and with human research students indicate that the earth's magnetic field plays its part in the sense of orientation. Some people have a much better 'location bump' than others: you can blindfold them, take them to a strange area, spin them around several times, and they can still tell you exactly which way home lies even on the darkest night. Birds migrating over vast distances are thought to be guided by subtle changes in the earth's magnetic field as well as by the more obvious navigational aids of stars and sun. Homing pigeons can be completely disorientated if tiny magnets are attached to them in flight. Ancient peoples and primitive tribes are thought to have been far more aware of magnetic fields than most modern people: like children, simple-minded people and animals, they relied more on their senses and less on their minds so that all their senses were more acute than ours. They had space for 'feeling' without analysis and they allowed those sensations to guide them. There is a theory that ley-lines are cracks of weakness in the earth's crust which affect the local magnetic field and that at first the ancients walked along them not to get somewhere in particular but merely because, like that homing drake, they were drawn along the line by a pleasant feeling which left them if they deviated from the line. As Charles Brooker explains it, these lines radiated from a central focus – like the pattern on a china plate shattered by a stone or hammer blow at a single point. Many people followed the lines and met up at the central focus, where the 'feeling' was even stronger and the place therefore became a temple of one kind or another, dedicated to powers that were greater than man and which he could not understand or explain. The moles of *Duncton Wood* had similar adventures and feelings.

Dogs on epic journeys use all their senses to the full, particularly this sensing of variations in the magnetic field and their sense of smell. Some say that a dog could smell and recognize a city like, say, Manchester, at least a hundred miles away. A smell on its own, however, is no good – the dog has to be able to associate the smell with something familiar. Desmond Morris adds another dimension to the dog's senses (*Dog Watching*) when he suggests that its nose has infra-red detectors as well as scent receptors so that a dog can also sense sources of heat, like living bodies buried in the snow. People can sometimes experience a sensation of warmth from a faint source such as an unseen living animal, but not necessarily via their noses.

The 'space for the senses' that the ancients knew also helps dogs (and cats and many wild creatures) to predict weather changes and earthquakes. Imminent thunderstorms can cause unsettled behaviour in some dogs long before the storm actually breaks and when it does break some dogs are reduced to trembling heaps under the bed. They are sensitive to the changes in atmospheric pressure that herald storms, and probably also the changed levels of static electricity. Many people are also weather-sensitive, feeling 'in their bones' (or through a headache) that, for example, rain is on the way. In the case of the storm, one cannot help wondering whether a dog's acute sense of hearing might cause it considerable discomfort, if not pain, when the thunder rolls; for the same reason many dogs react frantically to the sound of a door bell or ringing telephone – the noise is almost unbearable to them, especially the higher frequencies that are inaudible to humans.

Every force in nature radiates energy and dogs are well tuned to receive the signals. In the wild it may be vital to know about weather changes, especially cataclysmic ones like hurricanes and torrential downpours, and dogs have retained at least this much of their lupine inheritance. So have humans – if only they would listen to their bodies. As William J. Long put it in *How Animals Talk*, published in 1919, animals are *alive*, and alive in a way we ought to be but are not. 'Each moment seems to bring a new message from earth or heaven and the animal must not miss it or the consequent enjoyment of his own sensations.'

Earthquakes are one of nature's most dramatic releases of energy and it is hardly surprising that dogs can sense their imminence. It is more surprising that humans are so *in*sensitive. There are many, many tales of dogs predicting earthquakes; in some cases their strange behaviour alerts their human companions (the Chinese have learned to take very careful note of such warning signs) and in others the dogs deliberately plead with their owners to take evasive action. Often half the local stray dogs and cats (and most other creatures, domesticated or wild) will flee from a threatened area many hours before its human inhabitants have any inkling of the trouble ahead. But companion dogs, even if they are free to disappear for their own safety, tend to be true to the pack and do their best to drag their humans with them.

There are also many stories of dogs being aware of the imminence of death. Thomas Hardy's wire-haired terrier Wessex, for example, was extremely distressed one day by a visit from one of his favourite humans, William Watkins. The dog kept touching him with his paw and would not leave his side while he was in the house. Watkins died an hour after leaving Hardy's home.

Abraham Lincoln's dog went berserk at the White House just an hour or so before his master was assassinated at the theatre. A little mongrel called Rags, the only voluntary inmate of Sing Sing Prison in the 1930s, was very sensitive to depression in humans and would pay them particular attention; he spent a whole night with one potential suicide, growling furiously to deter him from hanging himself.

Dogs do seem to be very aware of hidden danger. William Long cites a personal experience in Nantucket, where he was sitting idly on a wharf on a warm summer day watching the hermit crabs scurrying about their urgent business and some labourers lazily unloading rocks from a barge with the aid of a derrick. He noticed an old dog soaking up the sunshine, sound asleep and quite motionless for more than an hour.

Suddenly the dog pulled himself up on rheumatic legs and sniffed the air alertly, turning his head this way and that as if he was expecting something. Nothing else had changed: the men still laboured, the pulleys creaked, the little wavelets lapped gently and the crabs scuttled as before, but Jones immediately understood that the dog was alarmed. At what? It stayed alert for a few moments then deliberately moved off a dozen yards or so and flopped back to sleep again. Almost as soon as its old body relaxed, a guy-rope snapped and the derrick crashed down exactly where the dog had originally been lying.

Luck? Perhaps, but it happens too often for chance. People, too, can suddenly have a feeling that something unpleasant is just around the corner. We call it 'sixth sense' – intuition, instinct, telepathy or whatever. In reality perhaps it is only the perfect co-ordination of all the senses tuned to their peak of perception, often when the mind is idle and not concentrating on the two or three senses we usually depend upon.

Telepathy is harder to understand and again it is something at which dogs seem to be adept. An old American Negro put it like this: 'Trust ol' Jum ter know when we'all's gwine fox-huntin! You jes' trust *him*. I speck he kinder pick de idee outer de air soon's we thunk it, same's he pick a fox scent. 'Tain't no use tryin' ter lie ter Jum, 'cause you can't fool 'im nohow. No, sir, when dat ol' dawg's eroun', you don' wanter *think* erbout nothin' you don' want 'im ter know.'

Every dog owner knows that their dog reads their minds, especially if the thought, however vaguely formed, is of a walk, or dinner, or packing a suitcase. If that is so, why doesn't a dog return home from its wanderings immediately its owner demands its presence? It often does – it comes home looking a little bit sheepish, almost sideways, as if its reappearance is of no consequence and it just happened to find itself there: it comes in its own time, well aware that it has been missed but retaining just enough independence to let you know that a dog, too, has a mind of its own. But every dog is an individual and some are much better than others at knowing their humans and being (or wanting to be) receptive to human communication whether verbal, physical or telepathic, just as some humans are apparently quite incapable of either issuing such communications or reading their dogs.

There are times when a dog's message is so obvious that even

the least sensitive person knows what it is all about. In 1854 a
Mr Hopkins of Cubley Lodge, Derbyshire, brought a case
against A.C. Howard Esquire of Brereton Hall, Cheshire, for
the recovery of £10, being the value of a dog which the latter
had killed. Mr Hopkins rented a farm, which had recently been
purchased by Howard. The farmer's dog got loose and followed
its master's son into the fields where it was spotted by his
landlord, who promptly shot it with a double-barrelled gun.
The dog was represented in court as 'sagacious and valuable'
and an example of its qualities was given. Apparently Mr
Hopkins had been having a rest on a sofa at home when, in the
middle of the night, the dog, Fid, scratched furiously at the
house door and barked so insistently that a servant let it in. Fid
went to his master and virtually dragged him off the sofa,
pulling him towards the door with some very peculiar noises.
Not surprisingly, Mr H. guessed something must be up and
followed the dog to the cowbarn where he found that two cows
had got loose and were 'goring themselves in a shocking
manner'. Ever since the incident, Fid had been a much prized
dog and the judge awarded him ten guineas (not pounds) plus
costs.

Many cases have been recorded of dogs rescuing people from
various life-threatening situations like drowning or fire. In the
case of the latter, the usual story is of a dog waking the family
in the middle of the night and being so insistent with its
pawings and whinings that the sleepiest and least sensitive
person cannot fail to realize that something is very wrong. Dogs
can also be heroic and self-sacrificing in fires, which gives the
lie to some people's assumption that a dog only warns of fire to
save its own life when it cannot get out of the house. There are
numerous incidences of dogs purposely going *into* a burning
building, or warning of a fire well away from their own home.
In 1985 a farm dog called Nipper rescued three hundred sheep
from a burning farm building and although his paws were badly
burnt he returned to fetch out the cows as well. Like so many
dogs, he had a strong sense of responsibility. He received a
medal from PRO-Dogs, an organization established in 1976 to
promote the image and interests of dogs.

A much older organization, the National Canine Defence

League (NCDL), has been giving due recognition to life-saving dogs since the nineteenth century and its records of medal winners are full of remarkable stories, involving the rescue of children drowning, people collapsing or injured in out-of-the-way places, and so on. Recently a Dobermann pinscher called Zak twice saved the life of his young master, once by raising the alarm when the family home caught fire and again when the boy was swept out to sea while swimming. Rex, a collie living in Hull, had an even more accident-prone young master whose life the dog saved at least three times, once on a busy road, then from a pond and later from a railway line. That was in 1936, and in the same year an Airedale called Bess saved three children from being flattened by a train.

Some of the more heroic rescues involve the sea. Boris was a London Alsatian on holiday in Devon with his master when they both found themselves cut off by the tide and marooned on a rock. A rescue party on the cliffs repeatedly tried, and failed, to throw out a line to them and eventually Boris plunged into a raging sea, swam to the cliff, seized the rope and returned to his master, who was then hauled to safety.

Dogs also enlist the help of complete strangers. A policeman was crossing Hackney Marshes early one morning when a collie raced across to him at full speed, setting up a heart-rending howl as soon as it reached him. It insisted that he follow as it headed back to the river, where a man's coat lay on the towpath. Unfortunately it was too late: the man's lifeless body was found floating in the water.

During the First World War the NCDL published an article that showed just how important dogs can be to people. The League received thousands of letters from soldiers and sailors and their families pleading for help to enable them to keep their dogs. Men away for very long periods of active service, in highly dangerous theatres of war, were deeply concerned that the family dog should be well cared for in their absence, protecting and consoling their lonely wives and there to greet them when (and if) they came home. Money was very short indeed and many families suffered considerable hardship. The League set up a fund to help.

In war, dogs have often kept company with individual

soldiers or with entire battalions, and they have played quite a part in boosting morale as well as carrying out their duties and often performing acts which in humans would be described as heroic. The stories of bravery are legion and many were gathered together by Major T.J. Edwards in his book *Mascots and Pets of the Services*. Some of the most outstanding dogs followed their battalions for several years and took part in famous battles and wars – the Boer War, the Peninsular Wars, even the battle of Marston Moor way back in 1644 when Prince Rupert, Charles I's cavalry leader, finally lost his constant companion, Boye, killed in the battle. Two particularly famous war dogs were immortalized on canvas: Dick of Rorke's Drift and Bobby of the Berkshires at Maiwand. Dick, a fox terrier, never left the side of his master, Surgeon Reynolds, who was one of only three officers in the isolated B Company, 2nd Battalion, 24th Regiment, The South Wales Borderers, when the Zulus attacked them in huge numbers in January 1879. The little company put up a famous defence, though they dwindled to a handful – including Dick, who accompanied his master throughout, leaving him only to take a nip at an occasional intruder. The scene was painted by A. De Neuville, with Dick right in the middle of the picture.

Bobby was also a terrier, small, rough-haired, white with liver-coloured ears. He was born in Malta and attached himself to the 66th Foot (The Royal Berkshire Regiment). He went with them to India and was stationed at Baluchistan when the 2nd Afghan War broke out. In the middle of a very hot July in 1880 a brigade, including the 66th, marched out to intercept Ayoub Khan, an Afghan chief with a large army swooping down on Kandahar. The odds were judged to be ten to one and the 66th was gradually whittled down until only eleven men remained, plus Bobby, completely surrounded by fanatical Afghan horsemen. One by one the eleven were killed but Bobby remained to the end, still standing in front of his men and barking defiantly at the enemy. He was taken prisoner and was held in Ayoub Khan's camp at Kandahar throughout the following siege of several weeks. The city was eventually relieved and Bobby proudly rejoined his regiment. In due course he returned to England and was presented to Queen Victoria. He showed her his war wound, a scar along his back which looked as if it had been seared with a red-hot poker, and Her Majesty presented him with the Afghan Medal. The scene of Bobby and the last eleven at Maiwand was painted by Frank Fuller. The heroic dog who had defied the Afghans was eventually killed ignominiously by a runaway cab in London.

Many, many more unsung unheroes died in battle or had to be left behind when the men came home. Britain's quarantine laws often meant that a faithful and much loved companion had to be deserted. Many soldiers tried to smuggle their dogs in with them, unable to face the cost or the loneliness of months of quarantine. The NCDL set up another fund to help pay the quarantine bills, in recognition of the debt a nation owed to its army's dogs.

ELEVEN

Man's Best Friend

The National Canine Defence League was founded in 1891 to 'protect dogs from ill-usage of every kind'. It was launched at Crufts, at the Agricultural Hall, Islington, by Lady Gertrude Stocks who was concerned at constant cruelty to dogs and abhorred the way so many of them were chained and muzzled for long periods. Six years later the League was protesting at the slaughter of 171 healthy dogs at the Brighton Dogs' Home (on advice of the Board of Agriculture) and its annual report said that the year's work included protesting 'not only against official callousness to the suffering of dogs but also against active and aggressive cruelty to them by those who should be the official protectors of our dumb friends from annoyance and indignities'. In that year, 1897, a law was passed which enforced the muzzling of dogs and the NCDL helped to pay fines imposed on poorer people whose only crime had been to take pity on starving strays and give them food and shelter, but who did not muzzle their protégés.

The muzzling laws, which were enforced until 1899, were made with good reason. London and other cities were full of strays which roamed the streets, had fights, and sometimes bit people. Rabies was still a problem in Britain then and an average of thirty people a year died the terrible death of rabies after being bitten by infected dogs. Many hundreds more lived in constant apprehension that they, too, might suffer because the teeth of a playful or angry dog had broken their skin.

W.H. Hudson observed the consequences of the new law with the eye of a naturalist. He had always hated to see 'so intelligent and serviceable a beast degraded to the position of a mere pet or plaything – a creature that has lost or been robbed of its true place in the scheme of things' and had written quite a diatribe against fashionably degenerate breeds 'in whose nature the jackal and wild-dog writing has quite or all but faded out': toy terriers, shivering Italian greyhounds, drawing-room pugs, 'pathetic' Blenheim and King Charles spaniels, and various others which Hudson claimed had 'rubbed themselves out by acquiring a white liver to please their owner's fantastic tastes'.

But fashions were already changing and the fox terrier was quickly becoming the most popular breed, 'assuredly the doggiest dog we possess, the most aggressive, born to trouble as the sparks fly upwards'. Hudson felt that such an admirable dog, and all other good fighters, should 'have liberty to go out daily into the streets in their thousands in search of shindies, to strive and worry one another to their heart's content; then to skulk home, smelling abominably of carrion and carnage, and, hiding under their master's sofa, or other dark place, to spend the time licking their wounds until they are well again and ready to go out in search of fresh adventures. For God hath made them so.' Yet the pet fox terriers' owners, whom Hudson described as gentle ladies and mild-tempered gentlemen, did not agree with him and preferred that they should be able to walk their dogs in the parks and streets 'without risk of injury or insult' – and when the muzzling order came in that is precisely what they were free to do. Dogs could frisk freely off the lead without any chance of sinking their teeth into the scruff of every passing lap-dog.

Hudson watched. He noticed that, in London at least, muzzling brought about a remarkable change in dogs – all dogs. Not only did it protect people from being bitten but it also effectively protected dogs from themselves. As they became aware of their powerlessness to inflict injury, they became less quarrelsome, and their confidence (and therefore their friendliness towards each other) increased. The bullies were prevented from bullying, the timid found courage and used it to 'challenge the fiercest among them to a circular race and rough-and-tumble on the grass'. Muzzling gave dogs the freedom to play uninhibitedly, though the more insistent fighters soon found ways of body-charging which could be almost as effective as a clash of teeth. In 1899 the Board of Agriculture decided that rabies had been completely stamped out in Britain and the muzzles were thrown away but, according to Hudson, those two and half years had completely altered the general nature of dogs. Writing fifteen years after 1899, he claimed that the majority of London's dogs still behaved as if they wore muzzles: the old days of many a glorious scrap were gone for good and he only rarely witnessed those old-fashioned dog-fights 'with two dogs in a tangle on the ground biting and tearing each other with incredible fury and with all the growls and shrieks and other warlike noises appropriate to the occasion'.

Perhaps what had really happened was that the strays and street curs of London had virtually disappeared during the reign of the muzzle. Loose, unmuzzled dogs had not been tolerated and the poor of London could not afford the burden of muzzling because it deprived their dogs of the ability to scavenge for themselves. The NCDL did what it could to help but there were simply too many dogs which, like the Baltimore ferals in the 1970s, had no real owner and were merely welcome friends who looked after themselves.

The League is still devoted to the welfare of dogs today and carries out its aims in many very practical ways. It maintains rescue centres all over the country, finds new homes for unwanted dogs (some of whom are playing new roles now as hearing dogs for the deaf, for example), tries to ensure that all dogs are properly identified so that they can be quickly returned to their owners when they stray, runs sponsorship schemes, and takes an active interest in any legislation which affects dogs. It still give awards to life-saving dogs.

The League's protective, caring work is just as necessary today as it ever was and there are others sharing the burden, trying to make amends for man's breaking of the canine contract. The RSPCA, for example, is the world's oldest animal welfare organization; it was founded in 1824 by a group of humanitarians brought together by an Anglican clergyman, Arthur Broome. They were determined to draw public attention to the cruelty which was widespread and commonplace towards animals, considered to be brute creatures with no emotions or sense of pain. This attitude had been reinforced by countless philosophers and moralists over the centuries and it was not until the eighteenth and nineteenth centuries that the first real concern for animal welfare began to be expressed openly by thoughtful and respected men. In 1795 the Quakers advised against 'the practices of hunting and shooting for diversion' and suggested that 'our leisure be employed in serving our neighbour, and not in distressing, for our amusement, the creatures of God'.

The RSPCA (originally without its Royal prefix) stated in its first prospectus that Christian benevolence and charity should be extended to animals and it was signed by several leading Christians including William Wilberforce. They were brave men: to show such concern for other living creatures, in an anthropocentric society, was to invite ridicule and opposition. That may be hard to believe today, when the majority of pets, at least, are valued and cared for by their owners who, by knowing pets, are much more aware of the respect due to farm livestock and wild animals as well. Yet even today the RSPCA receives a hundred thousand dogs a year into its homes – lost, straying, abandoned or abused – and their work on behalf of other animals, especially farm livestock and wildlife, seems never to abate. New owners are found for the majority of the dogs but many are too sick or badly injured to be saved and have to be destroyed, humanely, along with many unwanted newborn puppies. In 1984, for example, more than fifty-six thousand dogs were found new homes but more than fifty-three thousand were destroyed, and it is estimated that, including the RSPCA's failures, about two hundred thousand dogs are destroyed in the United Kingdom every year, not because of age or infirmity but because they were owned by irresponsible and uncaring people.

Recently the RSPCA claimed that two thousand dogs were being put down every day in this country, for one reason or another. San Francisco's SPCA, on the other hand, claims that ninety per cent of its healthy animals are re-homed and they are aiming for a hundred per cent by 1990. They have a very active programme towards this end and are liaising with all sorts of welfare groups (human as well as animal) to help people who would love to give a home to an unwanted dog. For example, they find ideal homes for older dogs (the Old Friendship scheme), giving them financial and veterinary support; they offer free lifetime veterinary care for the pets of low-income pensioners; they ensure the delivery of pet-food to housebound owners; and they have a full support programme for animals placed with people in institutions or with seriously disabled people in their own homes. Somehow they find the funds and time not only to place dogs in new homes but also to give them continued support thereafter.

Many of the cruelty cases handled by RSPCA inspectors are horrifying, particularly those involving 'sports' like dog-fighting, or deliberate torture (often by adolescent boys), and such cases are noticeably and alarmingly on the increase. Many more, however, are due to neglect and ignorance as much as vindictiveness or deliberate abuse. Extreme cases of emaciation are often seen and usually the owner can offer no satisfactory explanation for a dog's pitiful condition. Sometimes the problem is poverty, but by no means always. There are many instances of genuine ignorance, like the man who tried to cure his dog of 'distemper' (diagnosed by a friend) by pouring petrol down its throat.

If a dog is sick and veterinary fees are too much for an already stretched pocket, the People's Dispensary for Sick Animals can help. The PDSA was founded during the First World War, in 1917, by Mrs Maria Dickin, who was working with families in the poorest areas of London's East End and saw that many animals were suffering too. She opened a free animal clinic in a cellar in Whitehall and was immediately overwhelmed with patients – people wanted to care for their animals properly but they did not have the means to do so. The organization's aim was to provide free professional veterinary treatment for animals owned by those who could not afford to pay private fees and it offers the same service today, like an NHS for animals but with no government funding.

The service is still in great demand: in 1985 it provided substantially more than a million free treatments for sick or injured pets of all kinds and extended its service to cover even more towns. Entirely funded by public donations, it costs about eight million pounds a year to run and has 57 animal treatment centres, 163 veterinary officers and nearly 200 nursing staff, which means it is the largest veterinary practice in the country today. It also offers a pet insurance scheme; it gives free advice to all pet owners and to those who are considering keeping an animal, and has an active educational scheme which seeks to promote responsibility towards pets. There are many, many stories of lonely pensioners whose lives would have been shattered if they had not had access to the PDSA when their companion dogs became ill.

Animal welfare is dear to the hearts of many British people and we tend to feel smug about our good record, but you do not have to be British to care. In Japan Miss Michiko Fujita, a real estate lady by day and a geisha girl by night, somehow finds time to care for five hundred stray dogs and two hundred stray cats at her Bow-Wow-Meoiw Mansion outside Tokyo, which she opened to the animals nine years ago. Seven part-timers help her now, and their salaries and the animals' food cost her about ten thousand pounds a month. Luckily she has the support of five hundred members of an association she set up to help fund the refuge. Like the RSPCA in the nineteenth century, she was going against the general view of society: the Japanese are quick to put down strays rather than cherish them and one local authority offered financial incentives to the public to bring strays in for destruction. Just before Christmas 1985 Miss Fujita suddenly lost her job and her animals faced the threat of being put down, but a French pet-food manufacturer came to the rescue with nearly forty tons of tinned food in the nick of time.

Japan's attitude to its dogs is a mixed one. In the seventeenth century Shogun Tsunayoshi passed a law that all dogs must be treated kindly and always addressed politely; he ended up looking after a hundred thousand dogs and had to levy heavy farm taxes to pay for their upkeep. David Watts often mentions dogs in his Tokyo reports for *The Times* and early in 1985 he told the story of Hachiko, the small dog which used to accompany his master to one of Tokyo's busiest commuter stations every day and meet his train on his return from work at the Imperial University. His owner, Dr Eizaburo Ueno, died suddenly in 1925 but Hachiko lived in hope and continued to meet his usual evening train for the next nine years.

In this small, sturdy dog the Japanese saw the qualities they most admired: endurance and loyalty. Today there is a statue of Hachiko outside his station at Shibuya and in March 1985, the fiftieth anniversary of his death was marked by a dog called White Treasure who became station master for a day and with great ceremony toured the ticket barriers, the platforms and the travel centre, and paid his respects to the statue. Both dogs were of the Akita breed and it is said that the Akita, originally a fighting dog, is regarded as a 'national treasure', much like a work of art or a fine mansion.

The Japanese have recently taken a huge interest in imported pure-bred house pets as status symbols: the dogs are thoroughly pampered but by law are exercised regularly and are kept strictly under control. Even so, JAWS, an animal welfare society founded in the 1950s by a British ambassador's wife, is overwhelmed by work in the 1980s. In 1984 more than half a million dogs were destroyed in Japan, eighty-five per cent of them family pets, and less than seven thousand were found new homes.

In Sweden, it is claimed, there is almost no such thing as a stray dog and there are very few mongrels. There is even a law *against* castration of dogs. Other laws ensure that all dogs are on the leash in public places, and their droppings picked up and removed by the owner. Yet apparently, despite the restrictions, the Swedish dog 'satisfies important psychological, social and physical needs for large groups of people and acts as an important link between people and with nature'. In Iceland dogs have little chance of being so valued: no one has been allowed to keep a dog in Reykjavik since 1924, and a third of all Icelanders live in that city.

In the USSR dog-owning is a more serious business and there are one or two ideas which could be adopted elsewhere. For example, veterinary services are basically free of charge whether emergency home-calls, clinic consultations or operations, and there is also an ambulance service for pets. In return for these services, the dog-owner pays a standard fee (a mere 15 roubles a year in 1982, regardless of the dog's breed or size) in partial compensation for the authorities' expenditure on dogs, including laying out special training grounds and walking areas, giving vaccinations, and keeping all dogs registered. Is there perhaps a case for increasing the British dog licence fee and offering reduced veterinary fees in return?

There are several organizations in the USSR devoted to helping dog-owners give their animals the best possible lives – general groups like the Dog Lovers Association and many breed clubs, not forgetting the Old Chap club devoted to mongrels. There are exhibitions and shows; the annual Moscow Dog Show at the Bitsa sports centre includes child-and-dog classes, hound classes in which dummy rabbits are chased by the hounds with their owners on horseback shouting 'Tally-ho!', and the popular 'Canine Olympics' with obstacle courses and intruder detention. The motto of the service dog show at Bitsa is 'Deftness, Self-control and Popularity'. Many clubs give specialist advice and run courses for dog-training instructors and animal photographers.

However, there is no other country in the world that has anything quite like Britain's Battersea Dogs' Home. Since its foundation in 1860, more than two and a half million dogs have found temporary refuge within its gates. In 1985 more than twenty thousand dogs were received, two thousand of which were claimed by their relieved owners. During that year the majority of dogs were sold to new owners, but, on average, about a quarter of the annual intake has to be destroyed because no homes can be found for them or because of their health. These unlucky ones are given a sedative and then an intravenous injection: they die quietly, peacefully and with dignity. With hundreds of new dogs arriving every week, there is no room to keep them for very long.

The Home was started by Mrs Mary Tealby whose friend, Mrs Major, had rescued a starving little mongrel from the streets. It was an age when London was full of pathetic strays – English pariahs – and in a few days the women had gathered up half a dozen neglected dogs in Mrs Major's Islington kitchen. Later that year they set up a fund and held a first committee meeting in the RSPCA's Pall Mall offices. They found a place for their dogs in the Holloway area but ten years later the Home moved to Battersea. The full history of the Home, with many individual stories of the characters it has sheltered, has been told by Lady Gloria Cottesloe in her book *The Story of Battersea Dogs' Home*, which cannot fail to move you to tears.

Perhaps one day someone will carry out serious research into why some human beings keep animals only to neglect them and starve them to the point of death. What is it in human nature that leads to such callous indifference? What is the relationship between such individuals and their fellow human beings? Do they abuse their children and their partners? Do they pick fights with their peers, or are they cowards who only attack those they can easily dominate? An American study suggests that an animal can be seen as a person's *alter ego*, and the animal which is abused may serve as an image of that person's self-loathing.

Are the men who enjoy dog-fights, badger-baiting and other debasing spectator sports kind family men at home? Are the youths who set fire to a dog or torture a puppy dutiful sons? Or is it being part of a crowd that changes human behaviour? All creatures behave differently in a group: they lose their individuality, which means that they lose their personal responsibility and often their moral values. People in institutions – prisons, camps, armies, hospitals – have different behaviour codes to those they practise in the security of the home. Dogs are the same: the family pet at home is not the same animal when it joins the local street pack, and the pet also changes when it teams up with another dog and becomes a hunting pack.

Family pets, even the best loved, often cause problems for their owners and usually the problems stem from the owner's lack of understanding of a dog's physical and emotional needs: bad dogs tend to be made rather than born. However, elderly dog owners have special problems because of their own physical deterioration. Andrew Cage is a PDSA veterinary surgeon in Dundee and he sees several physical problems for older dog owners. They are much more frail than they used to be and when the little puppy that a well-meaning relative gave granny for Christmas begins to grow and mature it can be strong enough to yank granny unwillingly into the path of oncoming traffic and other hazards, and be difficult to control at home for basic care like grooming and dosing with medicines.

An old person's fraility also means that they are less mobile so that the dog gets less controlled exercise and either becomes fat or is allowed to stray. Lack of mobility also deters the owner from visiting the vet's surgery and the dog's health problems increase unless the owner can afford a house visit. Another problem of age is failing eyesight, which can lead to accidents in the home when the dog is easily tripped over, especially if it is aging itself and too arthritic to leap smartly out of the way. Also the owner is less likely to observe the condition of the dog's coat, or spot that it has fleas or worms, or notice early signs of illness in it. If senile dementia is added to the physical handicaps of aging, the situation can rapidly deteriorate as the owner becomes more and more confused and irregular in habit. Then there is the emotional stress of worrying about what will happen to the dog if the owner is taken ill, or dies, not to mention the terrible fear that the dog, often a sole companion and solace, will die first. A dog can be the most important thing in an old person's life.

Old people are far more likely to spoil their dogs than to neglect them, often feeding the dog and going hungry themselves, but spoiling can be as abusive as neglect and the dog can become grossly fat and lethargic, with all the consequent problems of arthritis, breathlessness and heart trouble. Then the owner faces the problem of coping with the dog's death. Veterinary surgeon and author Bruce Fogle points out that we still know very little about people's grief for a dead companion animal and vets need to exercise considerable tact and sympathy, especially if euthanasia of the dog is involved. Guilt can be a destructive emotion.

Most of the problems of aging dog-owners are soluble and help is available. For the many families who believe they have 'problem' dogs, however, help is less easily found. Vets can give advice and prescribe treatments but, surprisingly, animal behaviour and psychology are hardly mentioned during the seven long years of veterinary training. When one considers how many human physical ills are the result of emotional and social pressures, it is astonishing that vets are not trained to understand similar causal influences in the dogs they treat. Like a human being, a dog is not just a body. Moreover, the dog's relationship with its human family can be important both to the dog and to the humans, and again it would be beneficial if all vets received training in understanding such relationships. It would also help if dog-owners knew a lot more about the natural behaviour of canids, wild and domesticated; quite often 'problem' behaviour is merely typical of the species and the fault lies not with the dog but with the owner who does not understand why a dog does what it does.

Here and there, specialists are available to help vets and owners sort out the kind of problems with dogs which can completely disrupt family life. Dr Valerie O'Farrell, for example, is a clinical psychologist practising at the Edinburgh University veterinary school. She began her career treating humans but she now finds that two thirds of her clients are dogs. Not that her training is wasted: she uses the basic principles of human psychology to treat disturbed dogs and is especially interested in seeing how the behaviour of the owner affects the behaviour of the dog. Because of the dog's highly social nature, it is profoundly affected by its relationships with the rest of its 'pack' and also by relationships among other members of the pack, to which it is very sensitive. If a husband and wife are constantly having rows, they affect not only their children but also their dog. Some dogs, like some children, become withdrawn; some, like Napoleon the dingo, seek to defuse the situation by drawing attention to themselves; others may take sides, or start destructive behaviour like chewing everything in sight, and others may become generally aggressive and unstable.

Each reacts to home stress in a different way, and quite often Dr O'Farrell finds she cannot help the dog unless the humans can learn to live together on better terms. She also finds that, while the attitudes and personality of an owner are relevant to dog behaviour problems, the owner's influence is not necessarily that which might be expected. For example, it might be thought that an aggressively dominant dog has an owner who is not firm enough in punishing it, but Dr O'Farrell suggests that the dog's behaviour is related to the owner's anthropomorphic attitude – failing to remember that a dog is a dog, not another human being.

If it can be accepted that dogs are descended from wolves, then every dog either needs or is a pack leader. Stronger

characters naturally seek to be leaders. The domestic dog
generally regards its owner as its pack leader and its attitude is
a mixture of respect and affection, but the born leader will try
(and often succeed) to assume that role over the owner. This
does not necessarily mean that the dog is aggressive towards
the owner – aggression and dominance should not be confused.
It is usually a much more subtle manipulation whereby the dog
contrives to gain its own way by emotional blackmail. An owner
who, in the dog's eyes, constantly curries favour is a pack-
fellow lower down the scale. Dogs, like humans, are expert
manipulators and very soon realize, for example, the irritant
value of persistent barking in gaining a desired result like being
let out or fed. The owner who treats the dog like a spoiled child,
worrying that the dog will not 'love' them if they do not give it
what it demands, is asking for trouble and the dog soon realizes
that it is in control.

Dr O'Farrell also finds that some owners are almost glad that
their dogs are 'problems'. That may sound perverse but the
dog's problem is usually the result of the owner's problems and
by passing them on to the dog the owner is superficially
relieved. It is like the woman who keeps taking her child to the
doctor's surgery with all sorts of minor or imaginary ailments:
what she really needs is someone to perceive her own problems
and help her overcome them. It is a cry for help, often quite
unconscious. Dogs, like children, can be useful as scapegoats
and as unwitting mediators on behalf of their owners.

The best relationship is when human and dog respect each
other and share mutual affection and understanding: they are
friends on as near equal a basis as is possible in a situation
where humans are always in ultimate control of the relationship
because they voluntarily supply dogs with food, shelter, company and security. In the first place the human opted to take in
the dog and finally the human holds sway over its future,
deciding whether the dog should stay in the family, go elsewhere or, the ultimate decision, whether its life should be
ended. That is a mighty power indeed and emphasizes the
enormous responsibility a person has towards the dog. It also
ensures that the relationship can never be equal: the human
must be pack leader.

Dr Roger Mugford has also specialized in problem pets and their owners: he is an expert on animal behaviour and knows a great deal about cats and dogs in particular, especially in the context of their role as companions to humans. His main consultancy is in Surrey but the demand from owners with disruptive dogs has been so great that he now has several other centres in different parts of the country. Cases are referred to him through veterinary surgeons: he does not accept direct approaches from owners but works in co-operation with the vet if medical therapy can assist his own behavioural therapy. Mugford, too, emphasizes the importance of an owner's affiliation with the dog. For example, a common problem is the dog which destroys half the furniture or rips up the car seats when left alone. This is often a result of too close an attachment between dog and owner and is best cured by a positive effort to reduce that attachment. Many owners find this difficult to put into practice: they like their dog's dependence on them and 'don't want to hurt its feelings' by any suggestion of rejection.

Mugford is concerned at overemphasis on the need to dominate dogs, particularly as declared and practised by some professional trainers. Show-ring training tells the onlooker a lot more about humans than dogs and it can be most revealing to watch local obedience-training classes in action. Good teachers are those who understand people as well as dogs and who can see what the real motives are which have brought people to their classes. The man with the disruptive boxer, for example, who had been coming to classes for months with little or no result to show for it, is subconsciously (or even consciously) encouraging his dog to snarl furiously at all dogs and all people, and he only half-heartedly restrains it as it lunges at a cowering border collie next in line. A somewhat paunchy man with the look of an ex-rugby player about him, he is secretly proud of his apparently belligerent animal which is enacting his own aggressive fantasies. A dog can snap and snarl, giving physical expression to stress, but a man is restricted by social considerations: he cannot bare his fangs or thump every person he dislikes or fears. This highlights Roger Mugford's comment that people sometimes tolerate behaviour in a dog that would be quite unacceptable in other people, and is indeed unacceptable *to* other people.

Another man in the class is very different. He is tall, thin, shy and hesitant, and his aging cocker spaniel takes no notice of him at all. They, too, have been attending classes for months and have made no noticeable progress. The dog is thoroughly bored with the whole business and the man is half-hearted and dull, quite incapable of giving his dog enthusiastic encouragement or realistic reproof. He is a typical hen-pecked husband and he has found a perfect excuse for escaping from his wife's domain once a week – 'Must go to the dog-training, dear'. He is not in the least interested in the dog and the feeling is mutual.

The third man is different again. His beautiful German shepherd dog is only eight months old but it loves the classes, longs to please and throws itself whole-heartedly into every task it is set. Its owner is just as enthusiastic, in a quiet way, and knows the value of play in training. The dog is enjoying itself and enjoying its owner's pleasure in its abilities. That it is a German shepherd, bred for intelligence and work, does help: it is born to learn. The best-bred German shepherd, however, can be a complete failure in the wrong hands and in contrast a very nervous young bitch is brought into the hall for the first time. She snarls and snaps at all the other dogs, but fearfully rather than aggressively, warning them to leave her alone. The owners have fortunately chosen a good teacher who realizes that the dog has lacked 'socialization': it had been relatively isolated from other dogs (and people) early in life and was already timid when its new owners acquired it. Alarmed by its anti-social behaviour, they were already compounding the problem by avoiding contact with other dogs, going for walks only where they were sure to meet none. The teacher wisely advised them to go out of their way to meet other dogs, so that the bitch could overcome her fear, and suggested that they should bring her to the classes as often as possible simply to watch and get used to the presence of plenty of dogs and people. Then, gradually, she would become familiar with the setting and the ever-changing group of animals, and would in due course be ready for the next step of actual training among the crowd. That teacher was well aware of the importance of early socialization, even if she did not know of Scott and Fuller's researches into the crucial puppyhood stage when social patterns tend to be formed. It was probably already too late for the young bitch to become totally confident and reliable but by avoiding other dogs the owners only made the situation worse and would have eventually found that the problem would rule their lives with the dog.

Even at the level of local obedience classes the secrets of police-dog, sheepdog and gun-dog training apply: know enough about the way a dog's mind, nature and body work to be able to understand why it does what it does; exploit its better natural tendencies; and above all maintain the dog's interest by treating training as if it is a huge game for both of you. Wolf cubs, children and dogs learn best through play.

In the formal setting of a class many men feel inhibited or feel that they must be seen to dominate their dogs in manly fashion. They only talk to the dog to give it a masterly command. Women, used to spending time with children perhaps, do not think twice about talking freely to their dogs, speaking with animation, expressing themselves with their bodies as well – gestures, hugs, crouching down to welcome a retrieve, lavishing verbal praise and communicating excitement verbally and physically – and their dogs respond to them. Some women are less relaxed: they only pretend to play and they are nervous that the dog will 'let them down' or make a fool of them in public, so they tend to nag with continual commands. Dogs soon switch off and decide to ignore their entreaties or half-hearted threats. A dog on a walk which is continually called back to its owner if it strays five yards in open countryside soon sees the pointlessness of the calling. If it is a dog of strong character it also soon realizes that it can dominate its owner, and the nagging only reinforces its mild resentment and disregard. Like an adolescent it begins to defy the cling of the apron-strings, however lovingly they are tied, and loses interest in a contest it has already won.

People who are brought up living with animals in the way that I was are lucky. My grandfather was always surrounded by animals and birds – he shared his breakfast (in India) with an assortment of several dachshunds, Afghan hounds, demoiselle cranes, red-legged partridges, a donkey, a llama and any other creature that cared to join the daily meeting. My mother, though circumstances have prevented her from accumulating such a free menagerie, has always attracted and ministered to wild animals and birds and stray dogs and cats. I was born, therefore, with a need to share my life with animals and to try to know them, understand their ways, respect them and see life from their point of view as well as my own.

Many people are brought up to look at life entirely through human eyes and they find it difficult, if the idea ever occurs to them, to 'think dog'. They may have a dog in the house, not because they feel an affiliation with dogs but because the children wanted a pet, or pets are good for children, or their neighbours have dogs, or whatever, and they rarely stop to look at the dog or think about its behaviour and real needs. They make use of dogs for their own purposes and forget to consider whether the dog is getting anything out of the deal.

That lack of curiosity is the way to a 'problem' dog and there should be many more of them about. Fortunately, dogs are resilient and highly adaptable, and they forgive us our lack of understanding; they still try to carry out their side of the contract and keep the alliance alive. Fortunately, too, there are many people who drop their inhibitions and can instinctively understand at least something of a dog's nature. There are many more who, though they do not really understand, are wholly grateful to the dog and do their best to do right by it. In the end, however, whatever the historians of dog domestication and development might suggest, humans need dogs much more than dogs need humans and they are just beginning to appreciate the fact.

TWELVE

Guides and Companions

Probably among all the domestic animals that serve man there is none which performs as many services as the dog; nor is there any animal as attached to man as this faithful guardian and companion. The dog excels in activity and intelligence as well as in attachment and obedience, and has such a good-natured character that apparently he recalls only the kind deeds and not the whippings. Whatever his master orders him to do he carries out without tiring; anything entrusted to him he guards with the greatest care: if we are in danger he stands by to help us . . . Especially for the blind this animal performs most effective services: he functions excellently for those who have been robbed of their eyesight. One can say that the dog which serves as a guide to these unfortunate ones fulfills a mission which places him at the head of his kind.

Jacob Birrer, *A Blind Man Teaches His Dog* (1845, Germany)

Eight and a half million men were killed in action during the First World War, and twenty-one million were wounded. Among the four million wounded Germans there was an anonymous blind man who walked one day in the hospital grounds with a doctor and the doctor's Alsatian. The doctor was called away for a while and the Alsatian, sensitive as most dogs are to the disabled and the young, decided to look after the patient. The doctor was impressed by the dog's behaviour and began to train a few dogs to act as blind men's guides. By 1923 a training centre had been set up at Potsdam and in ten years it trained several thousand dogs.

Dogs helping the blind was nothing new. A whole century earlier, a Viennese *Textbook for Teaching the Blind* had described the use of poodles and shepherd dogs as aids for the blind, the dog wearing a loose brace around its body with a stick attached. The blind man grasped the other end of the stick in one hand and used his cane in the other, and through the stick he could feel every movement and deviation of the dog. Training of the dog was initially by a sighted person and the aim was to make the animal alert to various dangerous situations. Eventually the dog would be fed and cared for solely by its blind owner 'in order to arrive at a mutual understanding and to establish a true and faithful attachment'. The whole system was almost identical to the one used today in training guide dogs for the blind.

In 1845, Jacob Birrer published *A Blind Man Teaches His Dog*. Birrer, himself blind, insisted that the blind person must carry out all the training. Poodles were often used in Paris as guide dogs but Birrer decided to try a spitz for himself. He gave detailed instructions on his training methods: he started on a well-known path and gradually progressed to places where there were barriers and holes in the street. He had an interesting way of teaching the dog not to yank him through half-open doors: he placed a bench across the hallway, with a small gap to one side, and, leaving the door slightly open, put the dog on a leash and stationed himself on the far side of the bench. If the dog dashed under the bench towards the great outdoors, Birrer deliberately knocked the bench over with an almighty crash so that the dog thought he had fallen. It did not take long to teach a caring dog to proceed more cautiously and find the gap through which the blind man could pass safely. One of the most admirable qualities of a guide dog is its ability to put itself in its owner's shoes, so to speak; it develops a good enough imagination to appreciate its owner's extra height when confronted with overhead obstacles, for example. It learns to 'think human' and manages to do so more successfully than most of us ever learn to 'think dog'.

Still in the nineteenth century, Abram V. Courtney wrote about his faithful dog, Caper. Courtney had left the Perkins Institute for the Blind and was determined to 'gain my living by my own industry rather than to eat the bread of charity'. Caper was acquired in Maine in 1851 and seemed to have a remarkable instinct for guiding his master around obstacles, refusing to let him proceed if there was danger ahead and leading him to whatever destination was specified. The dog was a mixture of Newfoundland and spaniel – the breed is not really important as long as the dog has intelligence, endurance, a steady nature and a desire to help.

That desire to help was shown by Paul, a Labrador whose brother Peter was blind: Paul had taught himself to be Peter's guide, gently steering him round obstacles. The pair turned up at Battersea Dogs' Home recently but were quickly reclaimed by their owner.

Despite the precedents, there was no concerted effort to train guide dogs for the blind until the German school was set up at Potsdam. Since then the idea and the techniques have found their way all over the world. In 1927 a wealthy American, Mrs Dorothy Harrison Eustis, who bred and trained Alsatians in Switzerland, visited the Potsdam centre and wrote an article about it in the *Saturday Evening Post*. Frank Morris, a blind American, was so inspired by the article that he persuaded Mrs Eustis to start training such dogs and the very first of them became Frank Morris's own guide dog, Buddy. Mrs Eustis soon set up *L'Oeil Qui Voit* (The Seeing Eye) as a guide-dog centre in Switzerland and also a training school in the United States. In 1930 she met two Alsatian enthusiasts in London, Miss Muriel Crooke and Mrs Rosamund Bond, and by 1931 the two English women had set up their own Alsatian training centre at Wallasey, affiliated with the National Institute for the Blind. Their first four partnerships graduated in October 1931 – Allen Caldwell with Flash, G.W. Lamb with Meta, Musgrave Frankland with Judy and Thomas Ap Rhys with Folly. Ap Rhys was never without a guide dog for the rest of his life and when he died in 1979 at the age of eighty-two he was in the middle of retraining his sixth companion.

It was not easy in the beginning. The British, dog-lovers extraordinary, were shocked at the idea of making dogs work. In 1931 there were no service dogs working with the police or the armed forces, and guide-dog trainers were frequently berated or even physically assaulted for their work, which the general public decried as useless and cruel. It was some time before people accepted that not only did the dogs bring real benefit to the blind but that also they seemed to enjoy their role. However, that early attitude should be remembered. Today there is plenty of enthusiasm for using dogs as guides, helpers and aids for the physically, mentally and emotionally disabled. It is to be hoped that the interests and welfare of the dog are not overlooked in the rush to help humans.

The Guide Dogs for the Blind Association (GDBA) which has given independence and freedom to so many unsighted people today breeds its own dogs and has found that Labradors, retrievers and Labrador/retriever crosses are the best breeds for most of their purposes, though Alsatians still work very well for those who can handle them and and some people prefer the quickness and devotion of collies.

Training a guide dog is necessarily a long, careful and expensive process and training a blind person to understand and use the dog also takes considerable time and patience. The dog must learn to restrain itself from much of what comes naturally to it: while it is working it must ignore other dogs completely (friendly or aggressive); it must ignore other people, too, especially those that offer titbits. Can a Labrador, of all dogs, be trained to ignore food?! It can. During training after a dog has been paired with its new blind owner, the couple practise in a restricted corridor. Tempting piles of food are placed at intervals near the wall and the new owner walks the dog down the corridor, firmly ordering it to 'Leave it!' if he or she feels the slightest deviation by the dog. Then comes the most difficult test of all. The dog's original sighted trainer, whom it knows very well, approaches with a handful of goodies and offers them directly to the dog, crouching near it and talking with great enthusiasm and encouragement. The moment is a crucial one in the hand-over period. The dog has probably been with its new owner at the centre for a couple of weeks and this ruse tests whether it has indeed transferred its allegiance from the trainer it has known for months. Has the new owner established a strong enough bond to ensure the dog resists the temptation?

The joint training period is a time of great stress for the dog and for its new owner. The dog is used to the centre's routines;

it has lived there for several months and knows all the staff and its many kennel mates. The blind trainees are in alien surroundings, among total strangers, and might never have known a dog in their lives. They are under considerable strain, learning the layout of the centre, learning to recognize the staff, becoming acquainted with the other blind students whom they may or may not get along with. On top of all that, they suddenly become totally responsible for a dog – keeping it in their room, feeding it, grooming it, exercising it, playing with it and training it, spending almost twenty-four hours a day with it.

Nor is all the training within the relative security of the centre. There comes a time when they have to test themselves on the busy streets of the local town, a place which is quite unfamiliar to them. They have to memorize directions given to them in the minibus and then they are left alone on the pavement with their new dog, entirely dependent on it. If they have not learned to trust their animal, they might easily panic at the very first kerb. Discreet help is at hand, of course: the instructors are always in the background but are careful not to interfere unless there is a real problem. One difficulty is that the dog is too readily aware of their presence, however much they keep out of its sight.

The general public in towns where the training centres operate are well used to seeing hesitant trainees and their slightly uncertain dogs setting off at timed intervals down the street but even in these towns many people do not know the basic rules of guide-dog work. The dog is linked to its owner by a rigid handle attached to its harness, which allows a sensitive person to feel every nuance of the dog's behaviour and movement. If they reach a particularly busy crossing where the dog cannot find a safe interval in the traffic, the owner lays the handle along the dog's back, maintaining control with a loose leash. This is the signal, to the dog and to the public, that the dog is no longer in charge and that the blind person would welcome human assistance.

A guide dog only works for, say, an hour or two a day in many cases and it knows that if it is wearing its harness and handle it is on duty. At all other times it is just like any other family pet and it is well aware of the separation of roles.

Without the harness it is free to lie around, play, befriend other dogs and people, and generally behave like any other family dog.

One of the most difficult aspects of guide-dog training is to pair the right dog with the right person: a bad mix can be disastrous to the confidence of both parties. Trainers and instructors have a particular person in mind right from the start of the dog's training and they need to take into account not only physical compatibility (a huge Alsatian may not be appropriate to a five-foot slightly built woman, though there are exceptions) but also psychological compatibility. There must be no insurmountable personality clash. There can also be complications at home: quite often, with first-time owners, the blind person's partner or parent has cherished their role as protector and guide, enjoying (even if half resenting) the blind person's dependence on them. When a guide dog seems to supplant them in that role there can be considerable jealousy.

The blind people I have met all say that their guide dogs have given them a real sense of freedom, independence and companionship. The latter aspect can be almost as important as the practical benefits: a guide dog belongs specifically to the owner it works with and the bond between them is a very special one indeed. When the dog dies (and inevitably its life is much shorter than its owner's) the blind person loses not just a guide but also a very close friend, and sometimes, in the rush to replace the guide, proper grief for the friend is not given adequate time or space to find its true expression, and the bond with the new guide can be adversely affected. It is a problem all dog-owners face: do you get a replacement quickly to fill the void and ease the pain, or do you wait until grief for an old companion has run its proper course and full respects have been paid to its memory?

Companionship is equally an important part of the relationship between deaf people and their trained 'hearing dogs'. This is a fairly new idea in Britain in its formal guise, though the hard of hearing have probably always depended on their pet dogs to some extent to act as extra ears for them. In 1982, Hearing Dogs for the Deaf (HDFD) was launched under the auspices of the Royal National Institute for the Deaf and its funds are raised largely through the efforts of the national charity, PRO Dogs. There is no government aid. The scheme is in its formative days but there is already a new training centre at Lewknor, in Oxfordshire, with a kennel block for a dozen dogs.

Loss of hearing is more traumatic than many people realize. It is through sounds that we first become aware of a new event or presence – a rustle in the undergrowth, the approaching drone of a plane or the distant mutter of a car, the sound of footsteps up the path or a cleared throat, the summons of a telephone or a door-bell. Helen Keller, who was born blind and deaf, remarked: 'You can touch a rose; you can smell it. You do not have to see or hear it to know it. But not to hear a fellow human being's voice is the greatest of deprivations.' Trained hearing dogs may not be able to make amends for that particular deprivation but they do act as living ears for those who are otherwise isolated in a world of silence.

The dogs are all unwanted animals from NCDL homes and other rescue centres, and many are out-and-out mongrels, which often make the best hearing dogs of all. (It is my personal prejudice that mongrels are more intelligent, more willing and more loving than just about any pedigree dog you could ever meet.) They need to be friendly, outgoing, good-tempered, intelligent, alert and full of natural curiosity. An inquisitive dog will investigate sounds; an intelligent one will be able to distinguish their relevance to the dog's owner. Training teaches the dog what to do if it hears a wide range of everyday sounds which its deaf owner needs to know about – crying babies, whistling kettles, alarm clocks, telephones, door-bells, knocks and so on – and the best dogs teach themselves to react to other, less common sounds as well, especially if they spell danger for their owners. Just like a guide dog, a good hearing dog learns to 'think human'.

The basic routine is that the dog learns what different sounds imply, locates the source of the sound, then finds its owner and touches them to draw attention and indicate what is happening. Each hearing dog is trained specifically for its owner's personal needs and the owner receives a period of hand-over training in their own home so that the dog really is a personal aid. *Favour*, the HDFD newsletter, is full of stories from deaf people whose lives have been transformed by their dogs and, again like the blind, the benefits are not just practical but also emotional.

There can be unexpected problems. A recent issue of *Favour* told of a disastrous voyage when Cherry, a hearing dog, and her owner went on a holiday trip to the Channel Islands. Their vessel was diverted to France because of bad weather. The strict British quarantine regulations immediately came into effect and Cherry was separated from her owner for six months (the collies which did such effective rescue work after the El Salvador earthquake in 1986 suffered the same indignity of quarantine kennels) which was a huge blow for both of them. Their working partnership was shattered and Cherry had to go through a refresher course to bring her back to her former high standards as a hearing companion. It was one of those chances that seem so remote that most people would not even think of them but boats and planes can be and are diverted from time to time and, however good a case might be made for the individual dog to be exempt from the rules, the risk and consequences of bringing rabies back into Britain are far too serious for exceptions to be made.

The English hearing dogs scheme was inspired by a symposium talk given to the British Small Animals Veterinary Association in 1979. One of the veterinary surgeons in the audience was Bruce Fogle, who has always been keenly interested in the special relationship between pets and people, particularly in cases where the animals can help those who are handicapped, disturbed or simply lonely. Like Roger Mugford, Fogle is well known to the general public through media appearances; he also writes books on pet care and behaviour, and discusses such subjects as the grief people suffer at the death of a pet. The symposium talk he heard was given by Professor Leo Bustad, at that time Dean of the School of Veterinary Medicine at Washington State University, who explained that there were already several schemes in the United States for training dogs to help deaf people. Fogle listened hard and devised a British scheme with the help of the RNID, PRO Dogs, Pedigree

Petfoods and various media contacts, and gradually HDFD took shape.

In 1981 Leo Bustad became a founder member of America's Delta Society, a non-profit-making professional association whose objectives are to study the nature and significance of the bond that exists between people and the living environment, with a particular emphasis on interactions between people and animals, especially where these interactions are of benefit to human mental health and physical well-being. By 1986 the Society's annual conference was able to attract more than a thousand animal experts and enthusiasts from many parts of the world who heard something like two hundred presentations on subjects ranging from pet ownership among children to 'pet-facilitated therapy'.

Bustad was also one of several distinguished speakers at the International Symposium on the Human-Pet Relationship held in Vienna in October 1983 to honour the eightieth birthday of Professor Konrad Lorenz, lifelong observer of animal behaviour, naturalist, ethologist, Nobel Prize winner and author of such well-known books as *King Solomon's Ring* and *Man Meets Dog*. There were about 350 delegates, from many countries, among them several British members of the Society for Companion Animal Studies (SCAS). From the many subjects covered at the symposium, it was clear that animal companions (a more honourable description than 'pets') are enormously important to all kinds of people in all kinds of situations and that dogs are the most versatile and vital of them all.

The dog's role in human society has developed and expanded throughout the millennia of domestication and today there is a rapid and perhaps inevitable increase in the exploitation of its basic role as a companion to include a wide range of therapeutic and 'service' applications. For example, there is a substantial project in the United States known as PACT (People and Animals Coming Together) which has shown that elderly people who have developed a close attachment to a pet often enjoy better health and general contentment than those without pets. An Australian study has confirmed the psychological benefits of the presence of a dog for elderly people confined to hospital. Dr Aaron Katcher, Associate Professor of Psychiatry at the University of Pennsylvania, has proved that a person's blood pressure falls significantly in the presence of a companion dog and that such companions could almost 'calm their owners into a kind of reverie'. Patients recovering from heart problems heal noticeably sooner if they have a dog at home.

PRO Dogs have set up a PAT (PRO Dogs Active Therapy) visiting scheme in which suitably friendly dogs, trained for the work, accompany their owners on visits to hospital wards, nursing homes and any other institutions which welcome them. The dogs' role in this and similar schemes has been described as 'adding life to their years', 'friendship at a stroke', or 'tail-wagging psychotherapy'. Whatever the phraseology, it is a fact that simply stroking a responsive dog helps people to relax and to come out of themselves. Elderly people who are unable to have their own pets with them in institutions get immense pleasure from the chance of contact and conversation with an affable dog and it is noticeable that patients who are normally withdrawn, sullen and non-communicative often begin to respond to people again in the presence of a dog. The dog merely has to be there. Dr Brian Sproule, a general practitioner and PAT visitor, who incidentally breeds pharaoh hounds, finds that his patients respond far better and are much more willing to chat with him if he takes his family dog along on his visits. Sometimes a dog will stimulate reaction from stroke patients who seem otherwise to be completely unresponsive and sometimes there are even more spectacular results, like the recent story of Frank Mattingley and his pet collie, Tipper. Frank was seriously ill in a hospital and just as he began to lose consciousness he whispered the dog's name. Fortunately his doctors had the sense to bring Tipper to his bedside, and Tipper's nuzzle and howl brought Frank out of his coma and saved his life.

Children also respond well to dogs and there are several instances of autistic or withdrawn children finding it easy to communicate with a dog and eventually, through the dog, they begin to communicate with people too. It is the same for many of the mentally ill or emotionally disturbed, and 'pet psychotherapy' plays an increasingly important role in Britain, as it already does in the United States. Dr Doreen Hutchinson, a Staffordshire psychiatrist, knows of cases where dogs have major psychological influences on their owners. Dorothy Walster, a health educationist with the Scottish Health Education Group (SHEG) and a SCAS committee member, has developed several ideas involving contact between elderly people and companion animals, both within institutions and within their own homes. Scotland has a Pet Fostering Scheme which relieves elderly pet owners of concern for their pets if the owner is hospitalized or disabled; volunteers known to the owner and to the pet take care of the animal while the owner is unable to do so, and many of the volunteers have set up close friendships with owners and pets. Some are themselves pensioners who perhaps live in sheltered housing schemes where pets are banned – a considerable deprivation for many elderly people and one which should not be lightly dismissed.

At Heathcote Hospital in Leamington Spa, geriatric patients' pets are made welcome. An article in the local *Courier* in May 1986 reported that there was one dog for every four wards, three of them having been donated to the hospital by NCDL as permanent residents and therapists. One, a Jack Russell called Sheba, had given herself the daily job of delivering morning newspapers to the bedside; another, Clare, made a point of climbing on to the beds to bid good morning to every patient in turn and she also provided entertainment through the window by pursuing the nurses on their weekly jogs in the hospital grounds. Dogs to stroke, dogs to watch, dogs to talk to . . . Nursing officer Mary Curran says, 'They can express their emotions to an animal far better than to another human. They can talk and moan and they won't be answered back. But it is the stroking that is the most important thing . . . Our patients here who stroke animals are much calmer. It is definitely part of the curing process.'

An American survey about the therapeutic use of pets by psychologists, psychiatrists and general practitioners revealed that ninety-five per cent of the respondents said they would prescribe a pet for loneliness, eighty-eight per cent would do the same for depression, fifty-five per cent for stress or inactivity and fifty-four per cent for other emotional problems. Pets were also considered therapeutic for physical illnesses like postoperative recovery, high blood pressure, terminal diseases, Alzheimer's and Parkinson's.

Dogs can certainly be of great therapeutic value and ideally it is a two-way process. Mrs Evelyn Cauwood of the Arthritis and Rheumatism Council receives many a letter from people who suffer from these potentially crippling diseases. Their main message seems to be that the extra work of caring for a dog is well worth it because the dog gives so much in return. A sixty-one-year-old woman, at one stage almost bedridden with rheumatoid arthritis, said that her dogs had given her 'the will to fight and keep going'. An eighty-year-old suffering from osteoarthritis acquired a Yorkshire terrier and found that 'he soon shifted my thoughts away from myself and on to the pleasures of a daily outing . . . the joys of seeing this eager little dog careering around – laughing all over his face – makes me feel on top of the world and I've been able to discard my stick!' Many of the letter-writers say that if it was not for their dogs they would never take exercise themselves; because the dogs need their outings, their owners are much fitter. That is a very positive effect of dog ownership but the writers all agreed that the greatest benefit of all is that their dogs bring them fun, affection and companionship.

It is not only the sick and the elderly who can benefit from contact with dogs. Caring for an animal involves taking on a responsibility, learning to take its needs into account as well as or before your own, learning how to communicate with it and earn its trust, understanding something about reactions to danger and fear, discovering that there are limits to what an animal can tolerate, and finding a willing ear for your troubles and a reassuring response when you are hurt or sad: these are all of positive value. A child can learn about the pain of parting, the joy of reunion and the value of uncritical friendship – in fact a child can learn a great deal about living in human society by sharing a life with a companion dog. It may well be (and research is in hand on the theory) that the child who has the benefit of a dog, which can teach tolerance and encourage the expression of affection, is less likely to become delinquent.

Prisons are one of the latest institutions in which dogs (and other animals) are finding new roles. Dogs are specifically prohibited from British prisons at present, however, and the schemes in this country involve animals like fish, cats and birds. At Edinburgh's Saughton Prison, for example, a few long-term inmates are breeding tropical fish on a commercial basis, exporting huge numbers of tilapia to Third World fish farms. The project presents a challenge to the inmates, gives them a sense of purpose, achievement and self-esteem, and enables them to gain expert knowledge and experience which might be useful when they are released. They also have a scheme for breeding budgerigars to keep lonely pensioners company. Angus Whyte, education co-ordinator at the prison, has studied the use of animals in prison systems abroad and sees three major advantages: the possibility of interesting commercial employment and alternative work, animals helping prisoners emotionally, and animals enabling prisoners to contribute to the general benefit of society or specific communities. In the context of dogs, the most exciting prospects in these areas are, respectively, the maintenance of boarding and breeding kennels; the provision of genuine and trustworthy companionship; the satisfaction of protective feelings and diversion from self-concern among the prisoners; and (Edinburgh's dream) the breeding and training of guide dogs for the blind.

In the United States there are some exciting projects well under way involving dogs and prisoners, to the benefit of both and of the community at large. At the Purdy Treatment Center for Women, a maximum security prison in Washington state, there is a unique and adventurous Pet Partnership Program. It began when Kathy Quinn, veteran of fourteen different institutions, managed to make herself fit for a more normal way of life by photographing and training dogs. She saw the potential in dog-training for other inmates and her ideas were supported by Delta's Leo Bustad. The authorities were eventually persuaded to give it a go. The aim was to train dogs as assistants for the disabled and the scheme was launched in 1982 with the co-operation of the state university, the corrections board, a local community college and plenty of 'dog people'.

By the summer of 1983 the first graduate dog emerged from

the enclosed life of Purdy to become an overnight media star. Glory, like other dogs in the scheme, had been donated to Purdy by a member of the public and she is now a stable support for her disabled owner. Purdy dogs are also trained as hearing dogs for the deaf and as pets for convalescent homes. All the training is by inmates under careful instruction, and once the women prove themselves competent and well versed in animal kowledge they are given a dog of their own to train, for which they take total and sole responsibility including grooming, kennel maintenance and feeding. The course is thorough and the women not only learn about dog behaviour and care but also about employment opportunities in dog-grooming, veterinary nursing, kennel work, training and dog-sitting. The main aim of the whole project is to provide practical job skills for the women as well as supply the community with trained dogs.

The benefits of the scheme have proved to be substantial. The authorities feel satisfied that they are providing vocational training for the women; the women reap all kinds of personal benefits from their relationships with the dogs, and with each other in shared work; and the local community gains beautifully trained dogs which the women are proud to hand over. Glory's trainer, Sue, said that the programme was 'the most positive influence I've had in the past five years. It has enabled me to realize things about myself and has taught me many new skills. Having access to these dogs has helped me to realize too that I am still capable of responding to living creatures and has put me in touch with feelings I was sure I had lost.' She might have added that the dogs provide the women with outlets for their physical and emotional needs for giving and receiving affection: their lives are greatly enriched by caring for an animal and by knowing that, in return, it will give them an uncritical, reliable and constant friendship.

The Purdy dogs are what the Americans classify as 'service' dogs, which include guide dogs for the blind, hearing dogs for the deaf, pet visiting programmes, therapy dogs and also wheelchair and mobility dogs. A mobility dog gives its owner physical support – a living, four-legged crutch – and a wheelchair 'assistant dog' is trained to 'extend and maintain the maximum level of independent functioning for its owner'. Such dogs must of course be very versatile and their daily work depends entirely on the lifestyle of their owner. For example, a strong dog may be asked to move the wheelchair, help its owner to stand up and support them as they walk. Most of the dogs open doors, retrieve dropped items, fetch specific articles like a cordless telephone or a can of beer from the fridge, or solicit help from other humans if needed. Assistance dogs work in partnership with their owners: they form a team and the dog not only assists the owner but consciously works to enable a disabled person to express their potential.

An important side benefit which many disabled owners have noticed is that a dog acts as a bridge between the disabled and the able-bodied. All too often, the able-bodied either ignore the physically disabled or treat them like imbeciles. Often from embarrassment they avoid eye contact, they keep their distance or, if a meeting is unavoidable, they keep it brief. Three researchers at California State University observed an amazing difference of attitude if a wheelchair person was accompanied by a service dog. Passers-by began to smile at them, and initiated conversations by talking to or about the dog. Suddenly they realized that in every wheelchair there was an ordinary human being, just like themselves. But for the dog, they would never have found that out.

Burton D. Pusch manages the Good Samaritan Center for Independence in Puyallup, Washington, an agency which assists the physically handicapped to maximize their own independence. He has a congenital disability himself and makes full use of his Purdy-trained dog in his professional work and his personal activities. He stresses the importance of a matched partnership between man and dog: 'When you think of a service dog and its master, think of a tool and its craftsman. Without the proper tool a craftsman cannot work. Without the craftsman, the tool cannot be wielded as it was meant to be. Equally matched they create beauty and art.'

It is to be hoped that the craftsman remembers that his tool is a living creature with needs of its own and deserving of the

utmost respect and consideration. Some people are rightly
expressing concern that in the rush to make use of dogs to help
the human sick, disabled, mentally ill and elderly, the welfare
of the animal might be overlooked. Dorothy Steves, animal
educationalist, is deeply concerned at the prospect. Many
people have little knowledge of a dog's real needs, especially its
emotional ones, and, as she says, 'Because of their great
adaptability and desire to please us, it is extremely easy to take
advantage of dogs.' Do we, as she claims, abuse them by
effectively 'making slaves of man's best friend, and this we
humans have no right to do'? Yes, we do, and we should be
deeply ashamed of ourselves. We should not abuse their willingness and their extraordinary desire to help and their admirable sense of responsibility towards humans.

Dogs have been used for centuries as 'comforters', as living
blankets for cold feet, as warmth for aching bodies, as physical
presences to 'draw out' sickness from people by touch and as
psychological healers. There is nothing new in pet-facilitated
therapy and indeed it could be said that the therapeutic role
epitomizes the special relationship – from man's point of view.
But what about the dog? What does it get in return?

At Delta's international symposium in Boston in 1986, William
A. Mason of the California Primate Research Center presented
a paper entitled 'The Animal Side of the Human/Animal Bond'.
He pointed out that much research had been carried out,
especially recently, into the importance of the emotional factor
for the human in the partnership and that it was generally
assumed, particularly with dogs, that similar ties of affection
were felt by the animal – but nobody had really bothered to find
out if that was so. How did a dog cope with the absence of its
human companion at work during the day, for instance? (A
Philadelphian study has shown that mongrels, especially those
from rescue homes, are far more likely than other dogs to
experience considerable anxiety at separation.) How did it feel
about trips to the vet, often quite distressing for it? What about
the real trauma of being placed in kennels while the owner is
on holiday? How does a dog react to a new baby in the family,
or a new spouse or a new pet? What happens when, without
being consulted, a dog finds itself moved to a new house where

it has to start all over again establishing its territory and creating new relationships with other dogs that have the advantage of being on their home ground? Why shouldn't your dog 'caninize' you in the way you seek to 'humanize' your dog? Do you ever consult, let alone consider, the family dog on matters which can affect its whole life so radically?

Konrad Lorenz, in his message of greeting to the Boston symposium, put it very clearly when he reminded the delegates: 'We should not forget that our relationship with pets cannot be one of just taking the benefits. I feel that it is man's responsibility as the most powerful element in creation to make sure that other creatures too can lead their specific lives in an adequate way.' He talked about the growing importance of pets in human societies which have become so urbanized that they are alienated from nature. Pets, for many people, are often the only remaining contact with the rest of the natural, living world, and close contact with a living animal is the best way for a person to learn about the natural environment and the human role in the global ecological system. In the past Lorenz has used the phrase 'integration with nature in general' and it is through that special agent, the dog, that man can perhaps make an honest gesture to reach across towards the rest of creation again. As Aaron Katcher suggested, summing up at a meeting in Paris in 1982, the dog seems to lie somewhere between man and beast and this enables humans to treat it in both ways at different times – a power we do not have over other people or over other animals.

Man is becoming sadly estranged from so many of the living creatures with whom he shares this earth. Perhaps the dog offers his greatest chance of reconciliation with that living world so that he can overcome his increasing sense of loneliness and, like the American Indian, can remember how to think with his heart and not just with his intellect. His companion, the dog, always so ready to take responsibility for the humans entrusted to it, can be the bridge and can show him the way.

Postscript

by Claude Morris

He was just a poor old mongrel that had lost his boss and mate,
And his sad eyes checked the people round about the Pearly Gate.
He couldn't go to Heaven – only human types can go –
The very best ones make it, and the others go below.

And he knew his boss was splendid – they had been through thick
   and thin,
And he knew that he could find him, if St Peter let him in;
But he couldn't live in Heaven, for it seemed he had no soul,
And he wondered what a soul was like – that kept him from his goal.

He reckoned that his boss would know, and fix it up O.K.,
The way he did, betimes on earth, where things oft went astray.
So patiently, the old dog sat, and waited on and on,
And heaven had no nights to tell how many days had gone.

At last St Peter saw him, and came and stroked his head –
'What are you doing here Old Boy? You're far from home,' he said.
'Oh, yes I know,' the old dog said, 'But I know my boss is here,
But I guess I'll have to travel, if he doesn't soon appear.

'He was the finest man on earth, as anyone could tell,
So he must be here in Heaven, where the best of humans dwell.'
'Now wait a sec.,' St Peter said, 'I'll try the Lost and Found –
They're overworked, but through the years, I've found them very
   sound.'

So he sent a telex there and then, to ascertain the fate
Of the paragon, who so it seemed, had passed the Pearly Gate.
And like a flash, the answer came – 'The man you seek is well.
But he didn't get to Heaven, he is down – well down in Hell.'

'He's a braggart and a boozer, and he knows his way about –
He's a liar and a brawler, and a thorough down-and-out.
He's a heathen non-believer, and a trouble-maker too,
Who skates upon the thinnest ice, as wasters often do.'

When the dog heard this description, to his eyes there came a light,
For he recognised his owner, and he cried, 'That's him alright.
It seems that I'm mistaken, and my values are upturned,
But where he dwells is Heaven, just so far as I'm concerned.'

Then Peter read a postscript on the telex – 'Don't forget –
He gave his life to save his dog – and he gave without regret!'

[Reproduced by kind permission of 'MERIGAL',
Merigal Dingo Education Centre, Bargo, NSW, Australia]

Bibliography

Beach Thomas, Sir William, *The Way of a Dog* (Michael Joseph, 1948)

Beck, Alan M., 'The Ecology of Feral and Free-Roving Dogs in Baltimore', see Fox, M.W., *The Wild Canids*

Bekoff, Marc, 'Social Behaviour and Ecology of the African Canidae', see Fox, M.W., *The Wild Canids*

Boone, J. Allen, *Letters to Strongheart* (Robert H. Summer, 1977)

Burton, Maurice, *The Sixth Sense of Animals* (Dent, 1973)

Chiarelli, A.B., 'The Chromosomes of the Canidae', see Fox, M.W., *The Wild Canids*

Clutton-Brock, Juliet, *Domesticated Animals* (Heinemann/British Museum, 1981)

Corbet, L, and Newsome, A., 'Dingo Society and Its Maintenance: A Preliminary Analysis', see Fox, M.W., *The Wild Canids*

Cornish, C.J., *Animals at Work and Play* (Seeley & Co. Ltd, 1896)

Cottesloe, Gloria, *The Story of the Battersea Dogs' Home* (David & Charles, 1979)

Crisler, Lois, *Captive Wild* (W.H. Allen, 1969)

Croxton-Smith, Arthur, *British Dogs* (Collins, 1945)

Davidar, E.R.C., 'Ecology and Behaviour of the Dhole or Indian Wild Dog', see Fox, M.W., *The Wild Canids*

Dunbar, Ian, *Why Do Dogs Do What They Do?* (TFH Publications Inc, 1979)

Edwards, T.J., *Mascots and Pets of the Services* (Gale & Polden, 1953)

Fiennes, Richard, *The Order of Wolves* (Hamish Hamilton, 1976)

Fiennes, Richard and Alice, *The Natural History of the Dog* (Weidenfeld & Nicholson, 1968)

Fitzpatrick, Percy, *Jock of the Bushveld* (Longmans, 1907)

Fox, M.W. (ed), *The Wild Canids* (Robert E. Krieger Publishing Co. Inc, 1975)

Fox, M.W., 'Evolution of Social Behaviour in Canids', see above

Gier, H.T., 'Ecology and Behaviour of the Coyote', see Fox, M.W., *The Wild Canids*

Golani, I. and Keller, A., 'A Longitudinal Field Study of the Behaviour of a Pair of Golden Jackals', see Fox, M.W., *The Wild Canids*

Graham, Richard, *The Good Dog's Guide to Better Living* (Jay Landesman, 1981)

Holmes, John, *The Farmer's Dog* (Popular Dogs, revised 1984)
Hudson, W.H., *The Book of a Naturalist* (Thomas Nelson & Sons, 1919)
Keeler, Clyde, 'Genetics of Behaviour Variations in Color Phases of the Red Fox', see Fox, M.W., *The Wild Canids*
van Lawick-Goodall, H. and J., *The Innocent Killers* (Collins, 1970)
Lee, Raymond, *Not so Dumb – Animals in the Movies* (A.S. Barnes & Co., 1970)
Leslie, Robert Franklin, *Queen Wolf* (W.W. Norton/Macmillan, 1975)
Linzey, Andrew, *The Status of Animals in the Christian Tradition* (Woodbroke College, 1985)
Long, William J., *How Animals Talk* (Harper & Brothers, 1919)
Lorenz, Konrad, *Man Meets Dog* (Methuen, 1954)
Lucas, E.V., *The More I See of Men . . .* (Methuen, 1927)
Macauley, Thurston (ed), *The Constant Companion* (Blandford Press, 1985)
Macdonald, David (ed), *The Encyclopaedia of Mammals: 1* (George Allen & Unwin, 1984)
Macintosh, N.W.G., 'The Origin of the Dingo: An Enigma', see Fox, M.W., *The Wild Canids*
Maloney, William E. and Suares, Jean-Claude (eds), *The Literary Dog* (Berkley Windhover/Push Pin Press, 1978)
Mason, I.L. (ed), *Evolution of Domesticated Animals* (Longman, 1984)
McEwen, Peter, *Dogs in London* (U.F.A.W., 1985)
McFarland, David (ed), *The Oxford Companion to Animal Behaviour* (O.U.P., 1981)
Mech, L. David, 'Hunting Behaviour in Two Similar Species of Social Canids', see Fox, M.W., *The Wild Canids*
Morris, Desmond, *Dogwatching* (Jonathan Cape, 1986)
Mowat, Farley, *Never Cry Wolf* (Secker & Warburg, 1964)
Nesbitt, William H., 'Ecology of a Feral Dog Pack on a Wildlife Refuge', see Fox, M.W., *The Wild Canids*
Quarton, Marjorie, *All about the Working Border Collie* (Pelham, 1986)
Ross-Skinner, Rosemary, *Horizon House: The True Story of an Alcoholic* (Muller, Blond & White, 1987)
Rothel, David, *The Great Show Business Animals* (Dent, 1973)
Schul, Bill, *The Psychic Powers of Animals* (Coronet, 1978)
Scott, John Paul and Fuller, John L., *Genetics and the Social Behaviour of the Dog* (University of Chicago Press, 1965)
Serpell, James, *In the Company of Animals* (Basil Blackwell, 1986)
Shaw, Vero, *The Illustrated Book of the Dog* (Cassell, Petter, Galpin, 1879–81, reprinted 1984 Bonanza Books)
Sinclair, Sandra, *How Animals See* (Croom Helm, 1985)
Soulsby, E.J.L., *Animals in Society* (U.F.A.W., 1985)
Sproule, Brian J., *Pharaoh Hound Management* (1982)
Stephenson, Robert O. and Ahgook, Robert T., 'The Eskimo Hunter's View of Wolf Ecology and Behaviour', see Fox, M.W., *The Wild Canids*

Taylor, David, *You and Your Dog* (Dorling Kindersley, 1986)
Tinbergen, Niko, *Curious Naturalists* (Basic Books, 1958)
Tremain, Ruthven, *The Animals' Who's Who* (R.K.P., 1982)
Walker, Stephen, *Animal Thought* (Routledge & Kegan Paul, 1983)
Wood, Rev. J.G., *The Natural History of Man* (George Routledge & Sons, 1868)
Wood-Gush, D.G.M. (ed), *Self Awareness in Domesticated Animals* (U.F.A.W., 1981)
Zeuner, Frederick E., *A History of Domesticated Animals* (Hutchinson, 1963)
Zimen, Eric, 'Social Dynamics of the Wolf Pack', see Fox, M.W., *The Wild Canids*

Articles

THE DELTA SOCIETY
Abstracts from The Delta Society International Conference, August 1986, Boston, Mass., 'Living Together – People, Animals and the Environment':
  Eddy, Jane *et al*, 'Service Dogs and Social Acknowlegement of People in Wheelchairs'
  Filiatre, J.C., *et al*, 'Intraspecific and Interspecific Communication of the Pet Dog'
  Hedhammer, Ake, 'Keeping Pets in the Nordic Countries'
  Mason, William A., 'The Animal Side of the Human/Animal Bond'
  McCrave, Elizabeth A., 'Correlates of Separation Anxiety in the Dog'
  O'Farrell, Valerie, 'Owner Attitudes and Dog Behaviour Problems'
  Serpell, James, 'Social and Attitudinal Correlates of Pet Ownership in Middle Childhood'
  White, Ken, 'San Francisco SPCA Programs for Pets in the Community'

'People-Animals-Environment' (*Delta* magazine, Fall 1984):
  Pusch, Burton D., 'Of Dogs, Tools and Art'
  Stenzel, Patricia, 'The Purdy Prison Program'

MERIGAL
Corbett, L.K., 'Morphological comparisons of Australian and Thai dingoes' (reprinted in *Merigal*, August 1986)
Manwell, C. and Baker, C.M. Ann, 'Domestication of the dog: Hunter, food, bed-warmer, or emotional object' (reprinted in *Merigal*, December 1986)

SOCIETY FOR COMPANION ANIMAL STUDIES – NEWSLETTERS

Cage, Andrew, 'The Elderly Pet Owner – A Veterinary Perspective' (8.85)

Cauwood, Evelyn, 'Letters from rheumatism/arthritis sufferers' (11.84)

Dufour, Barbara, 'French attitudes to dogs', Paris, 1982 (4.82)

Lorenz, Konrad, 'Address to International Symposium on the Human-Pet Relationship', Vienna, October 1983 (1.84)

Mugford, Roger, 'Destructive behaviour and over-attachment' (1.84)

Reilly, W.A., 'Health Risks Associated with Dogs' (8.85)

Serpell, James, 'Pets and Children' (10.86)

Steves, Dorothy, 'Use Verging on Abuse' (7.84)

SCAS/SHEG Meeting, Edinburgh, 6 December 1986:
   Hutton, J.S., 'Childhood Experiences of Young Offenders'
   Whyte, Angus M., 'Animals in Prison'

Addresses

Battersea Dogs' Home
4 Battersea Park Road, London SW8 4AA
01-622 3626

The Delta Society
Century Building, 321 Burnett Ave. South, Renton, WA 98055, USA

The Guide Dogs for the Blind Association
Alexandra House, Park Street, Windsor, Berkshire SL4 1JR
0753 855711

Hearing Dogs for the Deaf Training Centre
Little Close, Lower Icknield Way, Lewknor, Oxon OX9 5RY
0844 53898

Merigal Dingo Education Centre
Arina Road, Bargo, NSW 2574, Australia

National Canine Defence League
1 & 2 Pratt Mews, London NW1 0AD
01-388 0137

People's Dispensary for Sick Animals
South Street, Dorking, Surrey RH4 2LB
0306 888291

PRO Dogs
Rocky Bank, 4 New Road, Ditton, Maidstone, Kent ME20 6AD
0732 848499

Royal Society for the Prevention of Cruelty to Animals
Causeway, Horsham, West Sussex RH12 1HG
0403 64181

Scottish Health Education Group
Woodburn House, Canaan Lane, Edinburgh EH10 4SG
031 447 8044

Society for Companion Animal Studies
Hon. Secretary: 7 Kingston Street, Cambridge

Index